The Romance of a Consecrated Life

A Biography of Alexander Beers

By
Adelaide Lionne Beers

Introduction by
Rev. Walter A. Sellew

First Fruits Press
Wilmore, Kentucky
c2016

The romance of a consecrated life: a biography of Alexander Beers.
By Adelaide Lionne Beers.

First Fruits Press, ©2016
Previously published by the Free Methodist Publishing House, [1922?].

ISBN: 9781621716044 (print), 9781621716051 (digital), 9781621716068 (kindle)

Digital version at http://place.asburyseminary.edu/freemethodistbooks/22/

For all other uses, contact:

First Fruits Press
B.L. Fisher Library
Asbury Theological Seminary
204 N. Lexington Ave.
Wilmore, KY 40390
http://place.asburyseminary.edu/firstfruits

Beers, Adelaide Lionne.
    The romance of a consecrated life : a biography of Alexander Beers / by Adelaide Lionne Beers ; introduction by Walter A. Sellew. Wilmore, Kentucky : First Fruits Press, ©2016.
        351 pages, [14] leaves of plates : illustrations, portraits ; 21 cm.
        Reprint. Previously published: Chicago, Illinois : Free Methodist Publishing House, [1922?].
        ISBN - 13: 9781621716044 (pbk.)
        1. Beers, Alexander, 1862-1921. 2. Free Methodist Church of North America--Clergy--United States--Biography. I. Title.
BX8419 .B4 2016   287.2092

Cover design by Jon Ramsay

asburyseminary.edu
800.2ASBURY
204 North Lexington Avenue
Wilmore, Kentucky 40390

First Fruits
THE ACADEMIC OPEN PRESS OF ASBURY SEMINARY

First Fruits Press
The Academic Open Press of Asbury Theological Seminary
204 N. Lexington Ave., Wilmore, KY 40390
859-858-2236
first.fruits@asburyseminary.edu
asbury.to/firstfruits

The Romance of a Consecrated Life

ADELAIDE LIONNE BEERS

REV. AND MRS. ALEXANDER BEERS

The Romance of a Consecrated Life

A Biography of
ALEXANDER BEERS

By His Wife
ADELAIDE LIONNE BEERS

Introduction by
Rev. Walter A. Sellew
Senior Bishop of the Free Methodist Church
of North America

PUBLISHED BY
THE FREE METHODIST PUBLISHING HOUSE
1132 Washington Boulevard
Chicago, Illinois

To
the many kind friends
who have made the publication
of this book possible:
In extending the
generous hospitality of wide
open doors; in the many choice
words spoken to encourage the writer
in her task of love; in paying of advance
subscriptions and contributing of their means;
in furnishing, correcting and arranging material;
in letters and tributes from which quotations
have been freely made; in the gracious,
unceasing and effectual prayers that
have ascended to the Father for
the success of the work;
this volume is
affectionately dedicated
by the author.

ILLUSTRATIONS

TABLE OF CONTENTS

INTRODUCTION

No class of literature makes so deep an impression on the average reader as biography, and no influences in life, excepting possibly that of the mother, have molded so many characters and shaped so many destinies, as has biography. The lives of statesmen, divines, generals, missionaries, scientists and eminent men in every department of life's activities, portrayed in biography, have moved millions to great deeds and have awakened slumbering talents which otherwise might have remained dormant forever.

It is therefore absolutely necessary that a biography, to be effective, must have a good subject. This condition is fully met in the book which is now presented to the reading public. Alexander Beers was no ordinary man. His life and activities were an inspiration to a large body of people, particularly students, who came under the influence of his noble, self-sacrificing life, and this volume will perpetuate the influence of those molding and inspiring activities which so strikingly characterized his life. His commanding figure, his affable and courteous manner and his striking personality can never be forgotten by those who came in contact with him. His vision of future events was so clear that he literally lived before his day, his great energy carried him through seemingly unsurmountable obstacles, and his strong love for the work of God won him many lasting friends.

Mrs. Adelaide L. Beers, who presents this volume to the public, is well qualified in every way to write it. Her many years of service in public life have fitted her for this task. Her practical nature and her intimate acquaintance with the outstanding facts of her husband's exceedingly busy life add to her other qualifications to write this brief history of his many activities in an interesting and readable manner.

I am confident that all who read this book will be amply repaid by the inspiration they will receive from its perusal, and my intimate acquaintance with both the author and the subject of this biography warrant me in saying that its production will be an interesting as well as a permanent contribution to biographical literature, and I take much pleasure in commending it to the reading public as worthy of universal perusal.

> "Be strong!
> We are not here to play, to dream, to drift,
> We have hard work to do and loads to lift,
> Shun not the labor; take it, 'tis God's gift.
> Be strong."

WALTER A. SELLEW.

Jamestown, N. Y., October 10, 1922.

PREFACE

The subject of this biography was unknown to the writer for the first twenty-two years of his life, and then not intimately until some time later. Since the sacred hour when the vows that made them one were taken, to the solemn moment when he went to be forever with the Lord, their lives had been so closely intermingled that when she attempted to portray the events of his life upon paper, she found it well nigh impossible to separate herself from his success and achievements.

Like two strands of finely-spun silk that had been so interwoven and intermeshed that the two threads could not be singled without marring the fabric. Together they had endured the suffering and sorrow and rejoiced when the victory came. No grief, no joy, had reached the one, that did not respond to the heart throb of the other.

For thirty-two years the lights and shadows of life's vicissitudes had fallen upon both alike. In perfect unison, their petitions had ascended to the throne of heavenly grace and both were blessed when the answers of peace were granted.

When the burdens of life were heavy, they helped one another to bear the load. When the road seemed hard and long to the one, the other intuitively found a way to brighten and shorten it. Together they sowed the precious gospel seed and rejoiced as one in the harvest reaping.

In the pages of this book the author has striven to reveal the character of the man whom she knew thus intimately and well; his great love for the beautiful in nature, painting, poetry and architecture, his great constructive ability as shown in the many buildings he planned and caused to be erected, his splendid talents as a Christian educator and his unusual success as preacher and pastor; his marked love for little children and the aged, his Christlike magnanimity to friend and foe alike, his wonderful fortitude during his long, wasting illness as confirmed by the appreciative words of many friends.

We are told also that he could adjust himself to the needs of all classes of society—the rich and poor, the high and low, the educated or illiterate, the young or old, were successfully ministered unto without compromising the principles of righteousness. Above and beyond all of these, his unswerving loyalty to truth and whole-hearted devotion to God shine with a purer luster in this volume.

Since no diaries had been kept to which the writer could have recourse, nor did Mr. Beers carry on a correspondence with friends that would have furnished letters revealing his views, his hopes, and his aims; consequently the writer found it necessary to quote freely from the comforting letters of condolence and the beautiful tributes given his memory by his many friends.

Much is said concerning the missionaries who were called to the foreign fields while students in the school Mr. Beers founded, but no attempt has been made to give any connected history of their lives or their work. The names are given of the pioneer missionaries only in the five countries where the work of the Free Methodist Church is represented, and the names mentioned of those who have been translated from "service to reward."

An explanation is due the reader as to the origin of the title of this book. The phrase was coined by Mr. Beers himself when advertising the autobiography of one of the bishops from the platform. Turning the leaves of the book, he turned to the bishop and said: "This book is not rightly named; it should have been called 'The Romance of a Consecrated Life.'" An alumnus of the institution recalled the incident and from this circumstance the title was chosen.

The fact should also be mentioned that Mr. Beers had begun writing his autobiography and left on record the greater portion of the second, third and fourth chapters which appear in this book. This incomplete work induced his wife to write his life history.

Will the kind reader exercise charity and pardon all defects?

CHAPTER I

PARENTAGE AND EARLY EVENTS

The sweetest lives are those to duty wed,
  Whose deeds, both great and small,
Are close-knit strands of an unbroken thread,
  Where love ennobles all.
The world may sound no trumpets, ring no bells;
  The Book of Life the shining record tells.
Thy love shall chant its own beautitudes
  After its own life working.
                    —*Elizabeth Barrett Browning.*

My heart leaps up when I behold
  A rainbow in the sky;
So was it when my life began;
So it is now I am a man;
So may it be when I am old
  Or let me die;
The child is father of the man.
                    —*Wordsworth.*

Great results are often achieved from small beginnings. The monarch of the forest springs from the tiny acorn. In oriental lands a grain of mustard seed grows to a tree so large that "the birds of the air come and lodge in the branches thereof."

At Bloomfield, Iowa, March 4, 1862, a devoted mother looked into the face of her new-born infant, and when the nurse placed him on the scales he was found to weigh but four and one-half pounds. No one at that time could have predicted that some day

15

Alexander, as he was named, would attain to six feet two inches in height and for many years of his life would weigh more than two hundred pounds.

Perhaps even at birth, when so diminutive in size, his mother may have foreseen his future greatness and named him Alexander as one of our preachers in his tribute writes: "We might say without embarrassment or exaggeration 'Alexander the Great,' the name seems almost prophetic and I have wondered at times if his dear little mother, who weighed less than one hundred pounds (of whom I have heard him speak again and again so tenderly and lovingly), as she rocked him in her arms did not have great ambitions for him and fond expectations of him, and was not this the reason she named him Alexander. Alexander Beers was a great-souled man. He possessed great personal resources, great and godly ambitions, great visions, and accomplished great things for God and humanity."

Those who knew him in manhood's prime will remember him as tall and robust, finely proportioned, his countenance bespeaking the nobility of soul possessed.

His father, George Ezekiel Beers, was born in Ohio; his mother, Jane Drusilla Underwood, came from West Virginia. His parents were honest and upright citizens who early instilled the principles of righteousness into the hearts and minds of their large family of twelve—six sons and six daughters. All of these excepting one, who died in infancy, became known as men and women of integrity. The dwelling was simple and primitive in which these promising sons and daughters were sheltered—a pioneer home on the prairie—but love ruled there and it was really a home.

> "Home's not merely four square walls,
>   Tho with pictures hung and gilded;
> Home is where affection calls—
>   Where its shrine a heart hath builded."

Strong affection existed between all the members of the household and bound their hearts indissolubly so that there was indeed "No place like home," however humble it might be. The atmosphere of this home where Alexander was nourished during his childhood was ever pure and wholesome. His parents were both members of an Evangelical church, but were cold in their spiritual devotion while rearing their children.

The mother was in a backslidden state, having once known the Lord, but had always kept a very tender conscience. She was restored to the favor of God very soon after Alexander was converted. The night following his conversion he was exhorting all his friends and neighbors in the schoolhouse to get saved. He looked back to the rear of the house and there sat his mother weeping. He called out without a thought of propriety: "Why, ma, I did not know you were here. Come to the altar right now and seek Christ." Without hesitation she arose and hurried to the mourner's bench and was soon rejoicing in her new-found joy. She was ever after this a most exemplary Christian and a great encouragement to Alexander. He was especially fond of his mother and always wrote her a weekly letter whenever he was absent from her. He visited her a short time before she passed away and found her too weak to rise from her bed. She placed her hands on his head and breathed upon him her dying benediction. He often referred to this sacred moment when preaching on "Mother's Day." Those who have heard him will remember the eloquent eulogy he ever paid to Christian motherhood and the touching tribute he gave to his own little mother. With what pathos have we heard him say: "How often in the heat of the battle when exhausted in the conflict have I been cheered and refreshed by the pressure of my mother's hand upon my brow." How he delighted in quoting from Joaquin Miller's "The Bravest Battle":

> "The bravest battle that ever was fought;
>   Shall I tell you where and when?
> On the maps of the world you will find it not;
>   It was fought by the mothers of men.

> "But deep in a walled-up woman's heart,
>   Of a woman that would not yield,
> But patiently, silently bore her part,
>   Lo! there is that battlefield.

> "No marshalling troops, no bivouac song,
>   No banner to gleam and wave;
> And oh! these battles they last so long,
>   From babyhood to the grave."

His father prided himself on his morality. He really was an exceptionally fine man, kind to his family, strictly honest and upright in all his dealings, and especially benevolent—this last being a prominent characteristic. All the widows and orphans in the neighborhood were remembered bountifully from the farm with fruit, meat and vegetables in their season. He expected to reach heaven through the merit of good deeds. Not until the latter part of his life did he feel the need of the Savior. But at last prayer prevailed—he saw himself lost and undone and realized that his own righteousness could never appease an offended Deity. He sought the forgiveness of his sins through the atoning blood and enjoyed great peace with God for several years before he went to meet the wife of his youth in the mansions above. When old and feeble he would tell Alexander what a great mistake he had made all his life trusting in his own self-righteousness. "Why," he'd say, "I am the chief of sinners saved by grace."

Alexander early evinced a great fondness for poetry. He would stand at his sister's knee when too young to read himself and learn from her lips poem after poem from the old *Toledo Blade* or some other paper. He admired his sisters very much and he thought that because they wore dresses it was much more becoming to him to be garbed in a similar fashion than to dress like a boy. There had been considerable talk in the family about getting him a boy's suit—his first—and finally his mother made him a pair of pants and a blouse. He had watched her sew and understood that an ultimatum had been declared that he must soon shed his feminine dress forever. He was very stubborn and resolved to resist as long as possible and was hidden away in the bushes when the fatal hour arrived. His sisters very soon found him and dragged the sobbing culprit out of his hiding place and brought him to his mother who robed him in a boy's suit, despite his struggles and protest. We can well excuse his weakness when we remember that he was not yet four years old and he thought his mother and sisters were the acme of excellence—they were his model.

One of his favorite pastimes was to take his snare gun and kill snow birds of which there were a great multitude flying about. He would carefully dress the bird, cook it and bear it in triumph for one of his sisters to feast upon; then he would stand off and say boastingly, "Who cooks snow birds for you?"

When Alexander was but a babe in arms, his parents moved to Kansas, near Topeka, on the banks of the Kansas River. Here there were many attractions and he early learned to swim, fish and row. In later years he furnished great amusement to his friends at the ocean, plunging, diving, floating on his back and riding on the highest billows. He seemed to have absolutely no fear of the water, being a real master of its forces. But woe to our lad on the banks of this river! Chills and fever came to the whole family and Alexander was a thin, spare, sickly boy. His health was constantly undermined by the ague, and consequently his early schooling was sadly neglected. He was ever religiously inclined and very conscientious. When but a small boy he would kneel down by a chair and pray, although family worship was unknown in his home. When eight years old his father sickened and seemed about to die. Alexander found a hiding place in the bushes and poured out his heart to God for his father's restoration to health. His sister, Emma, was also praying under another bush. Their prayers were answered and the father recovered. One time when he yielded to temptation and took a big lump of sugar from an old man and a cord from his boat, his conscience gave him no rest until he had confessed and made restitution.

When a child he was never idle and ever through life he was a great worker. As a boy he herded the cattle on the prairie, watched the burning coal pits and when he fell asleep on the watch he took his merited punishment from his father very gracefully, clinging so close to his father's knee with words of endearment, "Oh! nice papa—dear good papa"— that the force of the whip was lost. He was full of merry moods and youthful pranks so that his father said he would either make a clown or a preacher. Very resourceful too, was our young lad. One day the cattle had wandered far across the Kansas River. At last he succeeded in finding them but it was a long, long way to the bridge where they might cross. What should he do? He made his decision quickly. Driving the herd into the river, he caught hold of the tail of a big steer and rode safely over. What cared he for the wetting he got after such a good ride?

When he was fourteen years of age a momentous change came into the life of our young hero. His parents had for some time been talking about moving to a "better country." The drought and the grasshoppers destroyed the fruits of their labor until farming became a drudgery and a failure. They had been reading about a beautiful state on the Pacific Coast where there was never a complete failure of crops. If one kind of fruit or grain failed to yield, then there were always sure to be several others which would bring forth abundantly. Reports also reached them that the trees were so loaded down with delicious fruit, prunes, peaches, pears and apples that many times this fruit would hang on the trees ungathered or waste on the ground in decay. Now Alexander was very fond of fruit, especially of apples and never in his life had he been privileged to eat all he wanted of them. He said, "There will be no apples go to waste when I get there, for I can eat them all."

Day after day they read the glowing accounts in the papers and conversed with the enthusiastic immigrants who passed through in their prairie schooners on their way to this wonderful land. The father said at last, "We must sell out and go to Oregon." Accordingly hand-bills were printed and scattered broadcast advertising the farm, the stock, the household furniture for sale. In later years interested audiences have listened many times to the preacher as he would give an account of this great auction sale in his sermon from the text, "Except a man forsake all he hath, he can not be my disciple." He described the auctioneer selling off the old plow that had caused him so much hard labor and the other farming implements. He chuckled and rejoiced to see them go. Now he would not have to work in the fields so wearily all day. And the furniture, too—what did he care? To be sure, his dear little mother buried her face in her apron and wept bitterly when they bid off the cherished cradle in which she had rocked all her babies. But there was one object that was very dear to Alexander, and when they led his pet horse out on the block and called for the highest bidder, he felt his heart strings begin to snap. "Why, they surely will not sell my beautiful Prince, with the glossy mane, arched neck and white star in the forehead. Did not all the people in the country know that Prince was the fleetest of foot—not a horse could pass him on the prairie. Should he never mount him again and ride like the wind in his exultant glee?" He felt he would surely die if he had to part with his loved steed. While these thoughts were passing through his boyish mind, the auctioneer was crying out the fine quality of the horse, and calling for bids until at last the boy heard him say, "How much do I hear?" "Going, going, gone." And the horse was led away by the fortunate bidder. Alexander rushed to a convenient hiding place and sobbed in an abandonment of grief. When he would make the application in his sermons on giving up all for God, he would show how easily we yield up the things we care but little about but the Holy Spirit calls for the more and more valuable to be given in our consecration until finally we reach the cradle in which all of our fondest hopes and highest ambitions have been rocked—even this must go. At last the dearest object is called for and then we feel it is crucifixion indeed to lay our pet idol on the altar.

When everything had been sold, and all the arrangements were made, Alexander started with his parents and several of his brothers and sisters on their long journey toward the setting sun. There was no railroad yet laid through to Oregon and their route was to San Francisco by rail and then to Portland by boat. He had long heard of the delicious pound pears that grew in Oregon, and while in San Francisco, before he embarked on the steamer, he eagerly ate one of those, although he found it hard and tasteless, having been picked long before it had ripened. No sooner had the ship set sail on the ocean than he had his first attack of mal de mer which continued throughout the trip and made him think that all of his trouble was caused by eating that noted pear. For several years afterward he could not endure the taste of the finest Bonny Jersey or Bartlett pear because of his unfortunate experience with seasickness.

His parents settled in Multnomah county, Oregon, near Gresham. Here he helped to hew out a home in the forest and assisted his parents financially by making shingles. Whatever he did he always wished to excel. If he made a shingle he felt he must produce the best shingle on the market. And true it was, he could always get a better price for his bunch of shingles that were marked with his special brand, than others who made an inferior article could. Farther on we will let him tell in his own language how he came to be known as the champion potato digger of Multnomah county; also of his conversion and call to the ministry. Even then God was watching over him and would soon show him that he had something greater, deeper, higher, than digging potatoes or making a superior shingle.

CHAPTER II*

There is a spot to me more dear
   Than native vale or mountain,
A spot for which affection's tear
   Springs grateful from its fountain.
'Tis not where kindred souls abound,
   Though that were almost heaven,
But where I first my Savior found
   And felt my sins forgiven.
                          —*William Hunter.*

The sacredness of a spot is always associated with an event, a friend, or with something that has left its impress indelibly fixed upon the heart. The most sacred memories do not cluster around the palace, nor are they enshrined with the rich or the titled of earth. The fond memories of Home, Sweet Home, will always be fragrant, whether that sacred spot be a palace magnificent, or a lowly cottage with a vine growing over the door, and the homely hollyhock blossoming in the fence corner. As soon as that magic word "home" is spoken, the heart leaps like a fountain, and thrills with ecstatic joy. There comes to the mind fond memories of a mother's gentle touch, of a father's wise counsel, of the association of brother or sister, within this loved spot.

There is, however, a place that to every child of

---

*The greater portion of the second, third and fourth chapters was written by Mr. Beers himself before he was taken ill.

God is more sacred and suggestive than that of home. It is that consecrated and hallowed spot where in humiliation, confession and forsaking of sins, the heart for the first time reaches up, through the promise to a divine Savior, and cries, Abba, Father.

There is absolutely no joy comparable to that that fills the heart of a child of God. His peace flows like a river, and his righteousness becomes like waves of the mighty ocean. The scripture in beautiful poetic language describes it thus:

"And ye shall go forth with joy, and be led forth with peace. The mountains and the hills shall break forth before you into singing, and all the trees of the field shall clap their hands."

To the mere professor of religion this language is not significant, but to the child of God, who knows the "joyful sound," it is most expressive. He fully knows what it is to have the peace that passeth understanding, and the joy unspeakable and full of glory.

This was my happy experience when on the 18th day of November, 1881, the Lord for Christ's sake pardoned all my sins. As I left the little schoolhouse, in which the meeting was held, and crossed the quaint old bridge and started to my father's rustic home in Oregon, it seemed to me that all nature rejoiced, the stars shown with a new lustre, and the moon seemed to join with me and all nature in a paean of victory. I was so happy in my new-found joy that I fully believed that all I would have to do in order to get others to embrace Christ was to simply tell them of the treasure that was mine. Great was my surprise when on telling my own father the good news, to find that he listened to it with comparative indifference. Still more astonished was I to find that my dear relatives were not only unwilling to listen, but some of them regarded even with suspicion the mighty work that had been wrought in my unworthy heart. It seemed to me that my neighbors would be delighted to hear my story of the transforming power of the gospel, when lo! to my astonishment I found them to be cold and unsympathetic, and some of them even hostile to the marvelous truth I was advocating. Nicodemus is not alone in inquiring concerning the mystery of the new birth. Thousands of others are constantly saying, "How can these things be?"

It is exceedingly doubtful as to whether any one is truly converted without the cooperation and faith of some one else. God has ordained that men shall be saved through the preaching of the gospel; He has also ordained that man, not angels, shall be heralds of the divine message of salvation through faith. He has farther decreed that the men who preach the gospel of His Son shall be supported by His followers. He has never been without a witness, and has always had those who were only too willing to pray and sacrifice that this gospel may be preached to others. There were a number living in our neighborhood who had been holding on to God in prayer for years for a mighty outpouring of the Spirit. Mrs. Cathey, long since gone to her reward, and her devoted husband, had been making earnest intercession for a revival of pure and undefiled religion. An old gentleman by the name of Rugg had spent a number of years in faithful prayer, that God might visit the new neighborhood. Father Rugg believed that in order to have his prayer answered he must work as well as pray, and sacrifice with the intercession. He believed that faith without works was dead, and that prayer without a corresponding effort was sheer mockery. He heard of the successful evangelistic labors of the preachers, Frank and Henry Ashcraft, then laboring in California. He communicated with them to ascertain whether they would come to Oregon and begin a revival out in the wilderness in this new country. On learning that they would come, he immediately set out to raise money to pay their expenses. There were few Christians to respond to the appeal, and yet he felt that these men of God must be brought. He owned two pairs of very fine oxen, that he had purchased to use in clearing his wilderness land. These oxen represented practically all the personal property Father Rugg possessed. He found where he could raise a sufficient amount of money by placing a chattel mortgage on his oxen. This he did without hesitation or delay, and the evangelists came. God honored Father Rugg's faith and sacrifice, and the meetings were successful from the beginning.

The first meeting was held in the Union schoolhouse, in Clackamas county, about eight miles from where we lived. The report of the marvelous conversions spread like wildfire throughout the country. After they had closed the first meeting in the Union schoolhouse, they were invited to come to Powell's Valley and hold another meeting. This was my home, and I went out through sheer curiosity to hear them preach.   I was deeply impressed under the serious preaching the first night I was there.   The next day I went to my little shingle shed on the hillside, and worked just as I had done months before.   I continued to attend the meetings, and my conviction became more intense. The schoolhouse was lighted by ordinary kerosene lamps.   I think there were about six of them that hung from the walls on the side, and one in front, over the stand occupied by the evangelists.   So intense was my conviction that it seemed to me that every one of those old kerosene lamps literally shown with the brilliancy of a great arc light, and every reflected ray seemed to focalize in my heart.   It did not seem to be a very lofty flight of the imagination for me to believe that everybody in the schoolhouse knew that the preacher was aiming his shafts of truth directly at me.   It actually seemed at times that somebody had been informing on me, and that the preacher looked right at me and discerned my heart throbs. After listening the fifth night, and spending the remainder of the night in great agony of soul, I went to my shingle shed, but did not do a very large day's work.   I felt that I must yield myself without reserve to Jesus Christ, or be eternally lost. I then and there most solemnly promised God that if He would spare my life to get to the revival service that night, that I would seek Him.   I was only too glad when night came, and went to the schoolhouse early.   I found about fifteen young fellows, with whom I was acquainted, assembled at the entrance to the school-house.   They were speaking derisively concerning the meetings and the evangelists.   I remember saying to them, "Boys, I do not know whether these men are sincere men or not; they are strangers in our neighborhood and I am not acquainted with them. I have had no opportunity of finding out their past lives, but whether they are right or not, I am sure that I am wrong and need salvation, and have promised Christ that I would seek Him with my whole heart tonight." Little did I think that others of the gay company were serious, but as soon as I declared my intention to become a Christian, at least five of them said, "I have been thinking of the same thing myself."

I do not remember the text that was preached from that night. I know that Rev. Frank Ashcraft preached the sermon, and I fully remember how the word of God pierced my heart as a sword. I thought the sermon was altogether too long, and hoped for the time to come when the invitation would be given for seekers to come forward. I stood at the entrance of the door, leaning against the jamb, with my hat in hand. The house was so crowded that night I could not get a seat. Father Rugg, Mr. and Mrs. W. G. Cathey, David Cathey and others went out into the congregation to invite sinners forward. I was very much afraid that they would come to me. I thought if I was solicited to go, my outside friends would think that I was weak and did not go on my own initiative. I desired to go voluntarily, and I wanted everybody and the devil himself to understand that I was not coerced. I made for the altar with all possible haste; I had to literally elbow the crowd back and push them aside, in order to get through. God helped me, and I soon found myself kneeling for the first time at a penitent form. This meant much to me, as I had regarded those who had knelt there as being weak-minded. To me it had always meant to abandon my manhood, and forsake my self-respect to thus humiliate myself. All these feelings, however, vanished as by magic under the tremendous excoriating conviction of the Spirit. It was a privilege to kneel at a Methodist altar, and if necessary before an assembled universe, if I could be saved from the stingings of a guilty conscience.

One thing I shall be thankful for until my dying day. I was not led into confusion by an army of doctors, each one suggesting something different that I must do in order to be saved. I am sure that earnest seekers become greatly confused in listening to the many suggestions by the would-be helpers. I had no sooner knelt at the penitent form until I was made divinely conscious that my sins were all taken away and that I was a child of God. I felt the peace of God steal into my heart, and was conscious that the Holy Spirit did bear witness with my spirit that I was a child of God. Frank Cathey, later a district elder in the Free Methodist Church, had been converted a few nights before. He was very anxious to help me through and knelt by my side, and commenced telling me how to yield to Christ. I looked up into his face and said, "Frank, I've done all that and the Lord accepts me now." About this time the evangelist appeared on the scene, and looking down into my face with those expressive, penetrating eyes of his, said, "Young man, how are you getting along?" I replied triumphantly, "I know that Jesus Christ now pardons all my sins, and that I am

a child of God." Rev. Ashcraft was not slow in de-
tecting the seal of the Holy Spirit, and asked me if
I did not wish to testify. I arose and before that
great congregation told them how the Lord had pardoned all my sins. Somebody struck up that old
familiar hymn so dear to the heart of every new convert:

> "The Lord has pardoned all my sins,
>   I am condemned no more,
> I want to know the deeper things,
>   'Tis better on before."

For the first time in my life I knew what it was
to be conscious of the "joy of the Lord," that deep
peace and heavenly tranquillity overflowed the banks,
and my joy knew no bounds. It seemed that ropes
were dropped down from the skies, and that all the
bells of heaven were ringing, and that liquid ame-
thyst and pearl were filling my little cup to overflowing. I went home praising the Lord and testi-
fied to all with whom I came in contact. Many
were serious, others criticised, and others ridiculed,
but through His abounding grace I was able to keep
my testimony and walk in the light of His countenance.

I was in my twentieth year when this great
change was wrought. My life was completely transformed and my future course literally revolution-
ized. The world had become a new world to me and
I looked at everything from a different perspective.
Before this I had gotten my bearing from the standpoint of making and keeping money, and getting
along in the world in a worldly manner. I now
found myself on Mount Calvary, and from the foot

of the cross looked out upon the limitless possibilities of a life hid with Christ in God. The Lord has been pleased to give me numberless blessings from that day until this, and this transformation that has come into my life was owing very largely to that prayer of faith and marvelous sacrifice on the part of Father Rugg, and others who cooperated to bring about the condition that led to my salvation. This dear man of God has gone to his reward, but his works follow him.

A touching incident occurred shortly after Alexander's conversion. He had been very zealous in his spiritual life in the home, asking the blessing at the table and keeping up family worship faithfully. The mother and several of his brothers and sisters had yielded their hearts to Christ. The atmosphere of the home seemed electrified with the presence of the Spirit. Finally one of the brightest boys had been saved the night before and it looked to the father as though the entire family would be brought into the fold. He was staid and precise in his church worship and did not at all approve of the shouts of praise and notes of victory that were so commonly heard in these revival services which his loved ones were all enjoying. Very seriously he considered the matter, then calling Alexander to his side, he told him in a kind but emphatic manner that he must either stop praying in the family or leave home. He pointed out the sad fact that the whole family would soon be ruined if Alexander persisted in such religious zeal. It was a critical moment in the young man's life. He loved his home, he loved his parents most tenderly, but he loved his

Savior more than all—yea, more than life itself. He gathered his few belongings into an old oil-cloth satchel, kissed his mother, who was weeping, and his sisters good-by, and started down the road "sorrowful but rejoicing" that he was counted worthy to suffer for Christ. Under a grand old tree he knelt on a carpet of moss and poured out his heart to his heavenly Father. He repeated again and again,

> "Jesus, I my cross have taken,
> All to leave and follow Thee,
> Naked, poor, despised, forsaken,
> Thou from hence my all shalt be."

God revealed Himself in tender compassion and these words were given him,

> "Oh Jesus, Jesus, Jesus!
> My all sufficient friend;
> Come fold me to Thy bosom,
> E'en to my journey's end."

Just then he heard the voice of his younger brother calling, "Alex, come back, come back! Pa says for you to come back home and you can pray all you want to." Gladly he returned and found his father waiting at the gate for him. He made a humble apology and invited him into the house. Alexander said, "Father, do you mean to say that I can pray all I want to?" "Yes," replied his father. "Let us pray now," said Alexander and again implored God's blessing upon them all. How signally these prayers for his parents were answered later, we have previously related.

Rev. F. H. Horton, of southern California, writes peculiarly fitting words of the transforming grace of God in the life of this crude, imperfect, unshaped

preacher and educator yet to be. " 'From sinking
sand He lifted me, with tender hand He lifted me.'
Such is the experience and testimony of every saint
on earth who has been redeemed out of the hand of
the enemy. But the altitude to which we have been
lifted varies with individuals as do the summits of a
mountain range. When we think of Brother Beers
as the exceedingly uncultured country youth, just
converted to Jesus Christ, with the fires of a new
and holy ambition to *know,* to *be* and to *do* burning
in his soul; then view him in mature manhood, a
powerful preacher, an eminently successful educator, an efficient and tactful administrator, we are
morally sure that *something lifted him.*

"He always impressed me as preeminently *large
hearted.* There seemed to be no human need that
did not appeal to him. In season and out of season
was his time to work for souls. The high or seemingly inaccessible position of a man could never discourage him from an honest attempt to give him
the light of life. He carried a supernatural tact to
give a man the special truth that he needed.

"Nothing could betray him into the snare of returning evil for evil, or of making a martyr of himself for anything which he suffered. How it does
make one magnify the grace of God to contemplate
a life so unselfish, so devoted to the cause of Jesus,
so humble and self-denying, so swallowed up with a
great passion to meet the true end of life.

"I always admired Brother Beers as a great,
strong, efficient preacher and a noble Christian character. But there was more than admiration. I loved
him as a brother. There was a throb of heart union

between us that was unspeakably precious. How I did long and pray for his recovery, but when the Lord took him I felt so satisfied that His highest purpose was fulfilled that I could not wish it other- wise. Once more God had *lifted him* and all was well."

Mr. Beers was a man of very deep emotions. As the Spirit would be poured upon him, he would often laugh with holy joy. When a young convert he was frequently filled with holy laughter and his father took him to task for this lack of religious de- corum—it shocked his sense of propriety. The son had great respect for his father's judgment and thought perhaps he had been transgressing the laws of God, so he decided to search the Scriptures and see what the Word said. He began with Genesis, reading very carefully, and soon came to the ac- count of Sarah's laughter and the reason she gave the angel for such an unusual demonstration on her part, "God hath made me to laugh so that all that hear will laugh with me." Here was his license for yielding to his irrepressible joy. When he gave this reason for his laughing to his wise father, he was silenced completely. How could he question God's word? However, it was a very difficult matter for him to understand and he was still greatly troubled over a circumstance that occurred in the family. They were all seated around a large table and Alex- ander asked a blessing on the food in readiness for them. The Spirit was poured upon his soul, the well of joy in his heart overflowed, and he laughed im- moderately, his father thought, but what was more alarming, Alexander's brother at the other end of the table caught the "fire" and laughed with him. The father took this breach of etiquette very seriously. He told several of his neighbors he feared Alexander was losing his mind, for the other morning he laughed right out at the table and there was nothing at all to laugh at—no joke—no one had said a funny thing, and furthermore he had set his brother laughing too.

Rev. August Youngren, a former graduate, tells this incident of Mr. Beers: For several months while a student at the seminary, he had charge of a Swedish mission in Seattle, The Strangers' Rest, and always preached there in the Swedish language. One evening Mr. Beers came in and sat on the front seat, while Mr. Youngren was speaking from the text, "Which hope we have as an anchor of the soul, both sure and steadfast, and which entereth into that within the veil." Mr. Youngren had great liberty in presenting this truth, and although Mr. Beers was unable to understand a word of the sermon, he did know the "joyful sound," he recognized the Holy Spirit and was graciously blessed. He laughed and shouted until the whole audience felt the power and were blessed with him. Apropos to this subject we quote from a letter to his wife, written at Alberta church, Portland, dated July 14, 1919, "God helped me to preach and then blessed me nearly to death after I sat down. I had to laugh and cry for joy. Brother Beare got blessed and laughed and cried with me."

We would have no one think, however, that Mr. Beers was immune from sensation of grief—that he never drank from the cup of suffering. His was a profound nature. Whenever the billows of sorrow swept over him, he was carried down into the very depths of woe; when fierce temptations assailed him, it seemed as if legions upon legions of evil spirits made a combined assault upon the citadel of his soul. Speaking of his own emotions, he said once, "The higher the peaks of joy I ascend, the deeper the abyss of sorrow I am compelled to know." A friend who knew him intimately says of him, "Though heart-broken often, he smiled in the face of God and drank deep of the divine spirit. He was a man, God's man. We shall not soon see his like again."

CHAPTER III

HIS CALL TO THE MINISTRY, AND FIRST EFFORTS

"Ours is a universe where progress is secured in the fruits and grains through chemical reactions. Steel is iron plus fire; soil is rock plus fire billow and icy plow; statues are marble plus chisel and hammer strokes; linen is flax plus the bath that racks, the club that flails, the comb that separates, the acid that bleaches.

"Manhood is birth-gift plus struggles, temptation, wrestling and refusals to go downward and determination to climb upward. The saint is a man who has been carried off the field on his shield, victorious over inbred sin and outside temptation. Men who drift are men who drown."—*Newell Dwight Hillis*.

That every person has a specific call to some definite line of work, I have no doubt. The call is not confined to the gifted, the ten-talent persons; but those that have but five, two or one, are called by our kind heavenly Father to work in His vineyard. The equalization of the labor is found in the statement: "Every man according to his several ability." God would not create an inanimate world and send it speeding on its way with a direct commission and deny the humblest person made in His image a clear call to a specific field of labor.

Shortly after my conversion a great desire came over me for the salvation of the unsaved. I found myself attending prayer meetings, protracted meetings, camp meetings and other forms of religious worship and was constantly urging all with whom I came in contact to be reconciled to God. I continued my work, however, in the shingle business, and found more pleasure in manual labor than I had ever realized before. The days and weeks seemed to literally kaleidoscope into each other and the year passed by with lightning rapidity. The second month after my conversion I stayed with an agnostic or an infidel by the name of Lew Allan. He was a man who had read extensively and was possessed with quite a philosophical turn of mind. He was thoroughly familiar with the sophistries of reasoning and would often puzzle me with many perplexing problems. One thing always served as a timely aid to my embarrassment; this was my personal religious experience. Again and again when I was cornered and would not know how to reply to the subtle line of reasoning, I could always fall back on my experience. This always put my adversary to silence for the time being, and left him nothing to say.

Before my conversion I had attended a few balls. I became disgusted with the dance and had given it up entirely a number of months before I became a Christian. A night or two after I found Christ, I passed a ball room and through the open door could see the young people making merry in the giddy waltz. I found in my soul a feeling of utter disgust, and it was a marvel to me that I had ever been so foolish as to take any part whatsoever in such a performance.

The infidel with whom I stayed planned to give a ball to the young people of the community. I be-

lieved this to be a snare set for my feet and was not
a little anxious concerning what I would do on that
night. I was fully convinced as to what I would
not do, for I was determined to have nothing to do
with it. His home was in the dense forest, with a
little surrounding neighborhood. My own home was
a number of miles away and it would have been impracticable for me to have made my way through
the thick forest and heavy underbrush to spend the
night.

One night I had a very peculiar dream. I thought
that the ball was given and that the young people
of the local community had all gathered, attired in
their richest clothing. The violinist, whom I had
known for years, was present with his favorite instrument. The giddy dance was soon on, and I
found myself sitting in a corner of the room engaged
in meditation and prayer. Suddenly a burst of the
richest splendor came from the East, and lo! every
mountain peak and tree-top and all the heavens
were illuminated with divine glory. I looked
quickly, and to my rapture, saw the Son of God,
coming in the clouds of heaven with thousands and
ten thousands of angels with Him. I saw the violinist, the dancing master, my infidel friend, and
all the merry dancers prostrate on their faces crying for mercy. So glad was I to see my Savior, that
I shouted aloud in my sleep; and the infidel was
awakened by my shouting and asked what was the
matter with me. I frankly related my dream and
it evidently took hold on him. The much-talked-of
ball never came off, and I have always believed that
my dream had everything to do with stopping it.

I read my Bible constantly, and prayed much during the day, even while engaged in my work. The more I became engrossed in the study of the Word and the more earnestly I gave myself up to prayer, did the conviction come over me that God had called me into the work of the gospel ministry. For days and weeks I would not even admit my call to myself, much less did I inform any one concerning my feelings. I continued to study my Bible and attended all the prayer meetings held in the vicinity. Indeed I soon found myself arranging for prayer meetings on my own initiative. These were well attended; and frequently souls were born into the kingdom of God.

Rev. Frank Ashcraft organized a Holiness Band, and I was elected leader. If I remember correctly, there were about forty young people who were associated in this religious work. I found myself greatly interested in the spiritual welfare of every member of the band. I had been very clearly led into the glorious experience of entire sanctification, and longed to see every member of that little band enjoying a like experience. I think the greater number at one time really experienced the blessing of holiness; some of them have become very efficient workers in the cause of Christ. Among them I would name Rev. D. M. Cathey, who for two years was pastor of the First Free Methodist Church of Portland, Oregon (Mr. Beers chose Rev. D. M. Cathey to officiate at his funeral) ; Rev. F. W. Cathey, an ordained minister, and for a number of years traveling elder in the different conferences; and Rev. A. Anderberg, who became a strong minister in the Baptist Church.

The conviction that I should give myself entirely to the work of the ministry became very intense. I was so impressed with it one day, as I sat in my shingle shed, shaving the shingles with an old-fashioned drawing knife, that I dropped the knife and turned around on my seat and said audibly, "Oh, Lord, must I give myself up to the preaching of the gospel?" To me the work of the ministry was the last thing that I could ever consent to do. I was of a very independent make-up and was conscious of the fact that I had ability to make money and did not wish to be dependent upon any one. The thought of receiving money in an ordinary collection, and being supported by the people was unbearable. I promised the Lord faithfully if He would only excuse me from doing the work myself that I would do all within my power to make money and help others. I consecrated to give a large per cent of all of my net income for the support of the work. The Lord was not satisfied with these promises, but impressed the scripture upon me, "For the gifts and callings of God are without repentance." I felt that He had called me to His work and I could not even retain the precious experience that He had given me unless I would consecrate my life to the gospel ministry.

I carried the responsibility of the solemn call so long in my own heart that I felt I must confide my convictions to some one. My own precious little mother was converted shortly after I was brought to Christ, and she was to me a great help in every way. I took a trip home for the express purpose of telling mother of my call. I started very early in the morning and reached my father's house between ten and eleven in the morning. Mother was sitting in the front room sewing and gave me the usual warm welcome on my home-coming. I visited with her for a little while and then withdrew from the room and went upstairs into the bedroom that I occupied while I was home. Mother was impressed that there was something of a serious nature on my mind and in a short time stole up to my room and sat down quietly on the foot of the bed. She soon asked me as to what was the matter with me and if there was not something on my mind that was giving me trouble. I broke down and cried like a little child and told her, that strange as it might appear to her, I felt called to the work of the ministry. She told me that she had been impressed with the strange conviction and encouraged me with the thought that God would help me. God only knows how much I owe to my mother's encouragement at this critical juncture of my life.

I felt greatly relieved and returned to my shingle-making with much joy. I had really settled the matter and had the blessing that comes with obedience promised. I told the Lord that I would hold myself in readiness to respond to the first providential opening for holding meetings. Little did I think that an opening would soon present itself. The following week the same post brought me two letters—one asking me to hold a meeting at Hillsborough in Yamhill county, and the other asking me to come to Mountain Home, a rural district in Clackamas county. My friend, Frank Cathey, was called about the same time, and we decided to go together. I was illiterate and did not wish to go to Hillsborough on account of a more highly educated class of people living there. I decided to accept the invitation to hold the meeting at Mountain Home, and Frank made his plans to assist me in this meeting.

Never will I forget this trip, nor the first meeting we held. Rev. T. S. LaDue lived over at Sunnyside, just across the border in Clackamas county, where he had organized a church. In the meantime, I had become a member of the Free Methodist Church, Brother LaDue having received me in full connection and the quarterly conference having voted me an exhorter's license the same day. We decided that we would go as far as Rev. Mr. LaDue's and stay over Thursday night and attend the prayer meeting. It was about twenty-seven miles from our home to the place where the meeting was to be held. We made the trip on horseback. A very peculiar temptation assailed me when I left home to go to the meeting. I was made to feel absolutely foolish and greatly embarrassed to think that I had permitted myself to be scheduled for revival services; I had great hopes, however, that I would gather special inspiration at the Thursday night meeting, and would be encouraged for the work. In this I was greatly disappointed, for there was no inspiration in it for me. Mrs. LaDue was called "the fog splitter." I banked very much on the inspiration I would gather from her prayers at the meeting. She seemed to have, however, no liberty and I went to bed that night with a heavy heart. I entertained the hope that the clouds would break and that victory would come around the family altar the next morning. We

all prayed at family prayers, but with no more results than the night before. The heavens above
were as brass and apparently there was no response
to our earnest petitions.

The weather had grown quite cold during the
night, and the ground had frozen. We saddled our
horses and started out for our destination. Our
horses were not shod and as they crippled along over
the frozen road, it seemed that Satan walked by our
side and whispered, "Fools, fools, fools." I was
greatly distressed at the thought of holding a meeting that night, and in my heart hoped that my letter had not reached its destination and that no appointment had been announced for us. Frank was
as sorely tempted as I was and was eager to go back.

On arriving within about three miles of Horse
Heaven, where the meeting was to be held, I stopped
to inquire at a farm house as to whether they knew
anything about the meeting or not. I was much surprised when the lady informed me that two very
green and awkward young men were expected to
hold services and that the entire neighborhood was
greatly amused and expected to turn out *en masse*
to be entertained. She also informed me that a number of the boys had carried the news to an adjoin-
ing neighborhood and that they were expecting a
number of wagons loaded with people to be present
on the first night of the meeting. When she told
me this, the Lord marvelously blessed me with a
feeling of holy courage and a determination to do
the best I could. I returned to the road and meeting Frank, told him of the announcement and of
the general interest. I also told him of the great

blessing the Lord had given me and that I felt myself quite ready for any emergency. He at once replied that he was very glad and that inasmuch as
he had not received such a blessing himself, he
thought it was the will of the Lord that I should
preach the first sermon. I was certainly willing, if
not ready, "to preach, pray or die" at that time.

We went to the schoolhouse a little early and
found a large crowd awaiting us. The building was
literally jammed and a number stood on the outside.
I was not a little puzzled as to what text to use. I
had listened to Rev. Frank Ashcraft preach, and
was captivated by his mannerism and the trenchant
way in which he drove home the great truths of the
Bible. I might as well be frank and confess fully
what I did that night. I had heard Rev. Ashcraft
preach from the text, "If we confess our sins, He is
faithful and just to forgive us our sins." The sermon had made such an impression on my mind, that
I had the outline clearly defined. I decided to use
the same text and follow the outline that he had
used. I did take the text, but this was about as far
as I could go. On looking at the sea of faces before
me, I became greatly embarrassed and had a serious
lapse of memory which caused me to forget every
outline I had in my mind. I spoke as best I could
for a short time, but in a very incoherent manner.
I did not feel nearly so much like preaching as I did
an hour before. In fact, I would have been very
glad for an opening to beat an honorable retreat.
The wall of the schoolhouse was behind me, my congregation in front and all around, and retreat was
impossible. In my embarrassment, I pulled the pa-

pers from the table, and dropped a number of books on the floor. It was a most merciful providence, however, that my embarrassment awakened a sympathetic feeling in the congregation. I was made conscious of the fact that there was no intention on the part of the audience to deride me or to take advantage of the embarrassing position I was placed in. Rev. Ashcraft was wont to say in a most emphatic manner, "Sinning is a business, and if you ever get religion, you must quit the business, lock up the shop and throw away the key." How glad I was to remember this; and I looked squarely at my audience and said: "I want to tell you most seriously that 'sinning is a business, and if you ever get religion, you must quit the business, lock up the shop and throw away the key.'" Not being able to say anything else, I repeated this statement the third time, very much to the amusement of Mr. Cathey, and concluded by giving my own personal testimony. I told the congregation that I had lived in sin for twenty years, and found Satan to be a hard task-master. I related how wonderfully the Lord Jesus Christ had saved me. I assured them that since my conversion I had joy and peace that the world knew not of. I closed by urging all in the congregation to submit themselves to Jesus Christ without delay. Mr. Jim Heckard, one of the brightest young men in the community and the teacher of the school in that place, stepped boldly to the front and kneeling at the penitent form, gave himself fully to Christ. His conversion made a deep impression on the entire community. I must confess that I was surprised, but greatly pleased to have this un-

mistakable seal to my humble ministry the first
night of the service. I was not unlike the good Pres-
byterian deacon who thanked the Lord for the un-
expected answer to his prayers.

I attempted to preach again the next night and
had some liberty. On the third night Mr. Cathey
preached and had special help from the beginning.
The meeting continued for about two weeks, Mr.
Cathey doing most of the preaching, and I was always on hand with a testimony or exhortation. A
goodly number were brought to Christ, and have
served Him faithfully all these years.

But a short time ago I met Mr. Heckard in Seattle. He was still faithful in the service of the Lord
and had become a very prominent Sunday-school
worker. His son, a little boy of ten years of age,
came forward and was thoroughly converted in one
of our meetings.

From Mountain Home we went to other places as
the way opened. At times we had great opposition,
but the Lord stood by and gave courage. At one
place the rowdies tried to break up the meeting,
and would throw clubs at us as we went home. I
think at times that we were in great danger. As I
left the tent one night, a rowdy followed me and
struck me a terrific blow on the top of the head with
a club and then disappeared into the darkness. I
was knocked to the ground and bled very profusely.
I have a scar from that blow today and cherish it as
a badge of honor that I received from doing the
King's business. We literally gloried in tribulation
and with a victorious shout pressed on in the face of
every obstacle.

In looking back over the lapse of twenty-eight years since I made my first attempt, I am deeply impressed that the courage I received for my life's work came very largely in answer to my mother's prayer. She always held me up before a throne of grace and encouraged me to be true. A number of years ago she was called to her eternal reward, but again and again, as I have engaged in the conflict, have I been encouraged with the pressure of my mother's consecrated hand upon my head, and I have been inspired by her faith and courage. If the Lord has helped me in any way to bring souls to Him, my precious mother will have a large part and lot in the rewards that are to be given by and by.

I will simply say in closing this chapter that while in the beginning the preaching of the gospel seemed to be the greatest cross, it soon became my crowning joy. I have no greater delight than when the Holy Spirit catches me up on some mountain peak of inspiration and helps me to declare the glorious truths of my risen Savior.

*   *   *   *   *

Mr. Beers has related the following incident many times which occurred before he entered school at Chesbrough:

The Father Rugg, who mortgaged his oxen to get funds to send for Frank and Henry Ashcraft to hold the meeting in which he was converted, had two sons. One was gloriously converted during the revival services, but the other was filled with unbelief and seemed to be an infidel. The Christian boy soon sickened and was nearing the hour of his death. He had a terrible conflict with the powers of darkness and was in great agony, both in body and mind. So great were his sufferings that his own mother could not stay in the room. The infidel brother said sneeringly, "I can not believe a loving heavenly Father would let His child suffer like that. Unless my brother has an easy death, I can never believe there is a God." The parents were holding on in prayer for the dying boy. Soon wonderful victory was given to him. He shouted aloud the praises of God and his countenance was illuminated with a supernatural glory that seemed to light up the entire room. The infidel was now convinced and bowed in humble penitence as the pure spirit of his brother took its flight, while the dear mother danced for joy.

Mr. Beers had been away holding meetings, but heard of this death and funeral. He literally ran about twelve miles, but was not in time for the funeral. He reached the cemetery just as the body was being lowered into the grave. Father Rugg stood praising God with streaming eyes for saving his infidel son even at such a cost.

On reading over Mr. Beers' manuscript, the author finds he has failed to give an account of his marvelous healing of tuberculosis, which should be inserted here.

While laboring in revival meetings, he had contracted a severe cold which soon developed into serious lung difficulty. When the doctors examined him they said that one lung was already gone and the other was badly affected. His voice was so weak he could scarcely speak above a whisper, and it seemed that his days were numbered. One evening he had attended a service in East Portland, in company with Frank Cathey, but had not been able to take any part. After the service was over they went to the home of Eugene Grantham to stop over night. On the way he told Frank that he thought that was his last service and he felt he was going home to die. After they reached the house, Mr. Grantham said he felt God wanted to heal Mr. Beers and he wished to anoint him. The three knelt down by a chair and Mr. Grantham prayed a short, simple prayer of faith, anointing him with oil in the name of the Lord. After he retired, Mr. Beers felt the cooling, healing power of God until he fell asleep. When he awoke in the morning it was at a late hour. The sunlight was flooding the room, but the shekinah of glory shone more brightly in his soul than any earthly light. Leaping to his feet he shouted aloud the praises of the Lord in a full, clear voice. All the soreness was gone from his chest and in its place was perfect soundness. He was perfectly healed. That day he visited the doctor's office in Portland and asked for a test examination. To the surprise of the doctor, both lungs were as sound as though they had never been diseased. He was greatly astonished at the speedy and wonderful change. Mr. Beers gave God all the glory and no one could ever gainsay his testimony.

Rev. Frank Cathey, who was a co-laborer with Mr. Beers in this first evangelistic campaign, adds his account of the meetings:

The attendance at these meetings was largely of young people. The older folks said, "We've been church members for years, and do you think we are going to let these boys tell us we have no religion?"

So they remained at home, but drove five or six miles to attend our next meeting.

The next meeting was some five or six miles from there in the Highland Baptist Church. This was a remarkable meeting. It was a strong infidel community, but the Lord came in great power. The altar was full of seekers, but we did not seem to be able to pray them through. An elderly Evangelical minister came along and we asked him to preach. He preached on faith and it seemed to be just the thing to break the spell, and the seekers broke through into victory. We were staying with a Mr. Farlo. He had recently been sanctified and was full of joy. One of the infidels in the neighborhood was greatly enraged because the Lord was getting hold of some of his family. One of his daughters sat in the meeting and wept like a child. He came to Mr. Farlo's home early one morning and began to curse us all. He sat on his horse just outside the fence, and Mr. Farlo was in the yard—we were still in bed. When we heard him raving, we jumped out of bed and got on our knees and prayed for Mr. Farlo. In a few moments Mr. Farlo was praying for the man, and then he began to shout while the man cursed. We dressed, went down and out in the yard to wash. He called us every mean name he could think of. We felt sweet as heaven. We were glad to be counted worthy to suffer for our Master. Within a year the judgments of God were visited on that home. He died a horrible death and the daughter, who was so moved but hardened her heart, disgraced the home.

Later we held a meeting at the Harmony school-

house. But it was not all harmony. It was largely
a Catholic neighborhood, and they greatly disturbed
the meetings. But in spite of it all, some were
clearly saved and sanctified, some of whom have
gone to heaven. One evening Mr. Beers was talking
with a young man who replied, "The Lord don't
have anything to do with me." Mr. Beers remarked,
"I believe it. I think the devil has full control of
you." Then he wanted to fight.

We held the next meeting at Springwater, or
"Horse Heaven." It was during this meeting I became so troubled with a pain under my shoulder
blade, I could not preach. We were in the habit of
calling and praying with the people during the day.
We started out, I slipped off in the bushes and had
a time of secret prayer. I prayed for the Lord to
heal me. Then I got so interested in others I forgot
all about myself, and after a while as we walked
along I noticed my pain was all gone. I praised the
Lord and was able to take my place in the meetings
the rest of the time. At this place, Horse Heaven,
the correspondent for the Oregon City paper sent
in a lengthy notice of the meetings, in which he told
how we said if any would come forward to the sanctification bench, the Lord would sanctify them and
take the mad all out of them. The paper stated it
was thought we were Mormons in disguise, for we
preached as near the Mormon doctrine as we dared
to out of a Mormon country. We took it all as persecution for Christ's sake and shouted the victory.
Souls were saved in every meeting. We held quite
a remarkable meeting west of Portland. We began
this meeting in a Baptist Church near the Schultz

neighborhood. When the services had been going on a few nights, Mr. Beers spoke on Romans, sixth chapter. He told the people that the baptism here did not mean water baptism, but the baptism of the Holy Ghost which destroyed the "old man." The preacher informed us he would not allow any such preaching in his church, and so closed the doors against us. There was a Methodist Church about three or four miles distant at Cedar Mills. The trustees invited us to hold our services there. So we went over to the Methodist Church. When the meeting had run for nearly a week and the Spirit was moving on the people, one of the trustees informed us that he had talked with the pastor, who lived at Hillsborough, and he thought we better see him before we went any farther with the meetings. We spoke of it publicly and remarked that as we were invited by the trustees we did not consider it our place to look up the pastor and beg to continue the meeting. So we announced the meetings closed. An unsaved lady arose and said, "It will not do to close these meetings now. There is a schoolhouse a mile from here, deeded to the use of religious services, and I move we continue the meetings in the schoolhouse." It was put to vote and almost unanimously decided. We held meeting the next night in the schoolhouse. The meetings ran in power for some two weeks or more. It was here that "Mother Campbell," the hub and backbone of the Salvation Army in Portland, Oregon, years afterward, was reclaimed and sanctified. The lady who moved that the meetings be held in the schoolhouse was saved, with many others. During this meeting, one evening the Spirit was poured out in such a remarkable manner that nearly every sinner jumped up and ran out of the house. One by one they returned. When asked why they ran out, they said they did not know.

We were invited to hold a three days' meeting at the May's church. We borrowed Rev. T. S. LaDue's road cart, heavy enough for a horse, and able to carry the family, then we borrowed a pony. He was not only small, but balky. It was muddy and the roads were slippery. Mr. Beers was the driver. We used a hazel stick for a buggy whip. We had just crossed a bridge covered with puncheons, logs split in the center with the split side up. There was no railing on the bridge. We got well up the hill on the other side when, lo! the pony stopped, then the cart pulled on him and he started down the hill after the cart, tail first. I leaped to safety before the cart struck the bridge. One wheel missed the bridge. But Mr. Beers so vigorously applied the hazel that Billy started and ran up the hill. We found that if we held the cart when he stopped on the hill till he rested, he would start up again, so I set my foot out against a spoke in the wheel and held it, but the wheel was muddy and slick and my foot slipped through between the spokes and back we went, my leg through the wheel. I yelled and we both caught the wheels with our hands, until I extricated myself. We spent the night at Mr. MacKenzie's, a fine Christian family. In the morning we started on. We soon found ourselves in the midst of a large mudhole full of water, and Billy stopped. We let him rest and then urged him to proceed. But to no avail. He had become established. Neither kind words nor the use of the hazel could move him. All we could do was for one of us to wade out, take him by the bit and lead him out. We were soon on our way, happy as two young evangelists, full of religion, could be. All went well until we came to a mill pond. The floor of the bridge was of lumber, but no railing around the edge. In the middle of the pond Billy thought it unsafe to go ahead and began to back. We leaped from the cart and kept pulling the cart around to keep him from backing off into the pond, until one of us could get him by the head. We had to lead him across the bridge and up a long hill. When we reached the top of the hill we got in the cart and started on. There were stumps and logs along the road. The wheel hit a low stump, then a higher one, and over the cart went in a mud-hole. We cleared the mud-hole, being young and active, but the satchel and laprobe, etc., went into the mud. We righted the cart, shook off the mud from our things, and shouted the victory. We reached the place of meeting in time for the evening service. It was a Southern Methodist Church. The pastor wore a stove pipe hat, smoked a big pipe, and carried a whip cane. We unmercifully scored such preachers and he was present to hear it. The pastor preached Sunday morning, on the prodigal's return. He represented it as illustrating the coming of a sinner to God. Mr. Beers exhorted. He said he did not think it meant that at all, but the return of a backslider. We had a big meeting, a hallelujah time, souls prayed through and we had salvation.

After the meeting we returned home, feeling we

had had a glorious time. We prayed, and shouted, and sang, and preached, and souls broke down and found God and were sanctified. More than one night we waked the people up where we were entertained, praying and preaching in our sleep. One of us would pray or preach and the other would say, Amen.

CHAPTER IV

ENTERS SCHOOL AT CHESBROUGH SEMINARY

"Build thee more stately mansions, O my soul!
As the swift seasons roll,
Leave thy low-vaulted past,
Let each new temple nobler than the last
Shut thee from heaven with a dome more vast;
  Till thou at length art free!
Leaving thine outgrown shell by
  Life's unresting sea."   —*Oliver Wendell Holmes.*

In June, 1885, the Oregon and Washington Conference of the Free Methodist Church was organized at Beaverton. This is a small town in Yamhill county, about eight miles west of Portland. The conference was organized in connection with the annual camp meeting held in a grove owned by Mr. Hocken. The meeting was a very good one from the beginning, and among others who were led out into a very clear experience of holiness was Mr. Hocken himself. He was a member of the Methodist Episcopal Church, and at once identified himself with the Free Methodists. From that time he was a member of our denomination until his death, and his home was ever a place where the preachers and pilgrims received a most cordial welcome.

Bishop Edward P. Hart had charge of the camp meeting, and organized the conference. I think this was the first visit Bishop Hart had ever made to our part of the country. He was accompanied by his excellent wife, who engaged most heartily in all the services of the camp meeting. Bishop Hart's strong, incisive, logical and eloquent sermons stirred the entire community. I was charmed with the personality of the man, and greatly edified under his ministry. Many Methodists who listened to the preaching remarked, "This is really old-time Methodism." It looked as though many would join us, but we were greatly disappointed when only a very few identified themselves with the new church organization.

Rev. T. S. LaDue, George Edwards, Ira F. Ward, J. C. Scott and John Glenn were the charter members of the conference. F. W. Cathey, Harry Vanderveen and myself were received on probation. I shall never forget the day when we were to take our preliminary examination. I was greatly concerned and had reason for my fears—that I would not be able to reach the required standing. Rev. John LaDue was appointed to examine us. Mr. Vanderveen and F. W. Cathey seemed to understand the subjects quite well. I was very largely ignorant concerning the elementary branches in which I was being examined. Rev. LaDue was very considerate, and had the happy faculty of getting out of me all that I knew, and as I look over it now, I think much that I did not understand. He asked me a few questions concerning English, geography and the more elementary outlines of theology. I was not able to answer the questions, but replied to each interrogation, "Brother LaDue, I don't quite understand that particular question you are asking me, but one thing I am certain of, and that is, on the 18th day of November, 1881, the Lord wonderfully pardoned all my sins, and now I am conscious of the fact that I am His child." The examination was conducted in the woods, on a moss-covered log, under a fine maple tree. Brother LaDue did not give us our standing, and I was very much afraid that I had failed. When my name was called I was greatly pleased to hear Brother LaDue's report, which assured the conference that A. Beers had passed a very satisfactory examination in the preliminary course of study. He commended most highly my knowledge of theology, as I had expressed it in relating my personal experience. By a unanimous vote of that body I was received in the conference as a probationer. I have been keenly sensitive of the honors I have received from time to time from the church of my choice, but can say most candidly that none of them have afforded me greater pleasure than the vote by which I was received on probation.

During the conference, Bishop and Mrs. Hart had a talk with me concerning the Chili Seminary, now known as the A. M. Chesbrough Seminary of North Chili, New York. At the time I joined the church, I did not know that we had a paper, and had never heard of the school.

Bishop Hart informed me that a certain number of students were permitted to work their way through in part. He also volunteered to write a line to Prof. B. H. Roberts, principal of the school, and find out if there would be an opening for me, the coming September, to work for part of my board. I waited with much interest and deep solicitude for a reply to this letter. I was much encouraged when in about two weeks' time I received a most kindly letter from Prof. Roberts, telling me that there was a place for me, and urging me to be on hand for the beginning of school which would be about the middle of September.

I now began to pray most earnestly that my way would be opened up financially. I not only prayed, but labored very hard with my hands and tried in this way to answer my own prayers. A Mr. James MacKenzie had a very large field of potatoes on the Clackamas River. He gave me the opportunity to dig them, and paid me well for my work. If I never have the credit of being a champion for anything else, I secured that fall the title of champion potato digger of Multnomah county. I digged and placed in sacks one hundred three bushels in one day. So greatly was Mr. MacKenzie pleased with the amount of work I did, he had an article printed in the paper concerning my feat. I worked from very early morning until late at night, and had no desire to join a union, or demand shorter hours and longer pay. After having worked hard during the day, I would sit up late at night, practising penmanship and reading my Bible. My joy knew no bounds at the thought of entering school. I was owing a little, and decided that I should not enter upon my studies until every dollar I owed was paid in full.

A brother by the name of J. J. Robertson was on my note for one hundred dollars, the amount of my indebtedness. I often made my home at Brother Robertson's, and he was a great source of help and inspiration to me during the early years of my

Christian experience. About the first of September, I went to pay a visit to Brother and Sister Robertson. I reached their home late at night, after they had retired. Brother Robertson got up and let me in, and was very glad to see me. It was his habit often to praise the Lord aloud, and to say Amen. Many a time in the morning, as he would start for the City of Portland, on a load of potatoes, or a load of hay, did he shout, "Amen!" until the neighbors heard him. As soon as I entered his home that night, he went back and commenced to search among some papers, saying, "Amen, amen," as he did so. He finally handed me my note for the one hundred dollars, receipted in full. I was greatly surprised and asked him what it meant. He replied, "It means that you are to get to the A. M. Chesbrough Seminary, and commence your work as quickly as possible." I at once recognized this as a definite answer to prayer and an unmistakable providential opening for me to enter school. Brother Robertson had been over to see a man by the name of Green McMurry, and also Flavel Sumner, and the three had decided to pay the note and also promised to give me assistance from time to time while I was in school.

Without delay I commenced to get ready for the trip. Money came in answer to prayer to pay my railroad fare from Portland to Rochester, New York. I spent a week visiting my friends, telling them good-by, and exhorting them to yield to Christ. The pilgrims insisted that I should preach a farewell sermon before leaving. I had never preached in my own immediate neighborhood, and it was a great cross for me to attempt it. I finally consented, and arrangements were made for me to speak in the Baptist Church on Sunday night before I was to leave. The news spread far and wide, and through sheer curiosity the people came and crowded the church. Many were not able to gain admission. When I looked out upon the sea of faces before me the Lord wonderfully encouraged my heart and gave me special inspiration for the effort. I was very clearly led to use as my text, Romans 8:28: "And we know that all things work together for good to them that love God, to them who are the called according to His purpose." I had great liberty, and the Spirit of the Lord seemed to fall on the entire congregation. A doctor was present that night, who had laughed at me much, and was a great source of discouragement to me in my Christian life. He had said many things by way of derision of my call to the gospel ministry. This night I really got the victory over him, and did not care for his criticism. Greatly to my surprise, after the service, this same doctor came forward and congratulated me on my effort and apologized for all that he had ever said tending to discourage me. He also dropped a twenty dollar gold piece into my hand, and assured me that he would follow my future career with his sympathetic interest.

The next day I was driven to the City of Portland to take the train for my long journey across the continent. I was not accustomed to travel, and was not a little apprehensive concerning the trip. Our railroad accommodations then could not be compared in any sense to our modern facilities for travel. Instead of being able to secure a berth in a sleeper, each passenger was supposed to take his own bedding and straw tick or mattress and make his own bed on the slats that were drawn out for that purpose on the car. I had my bedding, straw mattress and lunch basket. My friends had bidden me good-by and returned back to their homes, and I was left alone at the station to wait for the train. It was quite a problem on my mind as to how I could get on the train with my lunch basket, bedding and straw tick. I heard the whistle and the train came around the curve at the little station in East Portland. I managed to get hold of my lunch basket with my right hand, gathered the bedding under my right arm, and took my old straw tick on my left arm. You can very readily imagine my embarrassment in trying to enter the car. The brakeman stepped down and asked me what I intended to do with that straw mattress. I informed him that I expected to use it as my bed across the continent. The coach I was trying to enter was a day coach, and the brakeman very sternly informed me that I could not enter the day coach with that bed tick and bedding. I insisted that I could, if he would only give me an opportunity. He was not disposed, however, to debate the question with me, but demanded that I throw the straw tick in the express car in the rear. I did this, and got back just in time to get on as the train was moving out from the station. I do not know what became of my famous straw tick, as I have not seen it from that time to this, but trust that some one found it and had many a sound nap on it.

I found myself in a car with about fifty young men, most of them rough in appearance. It appeared to me that they had taken all the suspicious young fellows and had placed them in a car by themselves. There were many foreigners and most of them were smoking and playing cards. I found myself facing a condition that seemed to me very serious. I knew that I must let my light shine and take up my cross, or that I would lose the blessing of the Lord out of my heart. Shortly after my ticket was taken up and I was quite comfortably situated in a seat, I commenced to look around for an opportunity to do a little foreign missionary work. I took my stand in the front of the coach, and there in the name of my Lord, lifted the standard of the cross. I told the young fellows how I had been converted on the 18th of November, 1881, and how I had been called to the work of the ministry. I told them that I was going all the way to New York, and that I expected to keep the victory and live my religion every day. They received the testimony in a most kindly spirit, and we had very little card playing or smoking in my part of the coach. I held meetings each day and urged all to be reconciled to God. One young man, a Swede, became greatly wrought on by the Spirit, and gave himself to Christ on the train. I was overjoyed over this trophy of the cross. That old rude coach was transformed into a veritable Pullman sleeper, and I was as happy as any person who ever shared the luxuries of a king's palace. When we arrived at St. Paul, I shook hands with every young person in the car, and bade them good-by.

From St. Paul I traveled largely alone, and did not become acquainted with any one. After I passed Chicago and Detroit, and got down near Buffalo, I commenced to feel that I was getting far away from home. I arrived at North Chili on Saturday afternoon and went up at once to the school. Prof. Roberts was not at home, but the colored housekeeper, after looking me over with more or less suspicion, finally, with some reluctance, invited me to come into the library. I found myself for the first time surrounded by hundreds of books, and at once felt that I would like to read them all through. In the evening Prof. Roberts returned from Rochester, where he had been spending the day, and gave me a most cordial welcome. I took dinner with him at his own private table, and shall never forget the kindly words spoken to me by both Prof. Roberts and his most excellent wife, who was associate principal with her husband. After supper and prayers, I was shown to a room in the dormitory. School was to open the following Tuesday, and I was very anxious to get a special blessing on the Sabbath that would help me in my school work. I was greatly disappointed when I awoke Sunday morning to find that I had left my laundry at my aunt's in Kansas where I had stopped on the way, and that I did not have a clean white shirt or collar for the Sabbath. I hardly knew what to do, and was almost overwhelmed with a sense of loneliness and homesickness that came upon me. I thought of the band of pilgrims in Oregon, of the grand sermon I knew that Rev. T. S. LaDue would preach that morning. I thought of the amens that would be coming from the heart and lips of my good friend, Brother Robertson, and of Sister Cathey's shouts of victory. I really longed for home, and felt that I was a stranger in a strange land.

How I realized that morning that the Lord is a present help in every time of need! I opened my Bible for encouragement, and the first verse that my eyes fell upon was the text I had used the Sunday before at home, Romans 8: 28. It seemed to be illuminated with a divine glory, and I read in it a significance that I had never realized before. "ALL THINGS WORK TOGETHER FOR GOOD." I dropped on my knees by my bedside, and in simple, childlike faith claimed that promise. But a short time after, a young man by the name of Baldwin, about my size, came into my room, and asked me whether I was going to church that morning. I told him that I had planned to do so, but informed him concerning my loss. He immediately went to his own wardrobe, and from his scanty supply brought me the necessary shirt and collar, and I was soon ready to attend the service. Just before I got ready to leave, Miss Carpenter, one of the teachers, came to me and asked me if I did not preach occasionally. I told her no, I did not really preach, but that I tried to exhort occasionally. She informed me that the preacher was sick and they had no one to take his place, and asked me if I would not occupy the pulpit. With quite a little hesitation I finally decided that I would do the best I could. What other text could I have used that morning, excepting Romans 8: 28, and I wanted to tell everybody how all things work together for good. My sermon was very simple, but the Lord wonderfully blessed me, and many expressed themselves as having been helped. This did me a great deal of good, and I was made to feel that I was just in the place the Lord wanted me. The various members of the faculty made me welcome, the old students who had been in the school for a number of years rallied around me, and I soon felt very much at home in my new environment, though far away from the old home nest that I had cherished for so many years.

The following reminiscences of her first acquaintance with Mr. Beers were given by Miss Adella P. Carpenter: "My acquaintance with the Rev. Alexander Beers began when he entered the A. M. Chesbrough Seminary, where I was then a teacher. He soon became an integral part of the school, assiduous in study, loyal to his teachers, courteous to and interested in all the students. To master mathematics he found a difficult task, but homiletics, mental science and like subjects were his delight. Called to be a minister of the gospel of our Lord and Savior Jesus Christ, he never forgot his calling. He was a brother in Christ to his teachers as well as to his fellow students. I well remember, one evening as many of us were standing together for a little social intercourse, how he came to me and said, 'Miss Carpenter, are you looking up?' I remember, also, the indorsement of the Spirit in my own heart, as I replied, 'Yes, Mr. Beers, straight up.' There was a time, one year, when he felt that he wanted more of the conscious presence of God in his soul. He urged the Christian young men, of whom there was a strong company, to pray for him. This continued several weeks with no visible results. One day he asked permission of the principal, Prof. B. H. Roberts, to be absent from school for a day. He started down the street toward the south, called upon and prayed with every family on the left hand side for a distance of three miles, and returning did the same in all the houses on the right hand side. He found families whom no minister had visited for years. In one home was a very old lady, blind, whose daughter, long accustomed to read to her mother, was too ill to perform her wonted task. How the blind woman rejoiced to hear again the sacred words of Scripture, the voice of song and prayer. Mr. Beers did not have to ask the boys any longer to pray for him. His cup of joy overflowed for weeks after this experience. He often preached at various places during his school days and the last year of his stay with us was the regularly appointed pastor at Rochester, New York, ten miles distant. Rev. B. T. Roberts and his wife were both living and were in close touch with the school while Mr. Beers was with us. He had the greatest reverence for them and close fellowship existed between them as long as they lived. The training he received, the example of God's saints, the personal knowledge of God which he had, the love that 'never faileth,' fitted him for his own fields of labor to which God called him later. Our memories of his school days are only pleasant memories."

As Mr. Beers entered the Chesbrough Seminary, it was necessary for him to join the primary classes in the school owing to the fact that he was sickly in health until he came to Oregon, and then was compelled to give all his time to manual labor to aid in the support of the family. His education had been neglected until he was converted. How humbly he took his place with the younger students in the class room will never be forgotten by those who knew him. He was so earnest and studious that he made very rapid progress and swift promotion followed.

CHAPTER V

HIS EDUCATION AND MARRIAGE

They tell me that in Pisa's old cathedral
　　All noises harsh and loud—
Grating of ponderous doors, shrill tones, the tramping
　　And murmur of the crowd—
Are caught up, softened, harmonized and blended,
　　Within the lofty dome;
Then echoed back in one great wave of music,
　　Sweet as a dream of home.

So all the harsh notes in life's mingled music—
　　The burden and the woe,
The stroke that almost snaps the quivering heart-strings,
　　The loss that grieves us so—
In heaven's o'erarching dome, of perfect wisdom,
　　Power and love shall be
Gathered and blended, in divinest marvel
　　Of matchless melody.　　　　　　—*Longfellow.*

The value and importance of first impressions are
often over-estimated. One can not picture the beauty
of the lily from a view of the unsightly bulb, and frequently the ignorant, uncultured youth, under
proper environments will develop a beauty of character which is both surprising and gratifying. This
great transformation of character began in the life
of a young man who entered the A. M. Chesbrough
Seminary in the autumn of 1884. Mrs. Emma Sellew Roberts, A.M., who with her husband was at
the head of Mr. Beers' alma mater, writes of her
first impressions and the later marvelous change in

the rude country boy she first met: "A great, big, awkward boy, who had come from far-away Oregon, stepped off the train at North Chili, carrying a big lunch basket and a rough looking valise. There was little that was pre-possessing in his appearance, but the look of strength in his face told the story of earnest resolution and lofty purpose. We soon learned that he was already in his nineteenth year, but was hardly able to read owing to early disadvantages. The spirit of God, however, had reached his heart and aroused great and holy ambitions to fit himself for life's responsibilities. One could hardly believe that this youth would become in the course of fifteen or twenty years a great preacher, a great organizer, the founder of a school and college, and a man so broad and intelligent that he gathered around him many from high and cultured ranks and various stations in life and was able to secure co-workers to assist him in his labors from great institutions of learning. That which Alexander Beers became, and what he was able to accomplish for the work of God, especially in the cause of Christian education, is one of the marvels of these latter days." A young lady who was a teacher in Chesbrough at that time was also compelled to decide that first impressions are not always correct.

Entering the church at North Chili, one Sabbath morning, in September, 1885, Miss N—— knelt in secret prayer as usual. When she arose she saw to her surprise a stranger was occupying the pulpit. He was tall, angular and awkward in appearance. There was little promise of a distinguished looking college president of after years. However, when he

faced the audience and announced his text, she realized that here was a young man of promise and one
filled with the Spirit. His subject was taken from
Romans 8:28, which was ever afterward a favorite
text of his. As she now recalls the first sermon that
she heard from the lips of Mr. Beers, it was discon-
nected and one could discover many grammatical
mistakes. But it was so fragrant with the blessing
of God that the saints were all graciously fed and
refreshed. After listening to Mr. Beers for over
thirty years, she has found that this was ever characteristic of his discourses, he invariably ministered
the Spirit in his simplest sermons. As Miss N——
became acquainted with "Brother Beers," as she
always called him then, she found him to be a very
spiritual man, which attracted her, but no thoughts
of anything further than a brother in Christ entered
her mind for three years. His studious habits com-
manded her respect. He was always well employed
—working with his hands for his schooling, and as
soon as his daily tasks were completed he could be
seen with a book in his hand, pouring over its contents in deep concentration. In a short time he
filled in the Sabbaths with preaching the gospel at
points near the school. Miss N—— had the privilege of teaching him grammar and soon noticed his
quick discernment, his fine mind and also his reten-
tive memory. His ability to memorize was remarkable. At one time when he was afflicted in body he
committed the eleventh chapter of Hebrews and was
healed completely by the words of faith he was
learning. The ease with which he could memorize
so much on so many different subjects, poems, ora-

tions, speeches and sayings of great men, was marvelous. Facts and figures were laid up in his mind for use in the future. When he was converted he was entirely ignorant of his Bible, but very soon he was familiar and conversant with Scripture and could repeat chapter after chapter of the sacred Word. When he traveled he usually carried clippings in his pockets which he studied on street cars and on trains. In his trips across the continent, which he took annually, he would have several books to read as he traveled.

This western brother soon became a great favorite of Rev. and Mrs. B. T. Roberts, the founders of the institution and also of the Free Methodist Church. This fact influenced Miss N—— favorably, for she knew very well that they were wiser than she in their estimation of character. But fortunately no serious thought hampered her mind nor interrupted the true and blessed fellowship with this very agreeable student. Mr. Beers was very diplomatic in winning the prize he so earnestly desired. If he had been at all premature in pressing his suit, no doubt it would have defeated him in his purpose. He ever sought to assist Miss N—— in every way possible and when she was called to bury her mother, he offered the most helpful and comforting words of condolence. They labored together most earnestly for the salvation of the students and many times helped to pray them through to God by their mutual intercession; so engrossed was Miss N—— in this work for the Master, that no troublesome thoughts were aroused to make her companionship with Mr. Beers embarrassing. He made rapid strides in his education and was soon enabled to take his proper place in the grade with his young companions. He ever took an active part in the literary societies and soon became noted for his skill in debating. Many former students will remember a debate that was given in the school on the subject, "*Resolved, that high license is better for the public welfare than low license.*" Since a very strong prohibition sentiment prevailed in the school, few students could be found who dared to brave public opinion and take the affirmative side of the question. Mr. Beers decided for the sake of argument to champion high license. This was unknown to Miss N——, and when she heard him argue so skilfully and eloquently that the judges gave their decision to the affirmative side of the question, she was very displeased with this western gentleman. She treated him very coldly for a time—in fact, this debate came near blighting the enchanting visions he had been indulging. With great difficulty he proved himself a stanch prohibitionist, who always voted that ticket straight, before the storm abated that threatened to wreck his fond hopes.

Since Miss N—— was teacher of music and Mr. Beers was preparing for the work of an itinerant preacher, it was not surprising that such an ambitious youth should wish to add the gift of song to his accomplishments. He went to her one day and asked her if she could teach him to sing hymns, as he wished, if possible, to be able to start his own hymns in his church services. She told him she would be glad to try and would consider it real missionary work, as he was preparing for the gospel ministry. She instructed him to get permission from the principals, since he was a student and her time belonged to them. When he presented his request to Mrs. Roberts, he encountered some difficulty. At first she shook her head, fearing perhaps where these lessons might lead, divining with wise sagacity that the institution might lose its music teacher. She was very kind, however, and could not well refuse such a reasonable request. She tried to dissuade Mr. Beers and said a few words to Miss N—— to discourage the undertaking, but the persistence of the young man could not long be denied, and she yielded the point contrary to her better judgment. The result was just as Mrs. Roberts feared, for the music teacher later on found a wider field of usefulness. The lessons began, but soon proved to be a most difficult task. Nature had been prodigal in bestowing her gifts upon this son of the prairie and forest, but it seemed she had forgotten to endow him with the art of song. After great perseverance, Miss N—— succeeded in teaching him to sing several hymns with his teacher—"At the Sounding of the Trumpet," "What a Gathering that will be," "We are Marching up on the King's Highway," so that he could carry these tunes very well. And he ever enjoyed singing these particular hymns which he had learned at the Chesbrough Seminary. However, he always leaned on her voice and made no effort unless she would carry the tune for him. An extract from a letter to his wife, dated July 14, 1919, says, "You are my song bird, my nightingale who sings in the night."

The music lessons were finally interrupted by an

urgent call from the west. Mr. Beers' mother was very ill and he felt that he must make her a visit. When he returned in the fall, the engagement of Alexander Beers and Miss Newton was announced. For a year and a half or a little more he served as pastor in the church in Rochester, New York, while she pursued her calling as teacher in the seminary. Dr. and Mrs. Roberts had made a trip to Europe and when they came back arrangements were made for the marriage. It seemed they could not do enough for the prospective bride and groom. Instead of say-ing, as many would have done, "We told you so," they made them a fine wedding. The ceremony was performed in the seminary chapel, November 29, 1889, by Rev. B. T. Roberts, who was assisted by Dr. Benson Howard Roberts and Rev. E. C. Best. After Father Roberts had pronounced a heavenly benedic-tion upon the happy couple, he introduced them as Rev. and Mrs. Alexander Beers. The spacious room was filled to overflowing with students and friends, who showered them with valuable gifts and vied with each other in wishing them great joy. A beauti-ful wedding feast was provided by the school and they soon bade farewell to their beloved alma mater and their dear friends who waved them a fond adieu.

Mr. Beers was ever a good judge of fine music and greatly enjoyed spiritual singing. He often said his heart was filled with music and when he reached heaven he would sing all four parts at once. As the bereaved wife now lingers on in her loneliness on the shores of time, she fancies she hears him joining in the glad anthems of the skies and her heart cries out, "Oh, dear one, you have outstripped your earthly teacher and are now singing as she has never been able to sing."

*   *   *   *   *

> "Love took up the harp of life
> And smote on all the chords with might;
> Smote the chord of Self that trembling
> Passed in music out of sight."

"Love is the keynote and vitalizing spirit of the Gospel. It is the crowning diadem of all religious attainment—the fulfilling of the divine law and the enabling power to manifest the Spirit of Christ to the child of God. 'Love worketh no ill to his neighbor.' Old grudges, bitter strifes, uncharitable fault-finding will disappear in the presence of love as the snow melts before the midday sun. Good will toward man will be manifested everywhere; it will be the very spirit, atmosphere and genius of the Christian life. It will be seen in all the activities of life and will be shown in the warm handshake, the pleasant smile and the hearty God bless you. May God grant throughout our earthly career that we may all breathe the spirit of this angelic sentiment and thus pray, 'Thy kingdom come, Thy will be done, on earth as it is in heaven.' "—*Extract from one of Mr. Beers' sermons.*

CHAPTER VI

OPENED UP SEMINARY AT SPOTSYLVANIA, VIRGINIA

Great men were all great workers in their time,
  Steadfast in purpose, to their calling true;
  Keeping with single eye, the end in view;
Giving their youthful days and manhood's prime
To ceaseless toil; matin and midnight chime
  Often upon their willing labors grew.
  In suffering schooled, their souls endurance knew,
And over difficulties rose sublime.

—Thomas Carlyle.

The founder of the Free Methodist Church, the Rev. Benjamin T. Roberts, was a deeply spiritual man, highly educated. He was especially cultured in the languages, reading Hebrew as fluently as the ordinary man does his English. Many times we have seen him on the camp ground on a hot afternoon when the people were scattered about, enter the pulpit and begin to repeat a chapter in the Hebrew language. Immediately the crowd would come thronging to their seats, attracted by this unusual tongue. Bishop Roberts saw clearly that thorough scholarship must go hand in hand with Bible holiness, if the newly formed church would take her place among the workers who were striving to evangelize the world. So in the very beginning he encouraged the founding of Christian schools in the denomination. With the aid of his efficient wife,

MR. BEERS AT 31 YEARS OF AGE

MR. BEERS AT 22 YEARS OF AGE

he had succeeded in establishing the A. M. Chesbrough Seminary after great self-denial and privations. He urged Mr. and Mrs. Beers to go to Spotsylvania, Virginia, and assume the management of a school which had been started by the Rev. W. A. Sellew, who was unwilling to be shut up constantly in the school room, feeling the call of the gospel ministry upon him. Mr. Beers hesitated long over the subject and had already made one visit to the place before he was married. Joseph Bittle had a farm upon which there was located a large building quite well suited to the needs of a school, located in the county seat of Spotsylvania, not far from the historic battlefields of General Grant's great engagements. The walls of the old brick house contained many conspicuous holes where bullets had rent the surface when the battle raged furiously all around. Mr. and Mrs. Beers decided to undertake the school work there, feeling that the Lord was thus leading them.

Leaving North Chili on the afternoon train, their first concern was to remove the rice from their clothing, which kind friends had rained upon them. At Rochester they were met by the private conveyance of Mr. and Mrs. Peters and taken to their beautiful home where they were entertained for several days. Mr. and Mrs. Peters had been like a father and mother to Mr. Beers while he was their pastor during the latter part of his stay in New York state. As soon as they had reached their room and removed their wraps, they bowed at the mercy seat in humble thanksgiving and consecration. They pledged themselves anew to devote their time, their talents, their all to God's service forever. After thirty years of wedded bliss, how blessed to look back upon that pledge unbroken and those vows to the Lord fulfilled. Their wedding trip included New York, Brooklyn, Philadelphia and Washington, D. C., and Fredericksburg, Virginia. While they were in New York and Brooklyn they were entertained at the home of Rev. James Mathews in a very kind and hospitable manner. At Philadelphia they stopped for a few days with Mrs. Emily Dickson, of sainted memory. Mr. Beers preached Sunday morning and was taken very sick immediately with what the doctor called intestinal grippe. This was a sore trial indeed; for a time it seemed that the disease might be fatal, but the Lord heard prayer and restored him quickly, and they were soon speeding on to their new field of labor. They stayed in Washington, D. C., but a short time, and were met at Fredericksburg, Virginia, by their good friend, Mr. Bittle. Time had been flying very swiftly and more than a month had elapsed since they left North Chili, New York. The twelve miles from Fredericksburg were passed with difficulty over a well-nigh impassable road, where the wheels sank continually in the deep, sticky mud until you could hardly discern the shape of the wheel. The poor horses had a hard pull, but after a long time, just as the sun was sinking in the west, they arrived at their new home on the last day of the old year, 1889. A warm welcome awaited them at the end of the journey and a bountiful supper had been prepared under the direction of Mrs. Bittle. From the moment they first met her, they found in Mrs. Bittle a wise counsellor, a loyal friend and a spiritual helper in all the problems that confronted them. Her prayers prevailed in many hours of darkness and brought the victory on Israel's side when Satan's hosts assailed.

When the new year of 1890 dawned, it found Mr. Beers in his new home at Spotsylvania, Virginia. Surrounded by entirely new environments, he faced new and grave responsibilities. Yes, it was indeed a New Year's day—new work, new friends, new hopes and new trials. But his heart was strong for the conflict, for God had heard his prayer and given him the companion for whom he had asked and he could now say in the language of Schiller: "Life is quite a different thing by the side of a beloved wife.... Beautiful nature! I now for the first time fully enjoy it, live in it. The world again clothes itself around me in poetic forms. I look with a glad mind around me; my heart finds a perennial contentment; my spirit so fine, so refreshing a nourishment.... I look to my future destiny with a cheerful heart; now when standing at the wished-for goal, I wonder with myself, how it has all happened so far beyond my expectation."

Mr. and Mrs. Beers found their new home very congenial and charming. A few students were soon gathered together and school work begun in the little chapel below their living rooms. After school hours they would take long strolls in the woods and out into the country, finding great pleasure in exploring the battle-fields which still bore evidence of the terrible scourge which had swept over them during the Civil War. On Sunday evenings Mr. Beers preached to the people who gathered in the little chapel. He soon learned that the whole country was cursed by drink. There was a saloon about a block from the chapel, which young men and even boys of tender age frequented. On court days, which came one day in the month, whisky flowed freely and men staggered about the streets. The writer can never forget seeing a young boy about sixteen years old so dazed by drink that he could not mount his horse without help. Mr. Beers began at once a vigorous warfare against this demon. Tobacco, too, was used freely by old and young. The elderly ladies all had their pipes and the young and old women their toddy. Even young children chewed or smoked tobacco. Here was work indeed to engage all one's strength and requiring great wisdom. Mr. Beers preached against these evils most uncompromisingly in every sermon. At last several prominent gentlemen, among them the judge of the county, waited on him and courteously asked Mr. Beers if he would not cease preaching against the use of tobacco. Mr. Beers replied, "Gentlemen, I tell you what I will do. If you will all stop using the filthy stuff, I will quit saying anything about it." It is needless to say they all passed out of the room in silence. The school increased in numbers and the Lord was working on the hearts of the students. Rousing temperance meetings were held in nearby places and the young people trained to sing rousing temperance songs. An inexorable rule was made that any student frequenting or even entering the saloon should be expelled from the seminary. On court days Mrs. Beers would gather the students out on the porch of the house and have them sing as only southern voices could, "Saloons, saloons must go!" This beautiful music attracted the attention of all who had congregated in and about the court house, for it was not so far away but that all could hear. It seemed very shocking to these southern people to hear their old-time custom of using intoxicants attacked so vehemently.

One of the patrons of the school, who was a very polite man when sober, always became bewildered when he attended court—too much booze addled his brain. On such occasions he would try to find Mr. Beers and would always say in a very belligerent tone, "I am a genuine Jeff Davis man and I hate the Yankees," repeating it several times if he had opportunity. One evening he came staggering up the stairs to their upper room, and when he came in he delivered his bitter speech as usual. Mr. Beers greeted him very cordially, paying no attention to his unkind words, gave him a chair and asked him if he liked music. "Would you not like to hear Mrs. Beers sing and play?" he said. The poor man eagerly assented. She sat down at the organ and began to sing a hymn while lifting her heart to God in prayer for this unfortunate man. Mr. Beers asked him if he ever sang. He said he did sometimes, and wanted to sing some old songs his mother used to sing. "Jesus, Lover of My Soul" and "Nearer, My God, to Thee" were sung and he tried to join in. But memories of his childhood completely overcame him. He became sobered and his voice choked with sobs. Mr. Beers put his arms about him and told him he had had no part whatever in the Civil War; that he was but a babe at that time. He assured

him that he did not hate him, that he loved everybody. The old man was completely conquered, and
after a nice chat he went away. Never again did
he tell Mr. Beers he hated the Yankees; instead, he
sought opportunity to express his gratitude for the
great work that Mr. and Mrs. Beers were doing in
the school, especially for the good his daughters
were receiving. Poor, dear man, may God bring
him through to heaven!

Miss Effie Southworth, who afterward went to India as a missionary, was numbered among the students. Her father, the Rev. Charles H. Southworth,
was secured to assist in a strong, powerful temperance campaign at the school and in several places
out in the country. A fire had been kindled and the
battle was on. Rev. Southworth was at his best and
gave his people very entertaining and vigorous prohibition addresses. The meetings were full of inspiration and the people were much aroused. One
morning Mr. Beers found the saloon keeper pacing
up and down the street, under deep conviction.
Seizing Mr. Beers by the hand, he solemnly vowed
he would never sell another drop of whisky and to
seal his promise on the spot, he entered his saloon
and began to pour all his liquor into the streets.
This action on the part of the saloon keeper created
a great sensation in the neighborhood and exerted
a powerful influence for righteousness in the entire
community. No more whisky could be obtained
there and the leaven of sobriety was spreading. Mr.
and Mrs. Beers were called to Seattle, Washington,
in February, 1893, to open up a seminary there, but
learned later to their delight that the entire county

of Spotsylvania was brought under the local option law and went bone dry.

To resume the subject, the tobacco campaign was not neglected. It seemed that Mr. Beers could not preach a single sermon without assailing this great evil. One of the young men, about sixteen years old, came to school one morning with a sealed envelope in his hand, bearing this inscription: "To be opened when you reach your room." We found enclosed a very unique will which read as follows: "I, ———, being of sound and disposing mind, do from this hour by the help of almighty God, promise to forever abstain from the use of tobacco in any form. Please pray for me, for I am finding the struggle very hard." We are glad to record that the vow so solemnly made that day was rigidly kept. This young man was soon clearly saved and consecrated himself to God's work. He afterward became an efficient and prominent missionary in the foreign fields.

A glorious revival broke out among the students and the Lord gave Mr. Beers some precious trophies for his crown of rejoicing. He would teach during the day and preach every night, and was ever ready to say, "This war is all my soul's delight. I love the thickest of the fight." A strong band of praying students was soon raised up who, together with Mrs. Bittle, assisted Mr. and Mrs. Beers faithfully in the work.

Mr. Beers had left the pastorate of the Free Methodist Church at Rochester, New York, where he was well supported, to assume the school work in Spotsylvania, without the promise of a dollar excepting board and lodging and what little came in from tuition. The school was small and the pupils very poor, so that the cash received was very meager. At the end of the first semester only a small surplus remained over and above all expenses. Mr. Beers needed a pair of shoes very badly and had planned to buy them from the small fund he had. About this time he learned that one of our Free Methodist families was in want. The husband had been sick for some time and could earn nothing, so they were in actual need of food. From the little amount he had saved, instead of buying shoes, Mr. Beers bought them a bill of groceries, which tided them over. The question now arose, "What should he do for shoes, since the only pair he had showed the marks of the cobbler's hand?" At this point he proved the verity of the promise, "Give and it shall be given unto you; good measure, pressed down and shaken together, and running over shall men give into your bosom." Not long after this he met Dr. and Mrs. Roberts who had recently returned from a trip to England. Not knowing Mr. Beers' needs, Dr. Roberts brought out a box of new shoes, which had been given to him in London to aid poor students. He said, "Brother Beers, here is a good pair of shoes. If they fit you, put them on and wear them. You see they are the very best kind of leather and would cost about two pounds in London." Is it necessary to add that the shoes fitted as if they had been made to order?—and faith whispered that our heavenly Father had ordered them especially for Alexander. But this is not the end—only the beginning of God's goodness in the line of shoes. Before the first pair

was worn very much, a brother-in-law said he felt
that he must give him some shoes, and presented
him with a fine pair made of alligator skin; these
two pairs were still good when other friends insisted on fitting him out with a pair of shoes, and
this expression of God's goodness continued for a
period of five years or more—just as long as Mr.
Beers told the story and gave God the praise, he did
not need to buy any shoes, nor could he wear out all
he had. But at last he felt embarrassed in telling
the incident, for it seemed like begging for more
shoes. When he ceased to testify to it, the flow of
shoes was cut off. The last gift that was made included a pair for his wife, with a tiny pair of baby
shoes tucked in the toes.

Many friends were made among the southern people and Mr. Beers was invited to preach in the different churches. Sometimes his wife would respond
in the services and shout God's praises as the Spirit
came upon her. Then the people would act very
curious and turn around to look at her as if she had
been guilty of some impropriety. One Sunday morning while Mr. Beers was preaching in a country
church, a good old lady felt the inspiration of the
Spirit come upon her soul. She arose and began to
shout, "Oh, glory, this is like we used to have twenty
years ago." Walking down the aisle with hands uplifted, she ascended the stairs to the pulpit, taking
Mr. Beers by the hand, rejoiced with joy unspeakable. The people were shocked with the interrup-
tion, but it brought great gladness to Mr. and Mrs.
Beers. The lady's daughter came around afterward
and made a very humble apology for her mother,

saying she was old and childish and did not often take *such spells.*

Their limited means gave Mr. and Mrs. Beers a fine chance to trust in divine providence, and they were never disappointed.

One bright autumn day the hand of sorrow was laid upon them. A telegram came announcing the death of her youngest brother, Rev. Burdette Newton, who was greatly beloved as preacher and pastor. He was assisting in taking down the large tabernacle at the close of a camp meeting held on his circuit in western New York. A small boy who was anxious to assist in the work thought he would climb the tree and untie the guy-rope; this caused the huge center pole to fall before any one could avert the calamity. It came down with crushing weight upon the beloved pastor, who never regained consciousness.

They must go at once to Norwich to attend the funeral. School had not yet opened for the new year and they were without sufficient money to make the trip. Mr. Beers borrowed twenty dollars of his book dealer, promising to repay it upon his return. After the funeral they started back to Virginia, but had not yet secured the promised twenty dollars. Kneeling together in their room in the morning, they asked definitely for the needed amount, then took an early train from Binghamton going south. The train stopped at Scranton, Pennsylvania, to allow time for breakfast. A man who sat at the farther end of the car arose and came where Mr. Beers was sitting, saying, "I do not know your circumstances, nor whether you are in need of money, but ever since I came in the car I have felt I should give you this." He placed several bills in Mr. Beers' hand, then passed out to breakfast. After a few moments of silent thanksgiving, Mr. Beers opened his hand and found four five-dollar bills—just twenty dollars—the amount they had asked for. Yes, this was a definite answer to prayer which had been offered in simple, believing faith.

The following pleasing incident occurred while Mr. and Mrs. Beers were living in Spotsylvania. One day they went to call on an English family who had joined the church and placed their daughter in the school. Among the children was a little girl eight years old named Evelyn. She had been very ill and was just able to toddle about with a white, drawn face. When the visit was over and they arose to depart, the little girl could not be found. They supposed she had been compelled to lie down through exhaustion. The house was located some distance from the main road, and when the large gate was reached that shut in the grounds, little Evelyn was found leaning upon the gate. She had gone on ahead to open and shut this gate so that Mr. Beers would not have to alight from his cart. He was greatly touched by the child's thoughtfulness. Reaching in his pocket he pulled out some pennies and tried to press them into her hand. He knew the family was poor and supposed Evelyn would be glad to get a little money. No, her chin began to quiver, tears fell, and in broken tones she said, "Mr. Beers, I didn't do this for money. I did it because I love you people." Oh, priceless words from a little child —a never-to-be-forgotten service—like the breaking of an alabaster box. Mr. Beers prized this act of devotion, often saying, "I would rather have a wild flower, plucked from the fence corner by a little child because it loved me, than to have many costly gifts given me through a sense of duty or conventionality." When relating this incident afterward in his sermon, Mr. Beers would show how real love to God never looks to the sacrifice involved in service to Him, nor shrinks from the suffering—it seeks only to bring joy to the Redeemer's heart.

Mr. and Mrs. Beers found the southern people exceedingly hospitable and warm-hearted. They were frequently invited to dine in the finest homes and showered with choice flowers. They greatly enjoyed taking Mr. Bittle's horse and buggy and driving out on the country roads, lined with grand old trees, with a profusion of wild flowers growing on either side. It seems now, after a lapse of thirty years, that the skies bore a richer hue, the moonlight was much brighter, the birds sang more sweetly than in any other spot. Mr. Beers was ever an ardent lover of nature, and appreciated to the full all this beauty of earth and sky. This love for the beautiful was very marked in his character, as a former teacher of expression says of him, "He always loved the beautiful in nature—God's handiwork—unsullied by the touch of man. In his living-room hung a picture which he prized highly. It was an enlarged printed photograph of the large trees in Oregon where he had lived as a boy. He added to the sum of human joy; and if every one for whom he did a loving service would bring a blossom to his grave, he would sleep today beneath a wilderness of flowers."

CHAPTER VII

WORLD-WIDE VISION: SEMINARY IN SEATTLE

I like the West, which seems to keep
The all-out-doorness in its sweep.
It greets the gray of every dawn
Then turns, and forges further on.
Large is its thought, and large its view,
It proves the old, it tries the new,
It thrives on wheat or thrives on chaff,
It takes its failures with a laugh,
Renews its strength to try them later,
Succeeds, and turns to something greater.
O, stanch of heart, O, broad of breast,
I like the West, the big, bold West!
—*Ida Tarbell*.

The beautiful golden days in the sunny southland were drawing to a close. The attendance of the school had increased until there were as many as could well be accommodated, and God's blessing rested richly upon the work. A clipping from one of the local newspapers will show the standing of the school at the beginning of the year 1891:

"The Virginia Seminary at the Courthouse, in charge of Prof. A. Beers and wife, opened about the 10th of September with an enrolment of twenty-one or two scholars, which up to this time has increased to twenty-eight. All are from the locality except five—they are from New Jersey, Illinois, Pennsylvania and Washington City. A new lot of school furniture and other necessary supplies have just been received, and with these facilities the school can easily ac-

commodate forty scholars. Prof. Beers is so well assured
of the future success of the seminary that he has engaged
another teacher to commence active work with the next session (December 9th). Mrs. Beers has a class of six in music and is giving entire satisfaction. The managers have in
contemplation the erection of a large and commodious
chapel in the spring, and as the school grows other improve-
ments will be added, bringing it up to all the modern requirements of a first-class educational institution."

There was, however, one hindrance in the way
which seemed an insuperable barrier to Mr. Beers'
continuing in the school work. The property was
located within the bounds of the New York Conference territory. Mr. Beers attended two of the annual sessions of the conference and tried to persuade that body to buy this property and establish
a church school. While many were in favor of doing this, the majority declined, urging that it was
too far remote from the center of their work and
that it was quite inaccessible—no railroads running
nearer than Fredericksburg, which was twelve miles
distant.

When Mr. Beers became convinced that it was
useless to try to get them to found a school there, he
accepted a position from the conference as missionary. The last year Mr. and Mrs. Beers remained in
Spotsylvania he filled this position with acceptability, while she carried on the school with some outside assistance. Mr. Beers was very loyal to the
church of his choice and felt he could not spend his
life building up an independent institution. Then,
too, he greatly enjoyed preaching the gospel without being hampered by other work. He was also
getting one hundred dollars a month with all his ex-

penses paid, which came as a needed relief after the months they had gotten along with so little money. At this juncture some time in January, 1893, a telegram came from Seattle, urging Mr. Beers to assume the principalship and open up a school in Seattle. Several weeks were spent in completing the arrangements and they were on their way to the Pacific Coast.

When Mrs. Beers married a western man whose relatives all lived on the Pacific Coast, she realized that he might some time take her away from the East where she had been born and educated. It seemed like laying aside every cherished plan and bidding a final farewell to every friend to leave New York and take up work among entire strangers. But as every true wife should do, she said very little and followed her husband wherever he felt he should go.

In June, the year of 1891, Bishop Benjamin T. Roberts had held the session of the Washington-Oregon Conference. Nils B. Peterson had presented five acres of ground to the conference for the erection of a church school, with the explicit understanding that the subject of foreign missions was to be made prominent always and that every effort should be made to send missionaries to all parts of the world. June 19, Bishop and Mrs. B. T. Roberts went out to Ross, a suburb of Seattle, where Mr. Peterson resided, and selected the site upon which afterward the school building was located. October 29, of the same year the ground was broken for the first building, which was to be built of brick, and the work begun. This building, three and one half stories high, had been completed and with its beautifully finished exterior presented quite a contrast to the rustic surroundings. In the rear was a forest whose beauty had been marred by the woodsman's axe, in the front and sides a rough, uncultivated five-acre campus.

Mr. and Mrs. Beers reached Seattle the first of March and went at once to view the buildings and grounds of their new inheritance. They learned that the street cars ran no nearer than Fremont—a half mile away—with no sidewalks. It was now the famous rainy season of Seattle and they found a good deal of difficulty in making their way up through the narrow trail leading to the seminary grounds. Some attempt had been made to clear away the dense timber, and huge stumps blackened by the logger's fire reared their unsightly arms on either side of the foot-path, or cow-trail as it was called. Reaching the one building, they were dis-appointed to find the interior covered with plaster and paint just as the workmen had left it, with no furnishings and no equipment in the room. But the greatest discouragement they met was the fact that there was a mortgage of more than fifteen thousand dollars on this one building. The first contractor had failed in the plan and this necessitated employ-ing other workmen to complete the work, making much additional expense. H. H. Pease, one of our pioneer Free Methodists, had contributed very heavily of his means, until he had placed his own home in jeopardy. He had also labored with his own hands for weeks and months on the finishing work. Surely when the books are opened on high,

FIRST DORMITORY ERECTED AND BRICK BUILDING IN WHICH THE SEMINARY
WAS OPENED

these two men, Nils B. Peterson and H. H. Pease, will share richly in the rewards that are granted for all the good accomplished in this seminary during the past thirty years.

The coarse, unadorned grounds, the empty, unclean building, the remote distance from car service, the very small local church membership and the little prospect of students did not form a very bright prospect for the future. But none of these discouraged Mr. Beers nor caused him to regret that he had come to take up the work. But the large indebtedness, the heavy mortgage, made him question seriously the advisability of remaining, even though he had come such a distance to assume the responsibility. He urged the trustees to excuse him and offered to refund the money which had been advanced to pay transportation; this, however, they were loath to do, and begged him to remain for the first three months at least. With a heavy heart and many misgivings, he organized a cleaning force and had the building thoroughly cleaned from top to bottom. Some interested persons had purchased a few seats and desks and placed them in the seminary chapel; here the people gathered on the following Sabbath afternoon to attend the first religious service in the new building. Rev. John Cripps, the pastor of the First Free Methodist Church in Seattle, was to preach the initial sermon in this institution. He called on Mr. Beers to lead in the first public prayer ever offered in the building. No sooner had he begun to pray than the heavens seemed to open above and the room was filled with the presence of Jehovah. Coming from the sunny southland to this country of much rain, Mrs. Beers had contracted a heavy attack of grippe. When the power of God descended, she was instantly healed, and what was far more important than her healing, this wonderful outpouring of the Spirit swept away all harrassing doubts from Mr. Beers' mind. Great assurances were given both that they were in divine order and that money would be given to lift the mortgage.

The school was soon opened with only a dozen students, all in the grammar grades, but before the close of the semester in June, this number had been increased three-fold, and the prospects for future patronage were very bright. For several years in the beginning of this work there was no stated salary. Mr. and Mrs. Beers received what could be spared from the tuition after the teachers' salaries and other expenses had been met. One Saturday afternoon they had no money to buy the necessary food for the coming Sabbath. Committing their needs to the Lord, they busied themselves with the preparation of rooms for students. When they came down to the kitchen at supper time, they found the table loaded down with groceries, fresh vegetables and meat. The Holy Spirit had spoken to a member of the school board and he hastened in with these supplies.

For the first few weeks a small boy about ten years old was the only boarder. The discovery was soon made that it would be impossible to keep this boy unless he could be induced to give up his bad habits. When the boy started home to spend the week-end, Mr. Beers talked very seriously to him about his faults and told him to ask his mother if she wanted him to take a good old-fashioned Methodist whipping; that he should tell her unless she consented to this, she need not send him back. He returned, however, Monday morning and reluctantly told Mr. Beers, "Ma says give me a Methodist whipping." Before applying the strap, Mr. Beers took the boy on his knee and said, "Now you know I don't want to whip you; you know I am not mad, don't you? Don't I talk to you just as I talk in prayer meeting?" Hoping to escape punishment, the boy replied, "I don't know whether you are mad or not." But finally, after Mr. Beers had continued talking with him, the boy admitted that Mr. Beers was not mad. The strap was applied faithfully and the lad promised that he would never smoke nor break the rules again. Taking his handkerchief, Mr. Beers wiped away the tears and then he knelt in prayer. After he had finished praying, the boy broke out in a childish manner, "O God, I thank Thee for Mr. Beers. He has been so good and kind to me. Bless him and give him money for his new building and make me a good boy, for Jesus' sake. Amen." The boy's reformation was wonderful and complete. He remained in the school until he had finished his high school work, always behaving in a very exemplary manner, and was ever a warm friend of the man who had chastised him so faithfully.

Many pleasing incidents occurred to break up the monotony of routine school work. The prohibition of the manufacture and sale of intoxicating liquors was a live issue in the school. One small boy, a day student, proved so unruly that it was necessary to apply the whip very frequently, with the full consent of his parents. Mrs. Beers says that Mr. Beers punished him at least once daily, but perhaps this is an exaggeration; however, the boy took advantage of all this talk about banishing liquors, and told his mother he thought the school should get rid of all *beers* and *lickers*. This was a bright saying in one so young.

A vigorous campaign was waged in the city, and Mr. Beers was urged to accept the nomination for mayor on the prohibition ticket. One of the daily papers commenting on this, exhorted its readers "to quiet their fears, for the *cold water* men are giving us beers (Beers)."

The first Thanksgiving day at Seattle Seminary marked the beginning of a custom which has been observed since that time, of providing a bountiful feast for the students who can not go home to spend the day with their own loved ones. In those early days the turkeys were usually donated through the solicitations of the president of the school. After a spiritual service at the church in the morning, a festive occasion was enjoyed around the well-spread table. The dining-room had been beautifully decorated and some guests invited. When full justice had been given to the roast turkey and its accompaniments, the company lingered to listen to an impromptu program of speeches and music. The boarding department was small and not favored with the array of talent found there in later years. A young man had been asked to make his first after-dinner speech. He had been preparing for some time, and Mr. Beers expected he would do very nicely. When his name was called, he arose and began, "While groaning under the burden of turkey and cranberry sauce—" At this point he was stricken with stage fright and had a lapse of memory, so started over again, "While groaning under the burden of turkey and cranberry sauce," and still he could not collect his scattered thoughts. His face became crimson and his fellow students were tittering with amusement. The third time he said, "While groaning under the burden of turkey and cranberry sauce," and sat down amid the cheers and laughter of all in the room.

A few months before Mr. Beers had left Virginia, a marked epoch came in his life. He had had the privilege of attending the dedication of Cox Hall at Chesbrough Seminary, North Chili, New York. The old building where he had received his education had caught fire and burned to the ground. Cox Hall, a more beautiful structure and more convenient in every way, had been erected. Rev. A. B. Simpson, of the Christian Missionary Alliance, delivered the dedicatory address. As usual, this great man was filled with the fire of missionary enthusiasm. While listening to his burning message, a flame was kindled in Mr. Beers' heart that was never extinguished to the day of his death. He returned to Spotsylvania, a transformed man—a man with a world-wide vision. The first Sabbath evening after returning home, he preached from the text, "I am a debtor." He seemed to stand in the shadow of Mount Calvary and be humbled into nothingness in the presence of the crucified One. He was abased, Christ was exalted. He had been taken from the depths of sin—lifted from the horrible pit of iniquity and placed in the paradise of purity and peace by omnipotent love. How could he ever repay his wonderful Savior—his adorable Lord. No recompense could be found to pay such an infinite debt. There was but one thing he could do, one way only for him to pursue, this path he was now determined to follow so long as life should last. There were millions of human beings—his brothers—who had never heard of the great salvation—millions passing out into eternity with terror filling their hearts—no hope in Christ and no comfort through the Scriptures. He must labor with all of his God-given powers to get the glorious news to these lost ones and induce just as many others as possible to help in evangelizing these nations. When he gave this burning message that evening, his wife caught the vision, too. Before this she had been absorbed in the work around her, like many other Christians who think "there is enough to do at home." But from that wonderful hour her heart was enlarged to love and yearn over the whole wide world. Since that time her theme has ever been:

> "Oh that the world might taste and see
> The riches of His grace,
> The arms of love that compass me
> Would all mankind embrace."

A former student, an alumnus and also a graduate of Greenville College, commenting on this transformation that came into the life of Mr. Beers and through him was communicated to his wife, says: "I've had a growing appreciation of Mr. Beers' judgment the longer I have known the choice he made of a wife. A frail, impaired body, and absence of all attempts at assuming beauty through adornment, he selected a woman of strong definite convictions and personal powers, combined with the noblest aspirations and truest affection innate in a loving disposition. She proved herself a mother to us all—the multitude of students that came under her influence were drawn heavenward by her womanly confidence in each individual. How persistent in effort and labor was the very detail of the training she gave, whether in music, in rhetorical work, or in the ordinary class room! But when by faith in God and earnest prayer and personal effort, she led so many to a knowledge of the Savior, her motherly travail brought forth its truest offspring.

"Mr. Beers appreciated the worth of his helpmeet and delighted in calling her his queen. Well for the man that realizes the asset to his liabilities that God has thus given him. For in helping her to reign in all her queenly influence he possesses his kingdom and unconsciously becomes himself kingly. But her strongest output has been in the missionary interests of her church. To this cause all her other efforts led, and in that devotion we find her longest vigil, her best thought, and her most prevailing prayers. So when I learned that she had received her missionary enlargement and her world vision of the missionary movement from Mr. Beers, I exclaimed, 'That was the biggest thing he ever did.' And it was biggest for himself, for her and for their life contribution to the cause of Christ. He had received his missionary baptism which gave him a life-long purpose, and when her force was added to that purpose, he had the assistance that with God's help and in His will made their contribution to those early years of Seattle Seminary a possibility."

In the first weeks of the school there was no one using the third story of the building. These empty rooms made a very fine place for secret prayer. Climbing the long flights of stairs day after day, where she could be alone with God, Mrs. Beers would pray that this school might be truly a missionary school, that many young people might go and carry the gospel to heathen lands from this institution.

The prayers for money to lift the mortgage were answered in a short time. Mr. Beers had been traveling far and wide soliciting funds until at last the needed amount was raised. In a little less than five years from the time the school was first opened, a momentous event was celebrated by the faculty and students of the seminary. Mr. Beers had labored indefatigably night and day to raise the money and pay off the mortgage. Many friends had contributed of their means and prayed very earnestly that the debt might be cleared. After much sacrifice and prayer the goal was reached on March 3, 1898. Inasmuch as Mr. Beers' birthday was the following day it was decided to have the formal celebration on that day—March 4. With appropriate exercises of praise and thanksgiving the mortgage was formally burned.

In the spring of 1895 the Washington-Oregon Conference was separated and two conferences were organized from this territory. Bishop Coleman held the Washington Conference at the First Church in Seattle, on the corner of Ninth and Pine. A committee was appointed to visit the seminary and report. Many of the preachers and laymen accompanied the committee and came to us in a body, headed by Bishop Coleman. The building was inspected from the basement to the third floor and then the good bishop called every one into the seminary chapel and knelt in prayer. The Holy Ghost descended in pentecostal showers and the scene that followed was indescribable. Shouts of praise and tears of joy were mingled with cries of victory. Many were weeping and running from room to room, up and down stairs, while others were standing in silent awe before Jehovah.

One of the brethren in the ministry who had known Mr. Beers from the time when the school was first founded, writes these words of appreciation concerning his work: "Brother and Sister Beers came to Seattle nearly twenty-nine years ago to take charge of Seattle Seminary (now Seattle Pacific College), which consisted of an unimproved campus site, one building without any furnishings whatever, which was to serve as chapel, class rooms, dining hall and dormitory, with no student body and a debt of more than sixteen thousand dollars on the property, with a total membership in what was then known as the Oregon and Washington Conference (now four conferences) of six hundred and one, and church and parsonage property valued at less than twenty-eight thousand dollars, and in the midst of the most fearful financial panic we have ever known. Under these most discouraging conditions Brother Beers and his noble wife, with faith in God, heroically accepted the heavy burden which they bore for nearly a quarter of a century, and during those years of hardship and self-denial they never murmured or complained. Brother Beers was a man with a broad vision and the splendid buildings and beautiful campus of Seattle Pacific College are the result of that vision and his untiring labors and self-denial."

Rev. B. Winget, former missionary secretary of the church for many years, also writes words of commendation: "He took a great interest in the young, both intellectually and spiritually. This is why, in the beginning of his ministry, he undertook what seemed to be a difficult if not an impossible task, i. e., to raise money to pay the indebtedness on the Seattle Seminary, develop the institution and make it a success. He was a reader of men and knew how to adapt himself to different classes, so as to secure much financial help and other assistance for the school. His large sympathy and love for the students caused them to esteem him very highly. He was one of the most successful, if not the most successful, of all the educators in the church in the manifestation of tact and ability in securing funds from persons outside the church to aid the school. The growth of the school on material lines, in additional buildings, etc., the increase of students, the high character of the work done in the institution, and the advanced work introduced into the curriculum all are a living monument to his honor and memory. Precious will be the memories of him and his work in the hearts of many of the young to whom he was made a blessing."

CHAPTER VIII

WORK PROGRESSES—HINDERED BY QUARANTINE

Forsaking, everywhere,
  The prizes cheaplier won,
The eternal morn of true and pure
  Shall light us on, and on,
Till, over summits dim,
  In purple glooms afar,
We see, through deepening glory, swim
  Our victory's morning star.
                    —*George Shepard Burleigh.*

The attendance of both day students and boarders had so increased that at the beginning of the following year, 1899, we were greatly crowded. Mr. Beers had raised sufficient funds for a girls' dormitory which was erected and added greatly to the comfort of all. A little later it became necessary to reconstruct the interior of the brick building which had always been used as a boys' dormitory. The heating system, and particularly the ventilation, was very unsatisfactory, so at considerable expense a new heating plant was installed and the old objectionable ventilating plant was removed. The old dining-room, pantry and kitchen were made into living rooms which gave much additional space for the accommodation of young men. Much space had been wasted in the first construction of the building in enormous halls and stairways. This difficulty was overcome and several comfortable rooms were

added. When this work was completed, it was like
a new building and was greatly enjoyed by our
young men, while the young ladies rejoiced in their
new building and all were made more comfortable.

In the beginning of the school work the faculty
was composed of Mr. and Mrs. Beers only. He was
principal, financial agent, preacher, teacher and jan-
itor, while she was preceptress, teacher of mathematics, languages and music, matron and cook. But
with the addition of students they soon needed more
help. Miss Mary A. Burrows has the honor of being their first assistant teacher in the school. The
writer remembers the day when she called at the
school and offered her services. She had been receiving the usual fine remuneration given in the public schools, but she felt her heart prompted her to
come and share the sacrifice that was being made to
establish a Christian seminary. She came as needed
help in an emergency and ever proved herself a
blessing among the students. Mrs. Ella Colson was
also one of the first helpers as matron, and with her
two gifted daughters took a very prominent place in
building up the institution. From time to time it
became necessary to add to the members of the faculty. Mr. Beers was fortunate in securing the services of Prof. Clarke W. Shay in the fall of 1893,
who remained with the school for seven years altogether, acting first as teacher, then when Mr. Beers
was sent as pastor of the First Church in Seattle,
he filled the position of principal with acceptability.
Miss Emma Freeland, who had recently returned
from Wellesley College, became a member of the faculty in the fall of 1894 and added much to the spiri-

THE BRICK BUILDING—THE FIRST ERECTED

tuality and missionary enthusiasm of the school. For one school year Cupid played his part successfully and in June wedding bells rang merrily. A beautiful wedding ceremony was performed by Mr. Beers in the seminary chapel of the brick building. No one who was permitted to be present at that time will ever forget the sacred solemnity of the occasion. Professor Clarke W. Shay and Miss Emma Freeland were made one and remained with us for several years, rendering most efficient service as instructors and principal. Many students will rise up and call them blessed for the salutary influence they exerted over their lives.

"Whoso is wise and will observe these things, even they shall understand the loving kindness of the Lord." We can learn much by using our powers of observation and understand God's wonder-working ways. Parents too frequently do not make the necessary effort to secure for their children the proper training under holy influences. To educate their sons and daughters in one of our Christian schools often requires great sacrifice and many times their eyes are blinded by commercial gain and the desire for present personal ease. This "vision splendid" which was given to Mr. Beers in the early days of his ministry gave him a powerful influence over both parents and children. In the many trips he made, he often discovered precious "diamonds in the rough" and was never satisfied until he had succeeded in securing them as students; then he began at once the work of polishing these gems. He took great pride and delight in the boys and young men committed to his care and multitudes today in our

own fair land and across the ocean can testify to the
strong sway for righteousness that Mr. Beers exerted over their lives. The general Sunday School
secretary of the church in a personal letter writes,
"I want you to know that I greatly appreciated
Brother Beers and always admired him. I knew
him for years before he knew me. I am thinking
now of the lives of the many young people he has
touched, both in the church and outside. His work
can not help but go on, both in the high ideals he set
up and the self-sacrifice he inspired in these lives."
Dr. Roberts in a personal letter to Mr. Beers recog-
nizes the holy effect of his life over young people.
He writes, "My heart rejoices in all the beautiful
service you have been enabled to render; in the fine
testimony to Christ that you have given to men high
in the business world—how great and important
this has been none can measure—and in the hundreds of young people whose lives have been inspired by you; in the thousands influenced by your
teaching. How God has helped, blessed and honored you in these great services, but above all I rejoice that you have kept under the anointing of divine love." The author quotes from another letter
which came to Mr. Beers during his illness, which
was sent by one of the graduates from the first college class: "I want you to know how greatly I appreciate your godly and noble influence on my life.
It may cheer you some if I stir up your pure mind
by way of remembrance. How many useful young
lives in this world owe you a great debt of gratitude
under God for what they are today. Always upper-
most in my own mind is the beautiful fragrance of

your Christ-like life as I look back upon it. I trust that a host of blessed memories may gather as roses to line your couch, and if you find an occasional thorn, it will but prove that Christ opens to view the sacred door of fellowship in suffering."

Quotations are given from four other personal letters: "I shall think of him as I walk over those dear old paths on the campus, made sacred because he walked there. Yes, many precious memories come rushing through our minds as we think of his life among us. Many shall rise up and call him blessed." "I am glad I ever had the privilege of meeting him, and knowing his love for righteousness and truth. It was through him that my husband was converted. I am sure that when the books are opened, and the rewards are given, Brother Beers will have many stars in his crown." "There are a few things that I look back on with pleasure. One is your good friendship; second, that you united my good wife and me in holy matrimony; third, that your name is on my diploma from the Seattle Seminary. I want you to know that I appreciate these things." "I shall never, never forget his holy, dignified life, above reproach in every way. His influence has been a great blessing to my own soul."

Several families had recognized the necessity of early Christian training for their children that they might have the advantage of pure environments. Their labor and sacrifice were rewarded in the spiritual and intellectual betterment of their sons and daughters. An illustrious example of what persistent determination and loving self-sacrifice may accomplish is found in the education of a notable family of ten children who were placed, one by one, in the seminary in the second semester of the school's history. The parents, their two daughters and one son had been brought out into the light of entire sanctification. There were six noble sons who must be saved and fitted for God's service. The last baby girl was born soon after the intrepid mother reached Seattle. They did not have sufficient means to pay the railroad fare from eastern Washington to the coast, but they possessed horses and several cows. Two large wagons were fitted up in schooner fashion and then filled in with as much provisions and clothing, bedding, etc., as could be stowed away. The horses were employed to draw these wagons over the mountains and through the vales, while the cattle were driven. They always stopped to rest on the Lord's day, excepting in one instance when they were compelled to travel a short distance to prepare themselves food. The trip was interspersed with trials and pleasures, and after about three weeks they reached Seattle in safety. No one will ever know the great sacrifice and privation that was endured by this noble family for the first few years after they arrived in Seattle. But they were upheld by an almighty arm and their faithfulness was honored in later years by the salvation of every child. One dear boy went to be with the Lord while he was but a child, and all of the others were called to fill some important position in life as Christian men and women. One son was principal at Spring Arbor Seminary and also at Chesbrough Seminary for several years, while another taught for a while at Greenville College and rendered efficient service as teacher in public schools for a number of years, and is now filling the position of principal of a school in western Washington. Five of these sons and daughters were called across the ocean to carry the gospel to the heathen. The dear missionary mother had the privilege, before she laid down her cross and received her crown, of visiting some of her children across the Pacific. One son has since gone to Japan, and one daughter and son now labor in China under a sister church board. It now appears that every member of this large family will not only make the portals of glory, but their lives will have been used for the salvation of souls and the elevation of humanity. Who can think that such blessed results would have been realized if these ten children had been placed in worldly schools?

Following this era of marked prosperity which the school had been enjoying, dark shadows were gathering in the sky and obscured the sunlight of divine Providence that had shown so brightly over them. The red scourge of small-pox broke out among the students and the school was under strict quarantine for about two months. More than thirty persons were afflicted with the disease and nearly every one was compelled to be vaccinated. Great cause for thankfulness will ever exist that there were no deaths. If the city had not insisted upon shutting the well persons with the sick, thus making it impossible for any one to observe the laws of quarantine, many would have escaped the contagion. But since there was no isolation possible, under the city's regime the boarders were compelled to pay their expenses even though they were held against their will and could not pursue their school work in any measure. Later on, however, Mr. Beers pleaded the case before the city council so successfully that five hundred dollars' damage was obtained from the city to reimburse those who had been so imprisoned.

At the time this sickness began, Mr. Beers was holding a series of meetings in Portland and vicinity. Mrs. Beers had accompanied him to assist in the services, but was soon taken with the dread disease and came down to the gates of death, where for days her life was despaired of. Nothing but the prayers of God's children kept her from crossing over. Mr. Beers made every effort to secure a nurse for her, but such terror filled the hearts of the people concerning this epidemic at that time that no one could be found who was willing to care for a patient afflicted with this disease. What was even more serious, there was no doctor in the city who was willing to take a case of small-pox. Consequently Mr. Beers became both doctor and nurse during three weeks of his wife's illness. Her bodily sufferings were very great, with no remedies to alleviate the pain. At times it seemed that she could not endure this any longer; then Mr. Beers would bow in prayer and plead with God until she was relieved. Truly the dear heavenly Father had great compassion upon these afflicted ones, thus left without human aid, and came Himself to the rescue. We will let Mrs. Beers relate her own experience during these days of peculiar trial: "It would be impossible to describe the beautiful music that burst upon my ears from time to time when my bodily sufferings were so great. It seemed like a wonderful orchestra from heaven was playing upon invisible instruments just for my solace and comfort. Sometimes these heavenly messengers sang to me, and one chorus that was repeated over and over was this:

'God's almighty arms are around me,
  Peace, peace is mine.
Judgment scenes can not confound me,
  Peace, peace is mine.'

and when the line, 'Peace, peace is mine,' was sung, my soul seemed to be floating out upon an ocean of peace, while billows of peace flowed over me and all sense of suffering was forgotten in the transport of the hour.

"The evening of the day on which I was taken, the health officer came out from the city and insisted on taking me to the pest house. The weather was cold and snowy and by this time I was in a high fever, and it would evidently have been certain death to take me in the open carriage in which he had come. He reasoned that I could expose no one until the following day, and thus my husband and friends would be spared infection from the disease. We were then at the home of Mr. and Mrs. Felix Gilbert of blessed memory. My husband had no choice if Brother Gilbert refused to keep me. There was no other place for me but the dreaded pest house. Going to Brother Gilbert, he told him the situation and said, 'It is just as you say, Brother Gilbert. This is your house, and if you so decide, I shall be compelled to let the officer take my wife away. I fear, however, that it will prove her death.' Father Gilbert was a strong, noble-looking man. Drawing himself to full height,

he said, 'No, sir, the officer shall never take Mrs.
Beers to the pest house from my home. If I take the
disease and my wife takes it, we will all die and go
to glory together.' As they were both aged, this
was a brave utterance and showed a courageous
spirit. I have ever thought since those days of trial
when I reach heaven and have looked upon the face
of my Savior, I shall hasten to Father and Mother
Gilbert, and again tell them how grateful I have
been all through the years for the loving shelter
they gave us during the six weeks of our quarantine.
When the crisis was past and I was convalescent, I
prayed earnestly that my husband might be spared
the contagion, but after nursing me for three weeks,
he found himself in need of a nurse. For a day or
two he bravely resisted the symptoms and the weakness that was stealing over him. At last he could
resist no longer and went to bed at noon, saying,
'It's no use. I shall have to yield to the disease.'
Before sunset he was in the throes of a raging fever.
I was still very weak and perfectly powerless to do
anything for him more than to bathe his face and
pray. He grew worse very rapidly, so that soon he
lay with purple face, swollen lips, moaning in great
pain, and too ill to notice me at all. We had many
friends in Seattle and Portland, but we were iso-
lated from them all. Not one could assist us nor
come into our presence. We knew they were praying for us, but oh! the loneliness and well-nigh despair that swept over me when I saw my husband
lying in this condition. Every hour I went into his
room to see how he was feeling, but each time came
back with a terrified, broken heart. Through all my

illness he had nursed me so carefully, so tenderly, refusing to put me in the pest house, even though the doctor said he might escape himself if he would. And now I thought he would die. What should I do? Oh, if I could only have medical aid for him or a skilful nurse. Oh, if some friend could only speak words of comfort to me or advise me what to do! At three o'clock in the morning he did not know me. I feared he would not live till sunrise. Too weak to kneel, I crouched in a heap on the floor and told my heavenly Father all about my terrible extremity. It seemed He stood close by my side. Has God not promised, 'I will never leave thee nor forsake thee'? I do not know how long I pleaded for my husband's life to be spared. But at last the assurance came and my prayer was answered. It seemed there were gold letters inscribed up above my head, 'I will heal him speedily.' Great peace filled my soul. I rested quietly until four o'clock, then I went to his bedside and found him with perspiration pouring from every pore in his body. His fever was gone, the muscles of his face had relaxed, and he was sleeping in a normal manner. At five I was compelled to change everything about him, it was so saturated, and at daylight he said, 'Please give me something to eat. I am as hungry as a bear.' He was really healed, but to prove that he had small-pox evidently, two of the pustules came on his face and several on his arms. However, he arose from his bed and felt as well as usual, although the health officer insisted on his staying in quarantine another three weeks."

CHAPTER IX

BUILDINGS ERECTED—TRIP TO NOME

Whoever sees 'neath winter's field of snow
The silent harvest of the future grow,
God's power must know.
                    —*Edward Bulwer Lytton.*

A child's kiss set on thy singing lips shall make thee glad;
A poor man served by thee shall make thee rich;
A sick man helped by thee shall make thee strong;
Thou shalt be served by every sense
Of service which thou renderest.   —*Mrs. Browning.*

During the early days of the school, Mr. Beers
had acted as pastor of a small band of pilgrims who
gathered every Sunday in the small seminary chapel
in the brick building. So sacred did the place become that when a capacious and comfortable church
was erected across the street, and another preacher
installed, the saints were loath to leave the spot.
Mr. Beers had been graciously blessed in preaching
to them and the young people worshipped with their
elders in sweet and blessed fellowship. His ministry in the students' Tuesday night meetings was
also crowned with the salvation of souls. In nearly
every service some of the students were saved or
sanctified. The standards of the Free Methodist
Church were held up faithfully in the school and
church services. With the steady growth of the institution, secular matters and temporal burdens

THE CIRCLE ON THE COLLEGE CAMPUS

pressed harder and heavier upon him. In the fall of 1902 Professor and Mrs. A. H. Stilwell came from Greenville to assist in the school work and have ever proved a great blessing to the school and to the community. Professor Stilwell continued in the school for, fourteen years. The heavy obligation resting upon Mr. Beers incident to the erection of an administration building, the girls' new dormitory and the dining-hall, compelled him to be absent a great deal in raising funds, and the trustees made Professor Stilwell principal, who will be remembered for his efficiency as an instructor and for his ever constant smile. The same year, Professor Omer A. Burns had graduated from Greenville College, June the 18th, and six days later had been united in marriage to an accomplished young lady from Belvidere, Illinois. They came to Seattle on their wedding trip and became at once honored members of the faculty. Their services proved invaluable and Professor Burns has continued in the school since then, at the head of the history department. While it is not practicable to mention all the self-sacrificing and capable teachers who were employed during the years Mr. Beers was connected with the seminary and college, there is one who has continued as teacher of Greek, German and English for so long a time, and who has always been deeply interested in the spiritual interest of the students, that justice could hardly be done to the work of Mr. Beers in the school without mentioning the name of Miss May Marston. She has remained in the institution from the time she entered in the fall of 1902, with the exception of two years only, which were spent at the

McPherson Seminary in Kansas. Mr. Beers ever possessed a lofty and laudable ambition to secure teachers who were not only well qualified as instructors of the topics assigned them, but were also truly God-fearing and consistent Christians. Scholastic attainments merely were not a sufficient recommendation. The teachers he employed must be men and women who would inspire the students to reach the highest altitudes of a true spiritual life and would ever seek to lead them also to the deepest depths of a whole-hearted consecration. Divine providence smiled upon his efforts to get the best, and at the time he left the school the members of the faculty were a strong body of godly teachers, well qualified as instructors in the grades, the preparatory course, and in all the college curriculum.

Although Mr. Beers was constantly employed in the secular matters pertaining to the school, he never forgot his calling. He loved to preach the sacred gospel and was never so happy as when he could dispense the Word of Life from the pulpit. So when the conference thought best to send him to the Free Methodist Church in Seattle as pastor, in the spring of 1902, he went joyfully. At this time Mr. and Mrs. Beers had but recently moved into their beautiful new home, which had been built from money received from her father's estate and which they were enjoying immensely. It now seemed a great contrast to them to move into the dilapidated old parsonage which was located underneath the audience room where the church services were held. They left the school in the care of Professor and Mrs. Stilwell, while Mr. Beers still remained financial secretary and president of the board of trustees. They were not compelled to worship long, however, in the old ram-shackled place. One of the bishops of the church said of Mr. Beers, that he could raise the most money with the fewest words of any man he ever saw. Certainly at this time he showed wonderful skill in securing funds, for he was so successful that he soon had a beautiful new church ready for dedication. The members of the church and friends were delighted with their fine new building, but the preacher and his wife still lived in the old barn-like parsonage. We would not have any one suppose, however, that their hearts were heavy because of their unpleasant surroundings—not so; no king in his palace nor queen with her ladies in waiting could be happier than they were as they labored on in the will of God. With indomitable courage Mr. Beers persisted in soliciting funds and soon had a new parsonage ready for occupancy, next door to the church. Here they spent many happy hours. In passing, it is fitting to note one auspicious event that occurred in the fine new parsonage. When his mother was dying, she had committed the care of his baby sister, Violet, to him, and Mr. and Mrs. Beers had cared for her since she was twelve years of age. She had been placed in the seminary and had acquitted herself creditably in her studies and was a great favorite among the students. The time had come for her to take that most important step— the one that marks the weal or woe of a young lady —and she was married in this new parsonage to a fine young business man from Portland, Oregon. Many of the students came down from the seminary to attend the beautiful ceremony that was performed by her brother.

With the building of the church and parsonage on his circuit, one might suppose that this pastor might have been satisfied with his labors in this respect; but no, "more and more" was his watchword. He saw an opportunity to build for the church an apartment house to rent, consisting of four flats, in which the church owned a half interest, and in due process of time had this building erected also. A friend who was an alumnus from the college and missionary to China, when called upon to make some remarks upon the occasion of his birthday, very fittingly called him "Alexander, the Great Builder." This poem will be found in the closing chapter.

In all of his work as builder, however, the spiritual interests of the society were not neglected. His regular congregations were more than doubled, the attendance in the Sunday-school was greatly increased, and the missionary society was in a flourishing condition. Many souls were saved and the work generally was prosperous. Among the trophies of grace secured, while he was pastor at the First Church, was a young man who was dying of tuberculosis. Mr. Beers found him in an old house where everything betokened poverty. The young man's sister admitted the pastor, but told him privately that her brother was an infidel and had become very much prejudiced against all preachers. Mr. Beers inquired if there was any article of food of which he was especially fond. She said that he had been asking for oranges and oysters, but they were altogether too poor to buy them. So before the pastor entered the room he purchased some large oranges and held one in each hand as he approached the bed. With a pleasant smile he asked the young man if he ever ate oranges, which at once disarmed the poor fellow of all his prejudices; in fact, he did not know that Mr. Beers was a preacher. He conversed very pleasantly on different topics with him for a while, and then said, "May I pray with you?" The young man hesitated and before he could reply, Mr. Beers said, "Now, I will guarantee that no harm shall come to you through my prayer. I promise to insure you against all damage." This so amused the young man that he said, "Yes, you can pray, but you must make it short." Fortunately Mr. Beers knew how to reach the throne by a short circuit, and when he withdrew, the young man seemed very tender. The next time Mr. Beers visited him, he carried a can of oysters in his hand, and found the sick man much more approachable. He was in such a dark spiritual condition and so weak physically, it seemed as if there was little hope for his salvation. But as Mr. Beers visited him day after day, he soon gained his confidence, pointed him to the Lamb of God, which taketh away the sins of the world, and had the inexpressible joy of seeing him pass over the river rejoicing in a bright hope.

Among the pleasing incidents that occurred while he was pastor at the First Church was one which at first appeared very unfortunate. While the family were at church one evening, a thief entered the front hall and stole Mr. Beers' overcoat. Smaller things of less importance were taken also, but the loss of the coat was a very heavy one, coming in mid-winter when it was so greatly needed. The morning papers called attention to this fact, and during the day an important telephone message came to Mr. Beers. A gentleman, who with his brother was an owner of the largest hardware store in Seattle, invited Mr. Beers to call at his office. As he entered the room, the good man arose and grasped his hand, saying, "I've called you down here because I had a warm thought about your welfare. Here, take this check and get you a new overcoat." This very generous check furnished him a much better coat than the one that was stolen. It was like the clothing worn by God's people of old—it seemed it would never wear out.

While Mr. Beers was pastor of the First Church in Seattle, he was taken very ill with appendicitis. The disease baffled the skill of the best physicians and his condition became very critical indeed. Friends advised an operation at once, but the attending physician did not. As the faithful wife prayed for divine guidance, she was constrained "to wait"—still he grew worse. Prayer was being offered for his recovery in all parts of the city. Two young ladies called and begged Mrs. Beers to order an ambulance and remove him to the hospital for an immediate operation. They pleaded so hard, she told them to go and ask their physician to call on Mr. Beers, and if his decision was an operation, she would follow his advice. While they were gone, Mr. Beers called his wife to the bedside and said the Spirit had been whispering recovery to him. He wished her to read from Job 29:20, "My glory was

fresh in me and my bow was renewed in my hand."
Also from Whittier's "Eternal Goodness":

> "I know not where His islands lift
>   Their fronded palms in air;
> I only know I can not drift
>   Beyond His love and care."

About this time a friend, who had formerly been a
physician, called and recommended a simple rem-
edy, which was gladly employed, and before the
young ladies returned the crisis was passed and he
was entirely relieved. His strength returned rapidly, and his bow against sin and wickedness was
renewed and became stronger than in former years.
Later, the physician who had attended him all
through his illness told Mrs. Beers he had realized
the gravity of the case from the first and felt confident very many doctors would have ordered the use
of the knife; the reason he had not done this was because he feared the operation would prove fatal.
How wonderfully God controls in the care of His
servants!

The summer of 1903 was remarkable in many
ways. After the General Conference, Mr. Beers
went on to New York City and visited the editor of
the *Christian Herald*. Dr. Klopsch took great interest in the seminary and gave a fine write-up in
his excellent paper. Mr. Beers was invited to preach
in the Bowery Mission, New York City, where he
had a very large audience with fine results on the
night of July 3. The next day there was a great
celebration of the Fourth, at Mont Lawn, which he
had the pleasure of attending, in company with Dr.
Klopsch and other noted people.

He found Mont Lawn a beautiful spot, where the children of the tenements and slums might enjoy for a time the benefits of fresh air, sunshine, green grass, abundance of wholesome food, clean beds, and are taught the blessed truths of the Scriptures. His heart was deeply touched as he listened to the tender verses they had committed and the pretty songs they sang, all breathing the spirit of love to God and our country, then closing with a graceful salute to Old Glory. This was a memorable occasion to him. The great work that he saw was being accomplished among the children conformed to his ideals of what should be done, and inspired him in his efforts for the elevation of childhood and youth.

While returning to Seattle he had a wonderful dream which we give in his own language, quoted from a letter dated July 6, 1903: "I had a fine night's rest last night. I was awakened after seven o'clock in the morning by a most refreshing dream. I seemed to be drilling in the ground for water. After considerable hard work, water as clear as crystal and sparkling like diamonds in the sunshine began to spring up in the air. First the drops were as large as birds' eggs, and then the most beautiful stream of clear water gushed high over my head. And as it leaped upward, it produced strains of the most enchanting music. My soul was charmed with the celestial strains and I awoke not to find myself in heaven, but lying in a dirty tourist sleeper. But the dream greatly refreshed me, after all."

It was in the early fall of the same year that he made his memorable trip to Nome, Alaska. Mrs. Mary E. Gilbert, of Portland, Oregon, had been urging him to go and collect a debt of several thousand dollars for her. She told him that he might have half of all he could collect from the creditor for the seminary. This was a sufficient incentive to make the trial. But Mrs. Gilbert had lost sight of the man and the debt had really become outlawed by the lapse of time. She felt sure, however, as the man who owed her was an old friend and formerly a Christian man, that if Mr. Beers could find him he could be induced to pay at least part of the amount. Mr. Beers did not like to make such an expensive trip on such uncertainties, so he continued to wait on God until he could see the way clearly. "A little child shall lead them," and truly in this instance a little girl did lead aright. While waiting for an elevator one day, he noticed a little girl crying, and inquiring the cause of her grief, he found she had lost her mamma. He then devoted himself to comforting and caring for the child. Presently the mother came down in the elevator and clasped her little girl in her arms joyously. She said, "Did you tell the gentleman where you live?" "I live in Nome," said she. In the conversation that followed with the mother, Mr. Beers learned that the lady was the wife of Dr. Rininger, of Nome, Alaska, and that her husband was the family physician of the very man Mr. Beers wished to locate. He also learned that the long-sought man was in good financial circumstances and could well afford to pay his debts. All doubts and fears were now removed and Mr. Beers embarked for Nome on the first boat that sailed. Reaching Nome, he found the man without any difficulty and with very satisfactory results. After he returned, he sent Mrs. Gilbert a check of $1,000.00, while the seminary was also enriched with a like amount. For two or three years Mr. Beers followed the matter up until the man finally settled with Mrs. Gilbert, although with considerable compromise on her part.

We must not pass on without noting some events that occurred on this remarkable trip. As was the custom in traveling, Mr. Beers "sowed beside all waters" among the passengers on the boat. At the table he sat next to an elderly white-haired gentleman, who was connected with the Smithsonian Institute at Washington, D. C. This man was very intelligent and a fine traveling companion, who claimed to be a skeptic. He was particularly fond of his wife, who was conspicuous for her wealth of beautiful white hair, and paid her the most courteous attention, being ever at her side. Mr. Beers had noticed this, and watched his chance to reprove the man for his constant fault-finding with divine providence. One day, after the gentleman had been criticising the heat in the South and the ice in the North, Mr. Beers said, "Do you not think God's goodness to you and me is very great? As for me, every time I look into the face of my good wife, I feel so thankful that God gave her to me that it more than repays me for all the mosquitos of the South or the icebergs in the North." Slapping his knee, the old man said to him vehemently, "Young man, I have as good a wife as ever lived." Mr. Beers replied, "We all feel sure you have, and it seems to me that you should be thankful that God has given you such a companion instead of finding so much fault with your heavenly Father." Silence reigned supreme. The next day the gentleman called Mr. Beers to one side and said, "Young man, that was a hard thrust you gave me yesterday, but I deserved it." We are glad to say there was no more fault-finding heard in his conversation. Several years later Mr. Beers met this same man in a depot at Seattle, in company with his son. He had been very ill and seemed greatly subdued. He told Mr. Beers that he was a changed man and said, "I am not troubled with doubts as I used to be. Please pray for me."

On the same trip one of his traveling companions, with whom he became quite well acquainted, was a Mr. Murphy who had made a fortune in Alaskan gold mines. He frankly professed himself an infidel. After several profitable conversations with him, they separated at Nome. Before embarking for home, Mr. Beers thought he would look up Mr. Murphy, but learned with regret that he was very sick at a hospital. He at once went to visit him, but was refused admittance by the nurse, who told him that no one was allowed to see him. Mr. Beers gave his card to the nurse to take to the sick man, and Mr. Murphy sent out immediately for Mr. Beers to come in. He found him very ill with typhoid fever and his recovery appeared doubtful. He urged the claims of God upon him and prayed for the sick man. Mr. Murphy, too, closed his eyes and prayed for mercy. He gave himself to the Lord as best he could in his weakness, and said he felt his sins were forgiven. A few weeks after Mr. Beers returned to Seattle, he received an urgent message from this same gentleman, asking him to call at his hotel. He had a wonderful story to tell Mr. Beers. He said he had never touched tobacco nor had any craving for it, since he gave himself to God in the hospital at Nome. Furthermore, he had returned to his home, where he had wines and liquors stored in the cellar, and had poured every drop into the streets. He was, indeed, a changed man.

On the same trip, while on the boat, Mr. Beers asked to hold a service on board. The captain gave consent rather reluctantly, saying he did not believe any one would come. Nothing daunted, Mr. Beers went throughout the length and breadth of the boat, inviting the passengers, the first, second and steerage passengers, to come. He even went down to the engine room, and urged all the men there to attend the meeting. The result was a large crowd and a great meeting.

Just before the service began, one of the deck hands was making the necessary preparations, improvising a pulpit, etc. Mr. Beers came by with his traveler's cap on his head and wearing a short frock coat. The boy never guessed that he was to be the preacher of the day, and called out, "Do you know who the minister is that is to spout for us today?" And then without waiting for an answer, he sang out lustily as he draped the box with the American flag, "Blessed is the man who sitteth on a hot stove, for he shall rise again." Making no comment, Mr. Beers went to his room, put on his preacher's coat, took his Bible and came back. The boy gave one glance at him, then disappeared down the stairway. After the meeting was over, he sought Mr. Beers out and made a very humble apology. This gave a fitting opportunity to talk seriously with the young man about his eternal interests. In a letter that was written to his wife, while making this trip, he says: "This is the eighth day since I bade you goodby in Seattle. They have been long days, but the Lord has been good to me, keeping me from sea-sickness, but not from home-sickness, and a great longing to see you. How I do miss you. I feel that I am in God's order. The first two days the devil tempted me sorely about my coming, but I have the victory now and God is blessing me. I am getting acquainted with men from Nome, who will help Seattle Seminary, I believe. We are now in Behring Sea, and will reach Nome tomorrow night, landing Saturday morning if the waves are not too high. I have had a pleasant trip thus far. The purser and all of the officers on board have been very kind to me, giving me the seat of honor at the table, showing me many kindnesses. The passengers also have been very kind to me, excepting a little religious persecution from some of them, of which I will tell you when I return." Altogether the voyage was very eventful both in going and coming. No doubt much seed was sown that will bring an abundant harvest.

Soon after his return, Mr. Beers prepared a lecture on his trip, which he delivered in the seminary and in places near Seattle. When he attended the executive meeting in the fall he was asked to deliver this lecture in Central Church, Chicago, and later on he went to Greenville College and Spring Arbor Seminary, and gave his lecture to the faculty and students. No one who listened to his thrilling description of the storm at sea, which he encountered, will ever forget this account. Every passenger had been ordered to his berth, but so great was the violence of the storm that it was only with great difficulty that any one could remain there. One man was thrown violently to the floor and seriously injured. Mr. Beers braced his feet and grasped the iron bar above his head, holding on for dear life during the fourteen hours the storm raged. Above the roar of the waves could be heard the screams of the frightened passengers. Many were praying, calling on God mightily for mercy, but Mr. Beers remained perfectly calm and unmoved. Though he thought the ship would surely go to the bottom, he knew he was safe in the arms of Jesus and had no fear. We give a brief extract from Mr. Beers' lecture. "Again and again the old ship seemed to shout, 'I think I will mount to the heavens,' and up, up, up, she was carried on the towering waves, until all hope was lost. Now we hear her sighing, 'I am so tired I want to lie down a while,' and down, down, down she would descend as if to a bottomless abyss. Listen! Again she shrieks, 'Let me turn over,' and over she goes on her broadside, without ceremony, while the captain and officers fear a watery grave. These dangerous movements of the ship continued until the storm ceased and the waters became quiet."

During the three years he was pastor of the First Church in Seattle, Mr. Beers never lost his interest in the school. The work there had been constantly growing until it had become so great that it was thought best for him to return as principal of the school with Professor Stilwell. The conference now appointed him pastor of the Second or Seminary Free Methodist Church, which position he occupied for three years, acting as principal at the same time. The people at the Seminary church were building at this time a fine, commodious edifice, which was nearly completed, but they had no home for their pastor. The members had contributed so heavily in building the church, they felt very doubtful about erecting a parsonage until some time had passed by. Here again was another chance to improve upon all the resources God gives. The society owned a nice plot of ground next to the church, which was very suitable for a manse. Mr. Beers saw that now was the auspicious time to erect this building also. He knew they were fearful in regard to the financial burden it would bring, should they now try to raise money for this object. To disarm them, he said in their official meeting, "If I go out and raise the money for a parsonage from the business men of Seattle and deed it to you, will you accept it?" Now they were eager to grant his request. One writer has said, "A Christian man is one who is always doing the impossible." Again this courageous man, with surprising faith in God, solicited funds from friends in the city and secured the necessary money to build a modern eight-room house completely finished and partially furnished, and presented it to the society free from all encumbrance. This gift received a very kind reception from the members of the church, inasmuch as Mr. Beers had secured the funds entirely from people outside of the Free Methodist denomination, with the exception of about two hundred dollars.

CHAPTER X

SCHOOL BUILDINGS ERECTED—MISSIONARIES EMBARK

Church of God, send forth the light
To the lands long steeped in night;
To the myriads groping there
'Neath the shades of grim despair.
Hear ye not their plaintive cry,
"Help us! save us! ere we die"?
Gird thee then with heavenly might,
Haste to send them gospel light.
—*Wilson T. Hogue.*

From the time of its inception, the Seattle Seminary had been permeated with missionary enthusiasm. "The Whole Wide World for Jesus" had been the battle cry, "Every student a home or foreign missionary," the slogan. The momentous hour when dear Miss H—— settled her divine call to India will never be forgotten. A wonderful blessing came on the entire institution from her glowing, exultant testimony. One of the teachers, too, had received a call while a student in Chesbrough Seminary. But as his heart was strangely enthralled by the thrilling testimony of this beautiful girl, he wisely refrained from telling any one he was called to India, too, until after their engagement was announced. They were married at the home of the bride's father in Centralia, Washington, but returned for a wonderful farewell at the seminary. The whole school went down to the depot to join in the parting song and to catch a last glimpse of Rev. and Mrs. M. C. Clarke, the first missionaries to go out from the Seattle Seminary to foreign lands.

Other students followed and the school soon bade a fond farewell to dear Jules and Lilla Eva Ryff, who embarked for dark Africa. The interest seemed ever to increase as the institution was frequently favored with visits from returned missionaries, who addressed the students on the pressing needs of their respective stations. Such addresses fanned their zeal and made them wish to go at once to foreign lands. In some instances it required wisdom to hold them to their work of preparation until the proper time came for them to engage in foreign missionary work. During the ten years following the outgoing of our first missionaries from the school, twenty students and three teachers went from the institution to foreign lands, averaging a little more than two every year. Of these, there were nine couples, seven of whom were wedded before leaving Seattle; one pair was married in India and the other in China. Since the year 1911, thirteen other students have gone to distant fields and two more are now anxiously waiting the time to embark for China. It would not be advisable to give a complete history of the workers in these pages as this has been done in other literature. Mention will be made of several important events only in their lives and the names given of the pioneers to the five countries in which Free Methodist missions are now maintained:

C. Floyd Appleton, who later married Miss Laura

Millican, was our first student to enter China; Rev.
and Mrs. August Youngren, the first to go to Japan;
Rev. and Mrs. Roy Nichols, our first representatives
in Santo Domingo; the names of the first students
to go to India and Africa have already been given,
and to Rev. and Mrs. Burton Beegle belongs the
honor of being the first students from Seattle Pacific College to take up work in Panama. Our precious Clara Leffingwell added not a little to the
number of foreign recruits. She had been laboring
in the China Inland Mission for several years and
had returned to America on a furlough. When she
visited the school, she fastened her attention upon
several promising young people whom she desired to
press into service. As the result of her pleadings
and prayers we lost one of our valuable teachers and
two students. She had a strong conviction that the
Free Methodist Church should open work in China,
and in conversation with Mr. Beers she enlisted his
sympathies and he felt that she was right in this
matter. Later when she attended the General Conference at Greenville to present the subject to the
church, the leaders thought that the finances of the
missionary treasury would hardly seem to warrant
an extension of foreign work to a new country. They
decided, however, if Miss Leffingwell could raise sufficient funds, that they would open the work as she
desired, and we all remember how faithfully she labored and the success that crowned her efforts.

Mr. Beers was now enlisted in her cause and felt
very clearly that God was leading the church to a
forward movement in China. While he was visiting
Mrs. B. T. Roberts, a mother in Israel, the conversa-

tion turned to the subject of mission work in China. Mother Roberts remarked that she thought it was God's time to open up the work there at once. Mr. Beers said, "If we wait until we see our way through, that will not be faith." As he arose to bid her good-by, Mother Roberts said, "I hate to see you go. I wish I could live with you always." He replied, "We shall live together some day." After he had gone, Mother Roberts said to a friend, "He is cut on too large a plan to suit some people." This conversation greatly strengthened Mr. Beers in his conviction, and when the General Conference met again he went before the Missionary Board and urged them to begin work in China without delay. Before leaving his home in Seattle he had presented this important question to Nils B. Peterson who, the reader will remember, gave the land upon which the seminary was built, on condition that it should be a missionary school. He learned at this time that Mr. Peterson was also greatly interested in work among the Chinese and was ready to contribute a large sum, providing the church would move forward at once. As he pleaded the case before the Missionary Board, he mentioned this fact and secured their promise that if Mr. Peterson would cooperate and assist them financially at this time, they would venture to undertake this new work. Forthwith sending a telegram to Mr. Peterson, he soon received the promise of five thousand dollars, or of property that was worth that amount. So the matter was definitely settled and the heart of our dear Mother Roberts rejoiced greatly when she heard the glad news.

Some passing scenes make a lasting impression never to be effaced. Such was an occasion that came in the life of a young lady who was called to Japan and betrothed to a young man in the school. The day was set for the marriage and the wedding trousseau nearly completed, when an urgent letter came from the missionary secretary, Rev. B. Winget, asking Mr. Beers to take an important message to the young lady. The board wished her to postpone her marriage and go at once to Japan, leaving the young man to finish his course at the seminary and join her in Japan a year later. This was indeed a severe test of her consecration. As Mr. Beers delivered Rev. Winget's message, she sat with downcast eyes for a few moments, while all color left her face. Then she looked straight at Mr. Beers and in a clear voice she said firmly, "I will go." What a victory over all selfish consideration. Her sacrifice was well rewarded as the missionary secretary decided to wait a little until the young man received his diploma and send them out as husband and wife.

Using the figure of the service flag, we had now fourteen silver stars on the flag. We felt highly honored when one who had graduated from our second class in the preparatory course decided to answer the call for foreign missionaries and embarked for China. Another silver star had been added. But when the sad news reached us that our dear Lily Peterson had contracted a fatal disease and was coming home to die, what sorrow filled our hearts! In loving submission she said, "God's will be done. It is all for the best." A few short weeks with her loved ones and her pure spirit went to be forever with God.

With sad hearts we placed the first gold star on the service flag. Upon the hill above the seminary is her sacred grave, with the inscription, "White precious Lily," as the Chinese always called her, which is the literal translation of her name. Also the scripture from Isaiah 49:12, "Behold, these shall come from far and lo these from the North and the West; and these from the land of Sinim." These inscriptions give a pathetic appeal to every one who visits the spot. The Chinese mourned deeply when Lily bade them a last farewell in China, and it seemed that a great gap was made in the ranks of our workers. The place was soon filled, however, for her sister stepped forward and offered her services as a missionary there so that the work might not be hindered.

> Send on the finest of your flocks,
> The child that sweetest sings,
> And ye, who have no child, send gold
> For missionary wings.

When we parted with Lorena Marston we felt we had given the best we had to God. Rena, as she was always called, was fair, sweet and womanly, and a well trained nurse. All hearts were filled with bright prospects for years of usefulness for her. A few months after she left Seattle for India, Mr. Beers was called to minister to her father in his last illness. She had felt only one regret in leaving her home, her loved father was not saved. He missed her very greatly, and it seemed to soften his heart and make him long for salvation. Now when he was very ill he welcomed Mr. Beers to his bedside and listened eagerly to his loving words of exhortation.

He willingly yielded himself to the Lord and left a clear evidence that he had gone to be forever with Him. God had been very gracious and Rena's fervent prayer for her father had been heard and answered. Only a few months was she separated from the father she loved so well. A happy reunion soon took place in heaven and she, too, went to meet her loved ones there. With sorrowful heart, another gold star was added to the service flag. A few months ago when dear Lilla Ryff joined the triumphant hosts above, the third gold star was placed on the missionary service flag.

The year of 1904-5 was an exceedingly important one for the seminary. The school had been favored with a steady growth and ever-increasing attendance until an administration or regular school building became a necessity. Up to this time the assembly room, recitation rooms, dining hall and young men's dormitory had all been combined under one roof—that of the brick building. Mr. Beers had been carrying on a steady campaign in public meetings and private circles and had succeeded in raising sufficient funds to warrant him in beginning this thirty thousand dollar undertaking. Presenting the matter to the trustees, they decided to arise and build. When Mr. Beers began planning the new school building, he remarked, "We will have one room—a chapel—for divine worship. No classes shall ever be held there, it shall be formally dedicated to God the same as we dedicate our churches." So when the architect drew the plans for the administration building, this chapel was incorporated in the western end of the building, a real sanctuary

THE ADMINISTRATION BUILDING, ERECTED IN 1904-05

with regular Gothic windows and pews, a beautiful pulpit with Gothic chairs and an altar where many souls have wept their way to God in all the years that have passed. Mr. Beers paid his workmen off regularly and progress was made only as fast as the funds would warrant. When he had the structure up, and the walls ready for plastering, he found himself lacking the money to go ahead. He estimated that the labor and material of the lathing and plastering would cost one thousand dollars. But he did not have this amount. Now the sisters of the Ross society had maintained their regular afternoon prayer meeting for a long time. Going before them one afternoon he requested them to pray for one thousand dollars to be used for this great need. Those who were present at that time will never forget this particular meeting, neither in time nor eternity. It would not be possible to mention all who were present, but the names of two noble ladies who seemed to be privileged above some of the others in their petitions should be given. Grandma Denny and Mrs. M. Wheelon besieged the throne of grace until the windows of heaven were opened and copious showers fell on all who were there. With great assurance they shouted, "I have it, I have it, it's coming, O glory!" It is difficult to describe the scene that followed; laughing and weeping for joy, running and leaping, shouting and singing the praises of God were all in order and all formalities were forgotten. All were made certain the prayer was answered and the needed money would be forthcoming. The cheering word was passed on to Mr. Beers and the plasterers began their labors. The time had nearly expired when the workmen must be paid and bills met; still the money did not come. The faith of these noble women did not waiver and the money was expected to come daily, yes, hourly. The day before Thanksgiving was the day of days. When Mr. Beers opened his mail he found a draft for one thousand dollars from S. E. Scott, Harrington, Washington. The summer before this, Mr. Beers had attended a camp meeting not far from Mr. Scott's home. At this time Mr. Scott was in an unsaved condition, and did not even come in to the tabernacle. He sat under the shade of a tree and listened attentively while Mr. Beers told of the needs of his school and of this fine administration building that was in the process of erection. He did not make himself known to Mr. Beers, who came home feeling that his efforts had been in vain. Not so!

> "Thou canst not toil in vain,
>   For cold or wet or dry,
> Shall moisten and mature the grain
>   For garners in the sky."

Several months had passed by, Mr. Scott had been reclaimed, and the matter of his tithe money troubled his conscience. For several years he had been withholding his money from God and he stated in his letter that now he was trying to pay up what he owed the Lord. So he sent this draft, not knowing anything about the prayer meeting.

In the morning when Mr. Beers went to the Thanksgiving meeting in the church, Grandma Denny was standing in the entrance. With a serious face, he asked her, "What about that thousand dollars, Grandma?" She said earnestly, "I thought it would have been here before this, but it's coming from a distance, I know." Pulling the draft from his pocket with great glee, Mr. Beers said, "Here it is, Grandma; here it is." With a shout of victory she bounded into the church and went weeping and running up and down the aisle like a young girl. Then followed a most wonderful Thanksgiving service.

Those who are familiar with the early affairs of the school will remember many other answers to prayer. The faculty and Christian students *really prayed their way through;* for competent teachers and suitable helpers; for promising young men and women who would become teachers and missionaries; for needed funds to carry forward the building operations which were continually in progress; for the conversion and sanctification of the students; and these effectual prayers were answered. Sometimes the cloud of glory rested so sensibly upon the student body that the regular routine of school work was suspended. One such memorable day will ever linger in the memories of those who were present. Revival services were being held by Rev. and Mrs. J. B. Freeland. There came a wonderful turning to the Lord. Nearly every student at the boarding hall was saved and the day students, too, shared in the general blessing. As we gathered in the assembly one morning for the opening of the school after a wonderful meeting the evening before, Mr. Beers called for testimony from the new converts. As they began speaking of their new-found joy, the whole room seemed electrified with the presence of the Holy Spirit. Several who had not yet attained the much desired blessing rushed forward and kneeling at the platform, began praying for mercy. Others bowed in prayer in the place where they were sitting. Some who were unwilling to yield to the claims of Christ started to leave the room, but overcome with intense conviction, bowed in humble contrition in the hall; and so there were various groups of earnest pleaders in the outside hall and others scattered about in the assembly room. Pentecost was repeated and the shouts of victory were mingled with the voice of weeping.

Every one in the school greatly enjoyed the new administration building, with its light, airy recitation rooms, its spacious assembly hall, fine laboratories and library, and the ever-sacred chapel. Many historic events occurred in this chapel. One only will be given here: The three couples who went out as the school's first missionaries were not married in the seminary chapel. There came a time, however, when the first missionary wedding ceremony was performed there. While charmingly beautiful in its simplicity and lack of lavish expenditures, it rivaled all the elaborate ceremonies in great cathedrals, embellished by all the costly adornments that wealth can buy. Loving hands had made snowy pillars and a great white wedding bell to form an arch under which the happy pair should stand. They brought a wealth of sweet flowers, made sweeter because they were plucked from their own gardens, and surely no decorations could have been more beautiful nor any bride more lovely than our own missionary. Mr. Beers performed the sacred ceremony and introduced the happy pair. For a short time they labored on a circuit in the Washington Conference, but very soon went to join the missionary force and are at this date teaching in a union training academy on the west coast of China.

Following close on the erection of the administration building, Mr. Beers raised money and in the year of 1907-08 built the second dormitory for young ladies. In this building he combined a spacious and comfortable dining hall and a beautiful reception hall below, with comfortable and spacious sleeping rooms above. Truly the God of Jacob was leading on the hosts of Israel. His people kept under the burden and cooperated with all their hearts and souls. It seemed that every step of progress spelled sacrifice on the part of the pilgrims.

The same donor who sent the one thousand dollar draft placed at different times in the institution three daughters and two sons, who were all converted in the school and received their diplomas from the seminary. Whenever news was brought to Brother and Sister Scott that another child was saved, they sent a large sum of money at once as a thank-offering—five hundred dollars twice and two hundred fifty dollars several times. Another gift much smaller and unique in its character is worthy of mention: One evening a message was brought to Mr. and Mrs. Beers while they were living in the third story of the brick building that a caller was standing outside at the entrance who earnestly desired to see them, but would not come in. Going down to see who the caller might be, they found a beautiful jersey cow staked down, with a note tied on her neck by a pink ribbon. The note read as follows: "Dear Brother and Sister Beers: We have come to be an inmate of your family if you will receive us. We already belong to an aristocratic family of thoroughbred jerseys. Nevertheless we are very fond of potato parings from the kitchen and will endeavor to adjust ourselves to your circumstances. We have come to help you. Yours sincerely, Pinkie."

While Mr. Beers was canvassing among the business men of Seattle to raise funds for the second dormitory, he had great success and received kind words from everybody excepting one man, a wealthy Jew. Nearly all of the large firms had treated him with great respect and responded generously to his appeal. Going into a large clothing store one day, he presented his subscription paper to this wealthy Jew who was the proprietor. He began to upbraid Mr. Beers, speaking sarcastically of the school work. Holding his hat in his hand, Mr. Beers listened respectfully until the Jew paused for breath, then he said quietly, "Is that all?" Somewhat abashed, the Jew said, "Yes, that is all." Now came Mr. Beers' opportunity to reprove the man in a very nice way. He said, "We read in the Bible, 'Woe unto you when all men speak well of you.' When I came into your store this morning no one so far as I know had spoken ill of me nor of my work. And if this woe was on me when I came in, you have taken it off, haven't you?" The man hung his head in silence. Reaching out his hand and grasping the Jew's hand, he said warmly, "May the God of Abraham, Isaac and Jacob bless you," then withdrew at once. A few days later Mr. Beers was passing the store, when the Jew ran out and said, "Come in, come in! You have a school out here at the foot of Queen Anne Hill, haven't you? Now I am sure you are doing a great deal of good. The other day I thought you were talking about some other school. I was mistaken in the place. I want to help you in this work." Taking the subscription paper from Mr. Beers' hand he put his name down for fifty dollars and immediately wrote his check for this amount. Then drawing Mr. Beers into the rear of the store, he fitted him out with a new suit of clothes. From that time on he was a regular contributor to the seminary and gave Mr. Beers several articles of clothing. Until the time of his death he continued to be a real friend to Mr. Beers and the institution, having been conquered by love.

In glancing back over the years that have passed since Mr. Beers received his wonderful world-wide vision, it is not difficult to discern the Almighty hand resting graciously upon him and ever leading him on from victory to victory. The success that attended his efforts has been recognized and appreciated by many. One says, "I am sure many have gone to glory from heathen lands, as well as from home lands, through the efforts put forth by Brother Beers and his wife. May God bless his memory." One of the alumni of the institution writes: "As an able minister of the gospel, he lived worthy of his calling, and when serving as pastor proved himself to be a faithful shepherd of the flock. A noble leader he was and because of the faithfulness of himself and devoted companion to the cause of Je-

sus Christ, many from East to West, and in other
lands across the sea 'will arise and call him blessed.'
He is gone from our midst, but his work and influence have made for him a living monument, yea,
many living monuments. Verily, the world is
brighter and heaven will be more densely populated
because our dear Brother Beers has lived."

Words of appreciation came from missionary students in heathen lands regarding the work of Mr.
Beers. From Africa, "How little we know what is
before us. It is less than a year since you wrote
your message of sympathy to me, and now you have
had to go through the same deep waters. But it is
the lot of mankind, after all; some live long and
others finish their work sooner. Brother Beers has
left a good memory on record. I shall always be
grateful to the Lord for having had the privilege
of being with him, and I know that I am only one
of the many who feel as I do." From China: "Regarding your dear husband and our esteemed friend,
the first verse that comes to me seems so appropriate. 'They...*rest* from their labors, and their works
do follow them.' He has gone, but the great work
for God that he helped to launch *is going on* and
shall not cease till Jesus comes. And when your big
family of home and foreign missionary children
come rejoicing, bringing in the sheaves, you and
Brother Beers will have your share in their harvest
also." From India: "I have over my writing desk
a photograph of the group taken in the early part of
the year 1900, and as I look at it from time to time,
it is hard to suppress the deep emotion that sometimes sweeps through my heart. A few of the num-

ber have crossed over to the 'other side.' Others are scattered far and wide through the remote corners of the earth. Seattle Seminary was one of God's means for preparing us for the places that He has designed that we shall fill. Had it not been for the Seminary, I fear that many of us would not be where we are today. God in His providence chose you and Brother Beers to make that institution what it was. To me Seattle Seminary is still the dearest spot on earth. While we were home on furlough, we located for a short time near those buildings because that place seemed the nearest like home to us of any spot in America." From Japan: "Your dear departed companion—our own Brother Beers —lives in the loving memories of thousands, whose lives he has enriched by his noble character and his boundless generosity." From a student formerly a missionary at Santo Domingo: "Brother Beers lived a beautiful and useful life, filled with the Spirit. There were many lives made better through his influence and many shall call him blessed. Personally he seemed like a father to us, so thoughtful of the interests of others, so appreciative of every little kindness, so thoughtful of others. While an intellectual giant and so many excellent qualities, yet very humble, which made him truly great. We feel that a *great* man has been called home and that heaven is the richer and this world poorer. We are very thankful that it has been our privilege to know him. We shall never forget him and his influence helps us to live better lives."

CHAPTER XI

TRIP TO SCOTLAND, ENGLAND AND FRANCE

And Nature, the old nurse,
  Took the child upon her knee,
Saying, "Here is a story book
  Thy Father has written for thee."

"Come, wander with me," she said,
  "Into regions yet untrod,
And read what is still unread
  In the manuscripts of God."

And he wandered away and away,
  With Nature, the dear old nurse,
Who sang to him night and day
  The rhymes of the universe.   —*Longfellow.*

Travel enlarges our conception of the universe and extends our vision from objects at hand to scenes far distant. When he first returned from North Chili, New York, to the Pacific Coast, Mr. Beers began to realize that his vision had been extended. He stopped for a few days at his old home in Topeka, Kansas. To his surprise the hill back of the house appeared much smaller. Had some one taken a mallet and flattened the top down? No, he had seen the Cascades and the Rockies; that was all; then, too, the Kansas River that he once thought so large, seemed now like a small stream, since he had looked upon the grand old Columbia and the mighty Mississippi.

For seventeen years he had labored incessantly. During this time he had never taken a vacation for more than two or three days; even then he was soliciting funds or seeking to promote the interests of his loved school. When he made his annual trips to Chicago, he could not find time to stop along the way and go sight-seeing, even though he loved and appreciated the wonderful works of God in nature. He often expressed a great desire to visit Yellowstone Park and other points of interest, but did not do so. During the great railroad strike on the Northern Pacific, he was forcibly detained in Montana and finally compelled to take a stage coach from Livingston to Butte in order to reach the Great Northern Railroad. For two days he rode with the driver on the top of the coach because the stage was crowded; the sun was exceedingly hot and he was affected by its burning rays. They stopped for the night at a small mining town, where the accommodations were small and very poor. The driver was a big-hearted man and had compassion upon this preacher who was so nearly overcome by the heat. He voluntarily gave Mr. Beers his own room, which was very comfortable, and showed him where it was as they drove into town. When Mr. Beers had deposited his baggage in this nice room and stepped back into the dirty-looking hotel, he heard a chorus of voices lamenting about the miserable surroundings. A physician's wife exclaimed, "Why, I'd rather sleep on a board outside than occupy that filthy bed." Mr. Beers was always very chivalrous toward womanhood and told the doctor that he and his wife could have the room where he had intended to stay. His generous offer was eagerly accepted, and now he must find another place. Looking about, he saw across the street a woman selling milk, and engaged her in pleasant conversation about his trip. When she learned of his dilemma, she said, "Now, I have a couch and if you care to occupy it, I'll make it up for you the best I can." He gladly accepted the invitation and was made very comfortable indeed. The lady provided him with a tempting supper and he rested as well as one might in a palace car. While he was partaking of the delicious breakfast in the morning, he ascertained that the lady was a Catholic. Before leaving, he asked her if he might pray. She seemed to welcome his prayer and refused to take any pay for his stay in her home, urging him to come again. This was a fortunate providence, as his compulsory detention had taken more money than he had planned for, and left him without sufficient means to reach his destination.

Mr. Beers finally became much exhausted. The years of unrelenting toil and almost constant travel in the interests of the school; the care and anxiety and heavy burdens borne were making him "old before his time." When the General Missionary Board chose him as one of its delegates to the World's Missionary Convention in Edinburgh, June, 1910, it was a strong incentive to ask for a vacation. The trustees very graciously granted him leave of absence, and kind friends made up a fine purse for him to help defray double expenses—for of course his wife must go, too, as otherwise he could not have been induced to make the trip. There would have been

A GLIMPSE OF THE BEAUTIFUL TREES ON THE COLLEGE CAMPUS

no pleasure in the journey if he should be compelled to leave her behind.

The fact that they must be absent from commencement exercises rendered it difficult to decide whether Mr. and Mrs. Beers should stay or go. The graduating class of 1910 was the largest in number of any class that had finished under their labors. Twenty-two fine young people received their diplomas that year. The personnel of this class was distinguished also; a number were soon to cross the ocean and carry the gospel to heathen lands; several of the young men were called to preach in the home land; elocution and music were also well represented in this class. Their hearts bade them to remain with this eminent class and the students were also very reluctant to have them leave, but reason said, "You are in great need of rest and change; you must go." They had never been absent from commencement before since the school was founded, but the voice of reason triumphed over all objections and they were soon hastening on their way to New York, which they reached in time to spend one day there before taking the steamer for Glasgow, Scotland, thence on to Edinburgh, the seat of the World's Missionary Convention.

The following day they went on board the steamer. The gang plank was lifted, the last farewell was spoken to friends who had come to wish them "bon voyage," and they slowly steamed out of the harbor. Looking through a field glass they watched for the last sight of their native land. The Singer Building, the Metropolitan, and other tall buildings disappeared; the Statue of Liberty faded from their

vision and soon they could not discern even the line
of the horizon—nothing was visible but ocean and
sky.

The pleasure and profit of the voyage were greatly
enhanced by the companionship of their agreeable
fellow travelers, among whom were Rev. B. Winget,
our former missionary secretary, Mrs. Mary L. Coleman, general president of the Woman's Foreign Missionary Society, Mrs. Rebecca E. Sellew, the wife of
our senior bishop, Miss Effie Southworth, who was
returning to India after her furlough, and Bishop
William Pearce. Several of the company were
afflicted with sea-sickness, but Mr. Beers proved himself a splendid sailor, enjoying the ocean on board
ship as well as when floating or diving in its depths.
From the time he left Seattle, he seemed to throw
aside every care and become young again. It was a
great satisfaction to his friends to note the benefit
and enjoyment he was deriving from the voyage. He
had labored so incessantly and carried such heavy
responsibilities, that mind and body both demanded
recreation and change.

Before leaving the United States, Mr. Beers had
secured letters of introduction from the congressional representatives in Washington, D. C., which
gave him prestige and favor with officials and persons in rank wherever he went. He was in Glasgow
a short time only, but long enough to give this eager,
observant traveler an opportunity to visit the great
university which was of deeper interest to him
than any other place in this busy commercial city.
Here he was cordially received by the head of the
institution and his visit made worth while, but the

goal, the objective of all the company, was Edinburgh and the great convention.

The travelers ascertained, however, that there was time to take the trip through the Trossachs and reach Edinburgh via Stirling, involving but little additional expense. Perhaps no part of the journey gave Mr. Beers more pleasure than the wonderful trip through the Trossachs. Riding in the high-seated coaches, filled with enthusiastic sight-seeing travelers, drawn by four spirited horses, guided and controlled by a driver dressed in a red-trimmed suit and jaunty hat, furnished an outfit conducive to the highest enjoyment of the tourist. Then, too, the ride from Glasgow to Stirling through "the charming, memory-haunted land," the Trossachs, a romantic glen, lying between Loch Achray and Loch Katrine, rendered the exquisite lines of Scott's "Lady of the Lake" most realistic.

Mr. Beers had a copy of this beautiful poem, from which he quoted as the driver pointed out the places made famous by the great poet. "The road leads through the forest beautifully, peacefully. The paths twine and retwine through this bosky birchen wood, with heather purple, knee deep on either side, and through the trees were caught swift glimpses of Ben Lomond, Ben Ledi and Ben Venue." Suddenly the very spot is reached in a wild rocky gorge where James Fitz James:

> "Dashing down a darksome glen,
> Soon lost to hound and hunter's ken,
> In the deep Trossach's wildest nook,
> His solitary refuge took."

and where the gallant gray stumbled in the rugged

dell—"Woe worth the chase, woe worth the day, that costs thy life, my gallant gray." The travelers were entertained frequently by a band of pipers who would spring up from the bracken and serenade them with their melodious bag-pipes. Then these lines became very vivid, "The clansmen springing from copse and heath arose, bonnets and spears and bended bows," as the plaided warriors answered the whistle shrill and, "That whistle garrisoned the glen, at once with full five hundred men." Also the place of combat between Fitz James and Roderick Dhu. The king had been greatly shocked by this sudden appearance of these armed men, but remained brave and undaunted. "His back against the rock he bare, and firmly placed his foot before," and calls out, "Come one, come all! this rock shall fly from its firm base as soon as I. * * * Three times in closing strife they stood, and thrice the Saxon's sword drank blood." When he reached the Brig o' Turk he recalled the lines:

"But ere the Brig o' Turk was won,
The headmost horseman rode alone,
Alone, but with unabated zeal."

The former students who were in the English classes will recall the very interesting lecture that Mr. Beers gave after his return, from Scott's masterpiece and his graphic rendering of the lines given above; also the sparkling manner in which he would picture the tender pathos of the royal knight's wooing:

"Sweet Ellen, dear, my life must be
Since it is worthy care from thee.
*   *   *   *   *   *

I come to bear thee from the wild,
Where ne'er before such blossoms smiled."

And when Ellen frankly tells Fitz James her heart belongs to Malcom Graeme, the gallant king gives her the magic ring and on through the beautiful narrative, closing with the restoration of peace to friend and foe alike by Scotland's noble king and the renowned quotation:

"Fetters and warden for the Graeme

*   *   *   *   *   *

His chain of gold the king unstrung,
The links o'er Malcolm's neck he flung,
Then gently drew the glittering band
And laid the clasp on Ellen's hand."

Ellen's Isle is one of the most beautiful and picturesque spots in all Scotland; this has been forever made famous by the poets' imagery. Since the writer was unable to make this trip, Mrs. Mary L. Coleman briefly describes the early morning row on Loch Katrine and the visit to this charming isle.

"Several of our party were loath to leave Loch Katrine without visiting Ellen's Isle. Our journey to Edinburgh must not be delayed; and the only possibility lay in taking the trip very early in the morning, before the tourist coaches were available. Mr. Beers with characteristic kindness and resourcefulness, secured a conveyance for those who wished to go. It was ready at the appointed hour, and we enjoyed a two-mile drive in all the freshness and beauty of a mid-summer morning in the heart of the Trossachs. At the right rose Ben An, at the left Ben Venue, and beside us flowed the clear waters that connect little Loch Achray with Loch

Katrine. Loch Katrine is said to have an area of about four thousand acres. Located three hundred and sixty-four feet above sea level, it has been for more than sixty years the chief water supply of the distant city of Glasgow. Scott's familiar lines picture well its beauty.

> 'Where, gleaming with the setting sun,
> One burnished sheet of living gold,
> Loch Katrine lay beneath him rolled,
> In all her length, far winding lay,
> With promontory, creek and bay,
> And islands that, empurpled bright,
> Floated amid the livelier light,
> And mountans that like giants stand
> To sentinel enchanted land.'

Mr. Beers proved himself a good oarsman, and a half hour over the blue waters brought us to the shore of the little island. To say that it lay like a jewel— an emerald—on the bosom of the lovely lake is to use a trite figure, but it well expresses the fact. Green with foliage from end to end,

> ' 'Twas all so close with copse-wood bound,
> Nor track, nor pathway might disclose
> That human foot frequented there.'

On the shore where our boat was moored, lay an old oak tree, long since fallen and decayed, looking, as Mr. Beers smilingly remarked, as though it might have been the identical 'old oak' from under whose shelter the 'Lady of the Lake' appeared in her light skiff at the call of the huntsman's horn. From the trunk projected a little silvery shaft a foot or so in length. Mr. Beers appropriated it, saying, 'It will make a fine paper-knife for Mrs. Beers.' A trifle, to be sure, but trifles often speak eloquently.

"We rowed across to 'the silver strand' as did Ellen in the story—'The beach of pebbles bright as snow,' to gather a few of them as reminders in the days to come of that delightful morning—ours to enjoy because of the kindness of a friend."

All tourists in making this trip through the Trossachs find themselves landed in time for six o'clock dinner at the luxurious Trossachs Hotel, which looks like a "Lady-of-the-Lake Abbotsford." There is no choice—no other place to sleep—and at first glance no other place to dine. Mr. Beers, however, was not to be outdone by this crafty arrangement. Procuring a row-boat, he took Mrs. Beers and three other ladies of the party and rowed across Loch Lomond, just as the setting sun turned the water into burnished gold and illumined the picturesque mountains, Ben Venue, Ben Lomond and Ben Ledi, with glorious shafts of light. He had discovered a little cottage nestling among the trees and toward this he made his way, feeling sure he could find appetizing food there. A real Scotch woman met him at the door. "Have you any milk?" said he. "Sure, I have some fine milk. I have just come in from milking our cows which are the best in the country," replied the woman. Mrs. Beers and the other ladies were sitting on the green sward admiring the beautiful scenery, and welcomed him as he came back with a pitcher of milk. Going once more to the good woman, he secured plenty of fresh, home-made bread and golden butter. When he went to pay his bill after they had all feasted until they were satisfied, the lady asked him if he thought one shilling was too much. "No, indeed, not enough," said Mr. Beers. "That feast was certainly worth four shillings." The company enjoyed the delight of the peasant woman upon receiving such a large sum as four shillings as greatly as they had the bountiful feast she had furnished them. "See," said she to her husband, "what the gentleman from America has given me."

When they had rowed back to the hotel, they found the other members of the party greatly dissatisfied because they had been compelled to pay a large sum for their evening meal, while the rich feast of bread and milk had cost these more fortunate ones less than a shilling apiece.

Passing through the Trossachs the party reached Stirling Castle. Two of the most impressive and picturesque castles of the world are found in Scotland at Stirling and Edinburgh. Stirling Castle is situated on the Firth of Forth, about thirty-five miles above Edinburgh, and it was for years the favorite residence of Scottish sovereigns. It played a prominent part in the history of Scotland, and is intimately associated with the name of Robert Bruce, who recaptured the castle from Edward the Second of England in the fourteenth century, after the battle of Bannockburn. The castle, like that of Edinburgh, is situated on a lofty height. On the esplanade before it stands a statue of Robert Bruce. The view from all sides is beautiful and commands, on the west, a fair range of mountains, including Ben Lomond and Ben Venue, while on the south the battlefield of Bannockburn stretches away before the eye. One has said, "This castle has looked down on more history, seen more armies advance and re-

treat, than any other one place in the world. Ben
Lomond lies blue and far to the east, the Grampion
Hills, gray and stalwart, to the north, the peaks of
the Highlands on the west." It is not the interior
of Stirling Castle that repays the visitor for his effort, but rather the view from the battlements over
the glorious and eloquent landscape of mid-Scotland.
Through a small opening in the wall, termed "the
Lady's Lookout," from which the best view is obtained, the mountains, the hills, the Vale of Mon-
teith, the ruins of Cambuskenneth Abbey, and the
proud Bruce and Wallace monuments that mark the
victory of Bruce at Bannockburn, form a picture
long to be remembered, which afforded the tourists
great pleasure.

In the old cemetery near this castle the company
came unexpectedly upon the monument to Agnes
and Margaret Wilson. This is sculptured from the
purest white marble—life size figures enclosed in
French plate glass. The elder sister sits reading the
Bible to the younger. A transcendently beautiful
angel folds her wings over and around the two girls.
The story of the martyrdom is recorded on the base
of the monument. As the band of tourists read the
pathetic story of the two beautiful maidens staked
down as victims to the rising tide unless they would
deny the Lord who bought them, every one in the
crowd was visibly affected—all eyes were wet. Mr.
Beers would relate this incident in his sermons with
effectiveness when dwelling upon fidelity to Christ.

From Stirling Castle the company soon reached
Edinburgh, where they were comfortably cared for
in MacKay's Temperance Hotel, located on Princes

Street opposite the Sunken Garden, with its marvelous flower dial and the towering historic castle
in the background.

One writer has said: "Princes Street in Edinburgh is the loveliest street in the world—a half
mile long but gardened all the way—broad and
straight, a wide, green-lawned, tree-forested, ter-
raced and flowered with a sunken garden near the
castle side." Above rises the castle in greater majesty than from any other point. There was no time
for sight-seeing, however, until the convention days
were over. The convention was exceedingly impressive and filled with thrilling interests, from first to
last. From the wonderful addresses given by Dr.
John Mott, Sherwood Eddy, Campbell White and
other notable speakers, Mr. Beers caught new inspiration for the great work which was committed
to his hand. The delegates from all parts of the globe
thronging the spacious hall in their native costumes
presented a shifting panorama of gorgeous coloring
and unique apparel not soon to be forgotten. When
the last hymn was sung by the myriad voices of the
vast congregation, and the last prayer had ascended
to the throne, and the last solemn benediction had
been pronounced, the great crowd of people from all
parts of the world separated to go to their respective
homes with a wider, grander view of the privilege
of spreading the gospel, and a greater, deeper inspiration to be worthy co-laborers in bringing the
nations to a knowledge of Christ.

At the close of the convention the company at
once started out to make the most of their short stay
in Scotland. The best view of Edinburgh can be ob-

tained from Calton Hill. From this point you can see the famous castle, Arthur's Seat and the Esplanade.

"From Calton Hill it is possible to catch the farthest glory of the encircling hills and the near glory of the ever glorious city." The monuments here of especial interest to Mr. Beers were those of Lord Nelson, the hero of Trafalgar, and our own beloved Lincoln and a freed slave to commemorate the Scottish dead in the American Civil War. The spirit of patriotism prompted him to visit the latter on our own nation's holiday. He found some fellow traveler with similar impulses had been there before him and had laid a wreath of fresh flowers at the foot. Other distinctive points on Calton Hill are the Old Royal Observatory, the city prison and Calton cemetery, with its Roman tomb of David Hume.

Arthur's Seat is situated on a hill lying southeast, rising eight hundred and twenty-two feet above the surrounding country. It is shaped like a lion, *couchant,* with head toward the north, and is named from the British King Arthur who from this height watched the defeat of his enemies, the Picts.

The Esplanade, in front of the castle, was of old the place for the execution of persons accused of witchcraft. It is said that no less than two thousand persons were burned at the stake here.

Edinburgh is a city of many magnificent statues. Princes Street is lined on either side with sculptural art, of which the statue of Sir Walter Scott is the most remarkable. It is in the form of a spiral Gothic cross, with a central canopy, beneath which is a seated statue of Scott with his dog "Maida" at his side. The niches are occupied by characters from the poet's writings.

A great lecturer and traveler writes of the scenery of Scotland and its castles: "Scotland has long been called the land of scenery and of song. The two are intimately associated. The scenery of Scotland has inspired many of her songs, and the songs have paid tribute in return by celebrating the beauty of the scenery in affectionate and eloquent phrase. The songs of Scotland breathe the life of the people and of the nation in a way that has won the sympathetic interest of the world. The prevailing note in Scottish song and literature is romance. The very name of Scotland is fragrant with romance. Its scenery is rich in romantic beauty and romantic associations, and its songs give eloquent expression to both. And so the traveler in Scotland finds the charm of her scenery happily voiced for him, and as he wanders from one spot to another he can recall the lines that enhance its beauty. It may be 'The Banks and Braes o' Bonnie Doon' or 'Within a Mile of Edinboro' Town.' Wherever he goes he may enjoy the scenery in companionship with the spirit of the poet who sang its praises. To most of us Scotland means Wallace and Robert Bruce in heroic chivalry, and Walter Scott and Robert Burns in romance and in song. Most of the scenes and places that interest the traveler are associated with one or another of these four names."

Edinburgh Castle, an ancient seat of Scottish kings, has a most magnificent situation on a rocky height above the city. On three sides the mountain on which it stands drops almost sheer. On the east it slopes gradually off.toward Holyrood.

Mr. Beers was interested in the room in the castle where James VI was born and the wonderful Regalia of Scotland in the crown room, in which were included the royal crown richly adorned with jewels; the sceptre of silver gilt made for James V with a great beryl taken from an Egyptian sceptre in the end; the sword of state, five feet long, which was presented to James IV by Pope Julius II, together with the golden rose; the royal jewels restored by Cardinal York to George IV and the coronation ring of Charles I. The company visited Holyrood and here saw the apartments where Mary, Queen of Scots, resided during that period of her life which was so crowded with passionate and tragic incidents—her two marriages to Darnley and Bothwell, the murder of Rizzio in her presence, and of Darnley with her approbation; the very room where Mary held her famous controversy with John Knox; the bed chamber of Mary and the apartments of Darnley with a little private stairway leading up to Mary's room; the queen's supper room and the blood stains in the audience room which marked the spot where Rizzio was murdered.

The picturesque location of Edinburgh on its group of hills with valleys between, its literary associations and general plan have sometimes given it the name of the modern Athens. It was not, however, its unique scenery that made the city of thrilling interest to Mr. Beers, but the heroic struggle that was enacted here for religious freedom and the martyrs' blood that has been shed that the pure

teachings of an open Bible might be given to the
common people. At St. Giles Cathedral he was
shown the stool which Jenny Geddes threw at the
preacher who dared to read the forbidden ritual in
the church, and also the very spot where it struck
on the wall. In Grey Friar's churchyard he saw the
place where the Solemn League and Covenant was
signed and read the inscription on the martyrs' monument which was erected in memory of twenty thousand Covenanters who sealed their adherence to
principal with their blood. Not far from these solemn scenes is the home of the great religious leader,
the brave, invincible John Knox. Reverently Mr.
Beers entered the prayer room which is sacredly preserved the same as when the great reformer poured
forth his agonizing petition, "Give me Scotland or I
die." One of the walls of the room is said to be—
and did actually appear to be—stained by the passionate breath of this great intercessor. Closing
the door, Mr. Beers shut himself away from the rest
of the company and engaged in private devotion.

CHAPTER XII

TRAVELS CONTINUED—LONDON AND PARIS

Thanks to the human heart by which we live,
Thanks to its tenderness, its joys, and fears—
To me the meanest flower that blows can give
Thoughts that do often lie too deep for tears.
                                    —Wordsworth.

Ah, who can tell how far away
    Some sentinel of God's good will
In forest cool, or desert gray,
    By lonely pool, or barren hill,
Shall faintly hear, with inward ear,
    The chiming bell of his dear school.
                                    —Van Dyke.

On the way to London Mr. Beers stopped off at
Stratford-on-Avon, Shakespeare's birthplace and
home, and visited the house in which he was born—
Anne Hathaway's cottage where the great poet went
wooing, and his tomb in the chancel of Trinity
Church. He also spent a few hours at Oxford University, getting but a brief glance as there are several hundred halls of learning in this eminent institution. He was, however, shown the dormitory in
which John and Charles Wesley lived while students
there. This room seems barren and cheerless without heat in the winter, but the guide informed Mr.
Beers that it was eagerly sought by present-day students who desire the fame of actually living in the
Wesleyan rooms.

In the world's metropolis, the company stopped at
Wild's Temperance Hotel, near St. Paul's Cathedral,
said to be London's most prominent building. It is
situated in the very heart of the city, the commercial
center of the British capital. It was designed by
Sir Christopher Wren and cost about $3,500,000
to construct. Almost all architects admit that
the dome which is 112 feet in diameter is the
finest dome in existence. Mr. Beers greatly admired the architecture of this cathedral and other
imposing structures that he visited during this trip.
He was peculiarly impressed by the grand, melodious chimes that were rung daily from the dome of
this cathedral. He said he felt like taking off his
hat and bowing in worship whenever the solemn
notes were pealing forth. In the crypt of this
church are many statues, among which is a large
and dignified monument to England's hero, Lord
Nelson. The lettering on the walls of the church at-
tracts the attention of all visitors: "Would you see
Christopher Wren's monument, look about you."
The religious service, however, in St. Paul's did not
appeal to Mr. Beers very favorably, being altogether
too formal, too ritualistic. He remarked to his wife
as they were joining in the worship one Sabbath:
"Oh, pray for me that my faith fail not." He found
a more congenial place of worship at Spurgeon's
Tabernacle and in Wesley's Church, the city Road
chapel. Going into Wesley's house, he sought the
sacred prayer room, closed the door and had a season of secret prayer. John Wesley lies buried in the
rear of the chapel, with a fitting monument to his
memory. Just across the street is the burial ground

of Bunhill Fields, where the immortal Bunyan is interred. His tomb is marked by a recumbent life-size figure of the great writer.

All travelers hasten to visit the world-renowned Westminster Abbey. This is a structure of singular beauty, built in the form of a cross. Its peculiar fame lies not in its beautiful architecture, but in its being the place of the coronation of sovereigns and the burial spot of royalty and nobility. Another strong reason for its fame is the reverence that attaches to the memory of the confessor, whose shrine stands in the central chapel behind the "high altar."

The morning the party first visited Westminster Abbey was a drizzly day—one that the English call "wet." In Oregon such precipitation is called "Oregon mist." It seemed very dark and gloomy within the walls where so many of earth's good and great were sepulchered. For a time Mrs. Beers did not notice that her husband was not enjoying the place as much as the others were, and when she did, she asked for the reason. He said, "I want to get out of here. This is one great sepulcher—it is filled with dead men's bones." On another day when the sun shone beautifully through the rose-stained windows with a burst of glorious illumination which is rarely seen, Mr. Beers wandered for hours through England's Hall of Fame with great pleasure and profit. The Poet's Corner, in the south transept, was one of his favorite shrines. Here he would recall the famous writings of Thackeray, Dickens, Chaucer, Spencer, the Wesleys and many others. The tomb of the immortal Livingstone also was a holy spot to him. He himself had long since been seeking for the "other sheep which are not of His fold." Among the many objects of interest to be seen in Westminster Abbey is the historic coronation chair made of oak for Edward I, standing in the Confessor's Chapel, containing the "Stone of Scone," the emblem of Scottish power. Tradition declares it was once used by the patriarch Jacob as a pillow, having originally come from the Island of Iona as the relic of Saint Columba. Edward 1 brought it to London in 1297, as a token of the subjection of Scotland and every monarch since his time has been crowned in this chair, excepting Edward V.

The tombs of Henry VII and his queen, Elizabeth of York, are among the finest in the abbey. Splendid recumbent effigies of the monarchs in bronze, of Italian workmanship, rest upon a tomb of black marble, and the whole is enclosed in a magnificent shrine of wrought brass. A wonderful range of sculptural art is found throughout the abbey, but Henry VII's chapel is the most remarkable of all, being ornamented with a surpassing wealth and minuteness of detail.

During Mr. Beers' stay in London, an eventful program of music was given in Westminster. The wonderful new pipe organ had been installed with an echo attachment, and he had the pleasure of listening to its majestic strains played by a master hand; sweet melodies, stately marches, imposing harmonies, filled the vast hall and rained down upon the head from the ceiling above.

It is interesting to note in this connection the origin of the expression, "Why rob Peter to pay Paul?" "St. Paul's and Westminster Abbey, the two greatest religious edifices in England, were rivals from early time, and out of this came the phrase, 'Robbing Peter to pay Paul.' Westminster was known as St. Peter's. In 1551 an appropriation was made there to clear up a deficiency in the accounts of St. Paul's. The people exclaimed, 'Why rob Peter to pay Paul?' "

Many points of interest in this great metropolis consume the time and energy of all tourists, but Mr. Beers seemed to be a tireless traveler and visited many more places than others are usually able to reach. Trafalgar Square with its marvelous statuary celebrating Nelson's victory over Napoleon, Kensington Gardens, Buckingham Palace at the west end of St. James Park, the Albert Memorial with its wonderful grouping of statues representing painting, sculpture, architecture, poetry, music, agriculture, commerce, engineering, mechanics and the life-size statue of the crown prince at the top, and many others were viewed and appreciated by him. He spent some time in the great museum, but as it would take a life-time of study to exhaust the stupendous array of exhibits here shown, a short visit is always unsatisfactory. Among the objects of interest that he noted were the Moabite stone, the Egyptian mummies, the Grecian marbles taken from the Parthenon at Athens and myriads of others.

No visit to London would be complete without a trip to Windsor Castle, twenty-one miles away, the chief residence of all British sovereigns. The tourist's visit here could never be forgotten. The chaste beauty of the Albert Memorial Chapel expresses in exquisite art Queen Victoria's adoration for the

Prince Consort. St. George's Chapel is strikingly
beautiful, and marks the burial place below its marble pavement of many royal personages. The magnificent dining hall, the grandeur of the luxurious
throne room excite the admiration of the traveler,
and the Round Tower has historic interest. It was
formerly a prison, its most notable prisoner having
been James I of Scotland.

The day Mr. Beers visited Windsor there was a re-
view of the Royal Guards in their red and gold uni-
forms, with gayly plumed lofty military hats, making one wonder how it was possible to support such
weighty trappings upon the head. The horses were
handsome, well-trained steeds, and the whole parade
was one of such splendor as could not be seen outside the realms of royalty.

No place in London, however, was of more importance to him than the House of Parliament. From
the Thames Embankment the best view may be had
of the notable buildings of Parliament. There, rising three hundred and eighteen feet high, is the
tower with its great clock, twenty-three feet in diameter, and its bell, Big Ben, one of the largest in the
world and weighing thirteen tons. They say it takes
five hours to wind up the clock. Below its sober face,
in the great stretch of buildings, the British government is conducted. The Parliament buildings look
their part. They are as beautiful and impressive in
exterior as they are luxurious within. The houses
were erected in 1840 from plans selected out of
ninety-seven sent in competition. The style of the
buildings is rich Gothic, covering eight acres, and
costing fifteen million dollars. These contain eleven

courts, one hundred stairways and eleven hundred apartments. This simple statement of facts conveys but little impression of the great beauty and what we might call the "human interest quality" of the Parliament buildings. One writer says: "One must go through the buildings again and again, must be present at some of the meetings of Parliament, and then mingle with the people at the tea hour on the terrace, to get a real impression of the meaning of the place."

Mr. Beers also visited the celebrated "Tower," which has been the scene of many sad tragedies in English history. The list of notables who have been beheaded in this grim place would fill pages. Prominent among them were poor Anne Boleyn, the unfortunate Catherine Howard and Lady Jane Grey. It was originally a royal palace, then a prison and place of execution. Today it is a museum of extraordinary historic interest. It is, too, a treasure house; the crown jewels, the most valuable collection of gems known, said to be worth fifteen million dollars, are shown here. The crown of Queen Victoria containing two thousand eight hundred and eighteen diamonds, three hundred pearls and other precious stones, is on exhibition, very strongly guarded.

Mention has already been made that Mr. Beers secured letters of introduction from our congressional representatives before he left America. While he was in Edinburgh, Scotland, the ambassador there called on Mr. Beers at the hotel and urged him to dine with him at the Embassy. While in London, also, our ambassador from the court of St. James, called and showed great kindness to Mr. Beers. Through the ambassador's influence, he was allowed to be present in the British Parliament when the great speech on "the king's oath" was made.

The time was drawing to a close and the voice of duty was calling Mr. Beers back to Seattle. Our party spent but two days in Paris, obtaining a brief glance only of this marvelously beautiful city. The stranger is impressed by the imposing effect produced by the wide and straight streets which are lined with elegant statuary and the buildings which have evidently been built with the thought of beauty in mind. No sky-scrapers are seen to break the symmetry of the whole, no narrow, crooked streets to mar the artist's design. The traveler marks at once the wonderful entrance to the city, at which stands the Arc de Triomphe, the largest triumphal arch in existence, which cost ten million dollars to construct, having been built for the entrance of Napoleon's victorious armies. On its wall blaze the names of three hundred eighty-six victorious generals. Extending from this arch is the world-renowned avenue, the Champs Elysees, which rivals Princes Street in Edinburgh, in its straight length, its exquisite statuary, its graceful trees, its sparkling fountains and profusion of flowers. The Palais de Luxembourg, the seat of the French senate, is a wonderful poem in architecture; rarely has the artist's genius reared a grander palace for the royalty of earth to occupy. The Palace of the Tuileries is now in ruin. One writer has said of these, "Shameful and departed ruin! I see the terrible trace of the vengeance of God in these calcined stones and I know not what Biblical Anathemas resound among this debris." These ruins mark the spot which was formerly the scene of the convention in which were heard the voices of Marat, Dante and Robespierre. The Place de la Concorde is the most beautiful and extensive place in Paris and one of the finest in the world. It is bounded on the west by the Champs Elysees and on the east by the garden of the Tuileries. In the center is the Obelisk, a block of red granite from Upper Egypt, weighing two hundred forty tons. Upon lofty pedestals placed around the square rise eight stone figures representing the chief towns of France. Mr. Beers took especial interest and found great pleasure in the Louvre, the most important building in Paris architecturally and on account of its treasures of art. The Louvre and Tuileris cover an area of forty-eight acres, forming one of the most magnificent palaces in the world, taking the tourists two hours to walk through the rooms without stopping. The ground floor is filled in with the most beautiful statuary. On the first floor are pictures and drawings which represent the greatest works of art in the world. On the second floor are the museums, also a supplementary saloon of drawings. Space will not permit us to enumerate the great paintings and the marvelous works of the sculptor's hand, which are to be seen in the Louvre.

The tourists visited Notre Dame, spending some time within its solemn precincts. Victor Hugo says of Notre Dame: "It is a vast symphony in stone, so to speak; the colossal of man and of a nation as united and as complex as the Iliad, and the romanceros of which it is the sister; a prodigious pro-

duction to which all the forces of an epoch contributed, and from every stone of which springs forth in
a hundred ways the workman's fancy directed by the
artist's genius; in one word, a kind of human creation, as strong as the divine creation from which it
seems to have stolen the twofold character, variety
and eternity."

The name of the great Napoleon is seen everywhere in Paris, sculptured in marble and stone,
molded in plaster, carved in ivory, gold, silver, wood
and bone. Wonderful pictures of the great general
and statues of him are in all parts of the city. The
French revere him and all tourists should visit his
tomb before leaving Paris. Mr. Beers lingered long
in this beautiful, renowned place. The sarcophagus
rests upon a mosaic pavement representing a wreath
of laurels upon which are inscribed the names of
eight battles in which Napoleon was victorious. It
is thirteen feet long, six and one-half feet wide and
fourteen feet high, built of Siberian porphry, weighing sixty-seven tons. Twelve colossal statues of victory surround the tomb, over which wave sixty flags
captured by Napoleon in battle. Above the crypt
rises a lofty dome one hundred sixty feet high,
painted with pictures of the twelve apostles and the
evangelists. The faint bluish light admitted from
above gives a sombre, supernatural appearance to
the tomb, and its remarkable surroundings greatly
enhance the solemn grandeur of the scene. As Mr.
Beers stood gazing upon the resting place of this
great general, who was made general of brigade at
twenty-four, he began to recite the lines concerning
Napoleon which he had committed long ago: "You

see him raising the siege of Toulon, putting down
the mob in Paris; crossing the snow-covered Alps
and taking command of the army at twenty-seven;
you see him before the majestic pyramids of Egypt;
you see him on the victorious battlefields of Ma-
rengo, Jena, Friedland, Wagram and Austerlitz;
you see him in Russia watching the burning of Mos-
cow and then making his terrible retreat in an awful
winter; you see him at Elba, capture and retake
France by the mere force of his genius; his wonderful personality and the love which he inspired in all
his soldiers; you see him defeated at Waterloo and
at last confined in the lonely, billow-dashed isle of
St. Helena, eighteen hundred feet above the sea,
where he suffered in close confinement for six years.
When at last the emperor died, he had one of the
most gorgeous and marvelous funerals of any monarch in the world. His ashes were conveyed to
Paris, where they now rest in this brilliant sarcophagus of rare and radiant marble, fit almost for a
deity dead."

Another place of great interest was the Colonne
Vendome, an imitation of Trajan's column in
Rome, erected to celebrate Napoleon's victories in
Russia and Austerlitz. It is made of masonry, en-
crusted with bronze plates, forming a spiral band,
representing battle scenes. The metal was obtained
by melting Russian and Austrian cannons. At the
top is a large statue of Napoleon in his imperial
robes. Mr. Beers used this monument, which had
been manufactured from trophies taken in warfare,
with impressive effect in one of his sermons. "It is
only by conquest that honorable monuments can be

reared to one's memory. Victory comes only after struggle, strife and battle. Would you have a name among the immortals? Then stand true in the conflict as did Paul, Luther, Wesley, B. T. Roberts and others, who reared themselves exalted monuments through trophies of grace taken in the terrible conflict with the hosts of sin.''

It was with regret that the tourists left Paris after so brief a stay. Returning to Liverpool, England, they were fortunate in securing passage on the great Lusitania through the influence of Mr. Beers' letters of introduction. Other travelers were refused and informed that the space was occupied. In closing this chapter, words of appreciation concerning Mr. Beers as a fellow traveler are given by Mrs. Rebecca E. Sellew.

"A great privilege came to me in 1910 in company with several other delegates, among whom were Mr. and Mrs. Beers, of attending the World's Missionary Convention held in Edinburgh, Scotland. Those few weeks of association with Mr. Beers in travel, sight-seeing, and during the convention deepened my regard for him as a Christian gentleman. He was always so thoughtful, so kind, so helpful in every way.

"One thing that touched my heart and will never be forgotten was his tender solicitude for his wife, who was not strong physically at that time. It seemed no hardship for him to remain with her if she was not able to go out with the others. He stayed with her several times when the rest of the party were out sight-seeing and it was done with apparent pleasure. Then again we found it profitable as well as pleasant to travel in company with Mr. Beers because of his knowledge of men and places. His well-stored mind, remarkable memory, and apt quotations made him a delightful traveling companion. His rich fund of information was a surprise not only to strangers, but to those of us who had known him for years. When we visited those places that have become famous through Scott's "Lady of the Lake," he was always ready with a quotation at every place, and many times entertained our company with extensive quotations from that beautiful poem. This was also noticeable when we were in France at the tomb of Napoleon. The guide remarked that Mr. Beers knew more about the tomb than he did.

"I feel sure that all who were associated with Mr. Beers on this trip will always remember the large share he contributed toward making it both pleasurable and profitable."

After a pleasant and uneventful voyage, Mr. and Mrs. Beers reached New York and hastened back to their home in Seattle. Mr. Beers had been refreshed and invigorated by his vacation and resumed his work for the college with renewed hope and courage.

CHAPTER XIII

COLLEGE WORK INTRODUCED—TWENTIETH ANNIVERSARY

There is a tide in the affairs of men,
Which, taken at the flood, leads on to fortune;
Omitted, all the voyage of their life
Is bound in shallows and in miseries.
On such a full sea are we now afloat;
And we must take the current when it serves,
Or lose our ventures.　　　　—*Shakespeare.*

The subject of this biography was known "as a man of large vision." He had many dreams for the advancement of God's kingdom in the earth. One of these was a Christian college on the Pacific Coast. He had induced many young people who graduated under his care to pursue their higher education in our college at Greenville, Illinois. But year after year, there were always some of the alumni from high school who could not bear the expense of this long trip from home and wished to take their college work in their own Alma Mater. This deepened his conviction and gave him the courage to enlarge the scope of the school. He secured permission from the Educational Board to introduce junior college work, and felt now that the divine hand was leading him on to higher things. There were some honest objectors, who sounded a warning alarm, but nothing daunted him.

The first year's college work was introduced in

September, 1910. Mr. Beers had secured a strong faculty, who were well qualified to give instruction in all of the studies of the college curriculum. One year only was added at a time until the full four years' course was complete.

Three bright young people received college diplomas in June, 1914. The junior college work was soon accredited by the University of the State of Washington and the number in the college classes kept increasing. In the second class, among others, diplomas were given to the honored African missionaries, Rev. and Mrs. A. M. Anderson, who wisely spent the time of their furlough in laboring diligently to secure a college degree.

An editorial printed in *The Cascade* in the spring of 1913 is given here: "Our land today boasts of a great and comprehensive educational system. Our colleges and universities have come to stand on a par with higher institutions of learning. We glory in this record, and yet we deplore certain tendencies prevalent today in many of our educational institutions. Our public schools have abolished the study of the Word of God from their curriculum, the universities are even now attacking its very foundations and are undermining the faith of the younger generations. Out in the world also are these tendencies to be seen. Men and women are trailing blindly after false doctrines because the true spiritual light is being 'hid under the bushel.' More and more are men of simple, earnest Christian faith coming to regret these facts. 'Only by true education,' they say, 'can false education be combatted.'

"How else may we counteract this fatal atmosphere than by implanting elevated standards of morality and spirituality in the hearts and minds of our future citizens and leaders? We, as young people, desire to secure our education under Christian influences and through Christian instruction, that we may cope successfully with the unbelief that is so widespread around us.

"Our own denomination already has eight schools within its borders and we feel that the hand of God is indeed in this work. For our purpose is not merely to create 'church accessories,' but to enlarge and deepen the spirituality and intelligence of the younger church militant. If we fail in this, we are robbing the Lord's vineyard of workers and leaving the harvest to the spoilers.

"Only one of the eight schools has been doing full college work in the past. We are certainly proud of the record of Greenville College and appreciate the inestimable worth of her service to the world. Yet our land is very broad and population is increasing rapidly in the West. Hence it has become imperative to provide work of collegiate grade for the many who can not bear the expense of traveling east to Greenville College, and who do not wish to attend worldly schools. Many of our own people are seeking western homes and yet they hesitate to place their children in an atmosphere harmful to their spiritual life. Such persons will rejoice in the determination of our board of trustees that full college work shall hereafter be carried on in this institution. There are only two of our schools on the Pacific Coast where already other institutions of national reputation have sprung up. Our Seattle

AS COLLEGE PRESIDENT

Seminary is pluckily endeavoring to place at your convenience, courses and teachers in the college department, equal in efficiency to those in older and more wealthy institutions.

"In modest pride we boast of our lofty mountain peaks and sunny valleys, of our sunshine and shower and of all the many other blessings with which we are favored. A restless 'onward' spirit pervades every nook and corner of this great country of ours. The development of the West has been phenomenal. The western spirit has become synonymous with advancement and progress. Must not our church educational institutions attempt to keep pace with this marvelous progress and development?

"The past has not been without its difficulties and hardships, but courage has never failed those who have guided the destinies of this school. Now that our seminary can register twenty winters of success, we stretch to our full height of manhood and feel the bounding pulse of youth within our veins respond to the call of greater courage. With the hope and faith of youth we see our college ship launched upon the future and we bespeak your frank support and earnest prayers for its safe passage to a final haven of security. The prospects are the best. Our college work is already well under way and we as college students invite you to swell our numbers and share with us the advantage of a Christian home and a Christian seminary and college in this great western city."

At this time a great opportunity came which Mr. Beers quickly seized. The original five acres of the campus seemed all too small for the large number of pupils who were now in attendance, including those in the grammar grades, high school and college work. Then, too, the view was obstructed by a row of dwell ings between the campus and Third Avenue. This greatly impaired the beauty of the campus. We had long felt the need of more room and wished that our territory extended to the avenue. At last there came a crisis. When the gentleman who owned the corner lot began to excavate for a large store on the very spot which properly should form an important part of our college campus—indeed, the site which Mr. Beers had selected for a future college building— there was no time for delay. Mr. Beers immediately interviewed these property owners and learned that all would be willing to vacate and the college buy an equal amount of land for them across the street to place their buildings on. The only difficulty he had now was with the gentleman who owned the corner. This man wished to put his store there and seemed quite obdurate at first. After considerable persua- sion and earnest prayer on the part of the seminary people, he consented to move his store across to the opposite corner. This remarkable transaction in- creased the campus from five to eight acres and gave a free, complete frontage on Third Avenue. It cost about twenty thousand dollars and involved a great deal of anxiety and careful dealing. Those who are now enjoying the beautiful and spacious campus will readily declare that it is worth double or treble that amount to the college grounds.

The introduction of college work rendered further equipment for the laboratories necessary. Sufficient apparatus to meet all the requirements of the Uni-

versity was now added. With characteristic fore-
sight Mr. Beers had secured recognition from the
University of Washington so that the college work
was soon placed on the accredited list and the students received full credit for all the work that was
done in the institution. Not only was the necessary
equipment provided for the laboratories at this time,
but many additional books were placed in the library. From the first history of the school Mr.
Beers had paid great attention to the library, believing that no institution could be successful without
the classics, and eminent poets were placed before
the students so that they would become acquainted
with the great literature of the times, not only of the
present but of the past as well. As the finances were
often limited, donations of books had been given in
various places from the private store of individuals,
with the result that many of these were not suitable
for the use of students. The idea was conceived of
appointing library days, when specially prepared
programs were rendered by the students for the public and everybody was asked to bring a book or
books as contribution. Professor Omer A. Burns,
an esteemed member of the faculty, who had ever
been a great lover of books, now proved himself a
real library benefactor. Carefully culling out all
that were not fitted for the use of students, he would
take them to the city and sell or exchange these for
other books that were indispensable. He himself
also donated many valuable books to this object.
Several benefit programs were held until at last the
library numbered a thousand or more choice volumes suited for recreation, reference or study.

It had required much labor and expense to furnish the new buildings which had been erected, but in a short space of time, with the aid of the faculty and friends of the school, beautiful furnishings had been placed in the large reception parlor and the dormitories supplied with comfortable and home-like furniture. Perhaps no one can ever realize the difficulties involved in all this undertaking. Only an individual who has labored to build up a Christian school under similar circumstances can appreciate the sleepless nights, the weary days, that must be realized before such a work is accomplished. Dr. Tiffany, of the Seattle Pacific College, refers to the difficulties Mr. Beers overcame, in his remarks which he made in the memorial service which was held in the college: "There are great difficulties attending the establishment of one of our church schools. The average career of an administrator of one of these schools is from about four to six years. Brother Beers has been connected with the Seattle Seminary and College for more than twenty years. This fact itself shows that he was a man of unusual ability, large faith, and heroic courage. He also filled other high positions in the church with great acceptability. He was a member of the Executive Committee of the Free Methodist Church for eighteen years, where his counsels were greatly appreciated, but the heavy burdens that he carried in the school work and in various offices in the church did not preclude his becoming a very successful minister of the gospel. His sermons were of very high rank and his preaching eagerly sought by the masses." One of our student missionaries in Japan also refers to the struggle and the conflict with very comforting words in a personal letter: "God has His wondrous hand on all these things. We may suffer, we may be buffeted, our names may be cast out as evil, our good may be evil spoken of and our sacrificing service for Him may be considered as naught, but glory be to God who has given us the victory through Jesus Christ our Lord. The greater the struggle the more glorious will be the victory. The hotter the fire, the greater the purity of the gold afterward. The deeper the valleys with their shadows, the higher the mountain heights with their brilliancy of sunshine and glory."

The responsibility of caring for young people in one of our Christian schools is very grave. It is a burden that is never lifted from the time the students arrive in the fall until they return to their own homes in June. But when Rev. and Mrs. E. F. Ward wrote to Mr. Beers from India asking him to assume the care of their two youngest daughters, Bessie and Louise, to look after their physical and spiritual welfare during school days and vacation days, summer and winter, until they finished the grammar grades and completed their high school work, it seemed almost more than he dare attempt. The older sister, Ethel, was already in the institution and would faithfully do her part in caring for the younger girls. After prayerful consideration, Mr. and Mrs. Beers wrote to Rev. and Mrs. Ward to send the girls to America and they would do the best they could in caring for them, with the help of the Lord. In the process of time they came—two darling girls just fresh from their mother's arms.

fourteen and twelve years of age. They were soon greatly beloved by all. From the first, Bessie and Louise filled a large place in our musical department, being especially gifted in music. They pursued their studies faithfully and grew to be young ladies who brought great pleasure to the faculty and friends.

Mr. Beers always insisted on their keeping a good Christian experience. When Louise had lapsed for a short time in her spiritual life and had been getting cold in her devotions, he told her most emphatically in one Tuesday evening's service if she did not retrace her steps and return to God he would buy her ticket and send her back to India. She knew that he would not speak thus unless he fully intended to carry out his purpose. She sought pardon at once, obtained a satisfactory experience in that very service, and was never known to lapse after that. A few days before Mr. Beers passed away, Mrs. Beers read to him the sad news of dear Louise's death. He mourned sincerely for her then, but how soon he was to clasp her hand, where parting never comes. She surely welcomed him with joy when he reached heaven, since he was always so like a father to her.

An approaching event brought great anticipation to the institution and its friends in the closing months of 1912 and the dawning of 1913—it would soon be twenty years since school was opened in March, 1893. Since the birthday of the president, Mr. Beers, came March 4, the trustees and faculty thought this would be a suitable day to call a general rally for a week's celebration of the twentieth milestone of the school. For several months Mr.

Beers had been securing speakers and making preparation for this illustrious event. The convention was opened by a gathering of the alumni and former students in the young ladies' hall, Tuesday evening, March 4, 1913.

A brief account of this convention was given by one of the teachers, Miss Rose Logan, and published in *The Cascade*, 1913: "From the fourth to the tenth of March a memorable convention was held at Seattle Seminary and College to celebrate the twentieth anniversary of the founding of the institution. To the faculty and students, the week was one of the greatest interest and inspiration. The various addresses were radiant with idealism, and stimulated all who heard them to live lives of greater usefulness and fuller service. Many suggestions were given those who intended to consecrate themselves to missionary work, to the ministry or to the practical, every-day duties of the Christian citizen. Those who were interested in the development of the Seminary and College were enthusiastic over the delightful reminiscences of the past twenty years, and felt keen sympathy with the prophecies of the future growth and success of the school. All the services of the convention held in the assembly hall, in the chapel and in the church were well attended throughout the convention. Those parts of the anniversary celebration which took place in the girls' hall were particularly enjoyable. Old friends, former classmates, missionaries, who in days past were students here, ministers whose earliest inspiration for their life work was implanted here, former instructors, and many guests met at a reception and exchanged news and incidents of other years, and foretold days of greater development for the seminary. The meeting of the older friends of the institution, the pioneers, occurred on Saturday night. Heart met heart on that occasion, tender memories were revived, friendships were made more fast through the ties of common interest in the welfare of a noble school. A feature ever kept before the convention was the necessity of raising the long-desired endowment fund. And on Sunday the interest in the financial success of the school culminated in the raising of over ten thousand dollars in cash and pledges.

"On Sunday afternoon the service was conducted by the students. Mr. E. A. Haslam, assisted by representatives from the various societies of the school; Mr. O. Haslam, Mr. Root, Miss Sharpe and Mr. Logan, presented from the students' point of view the importance of Christian education as a preparation for the active service of life. The convention fittingly closed with the rendering of the oratorio, 'The Holy City,' by the Seattle Seminary and College chorus. The convention from the first session until the last was a most inspiring one. Addresses delivered by Bishop William Pearce, Revs. C. S. McKinley, William Boddy, J. D. Marsh, A. Youngren, W. N. Coffee, E. W. Achilles, H. V. Haslam, A. N. West and Judge Milo A. Root will live long in the memory, and the new ideals gained will always be cherished by every student, teacher and friend of the institution."

Former Bishop E. P. Hart had been expected to address the student body Thursday morning, but circumstances prohibited his being present. Bishop

William Pearce gave two fine addresses during the convention, "Christ and Culture" and "The Path to Excellence." Rev. August Youngren, from Japan, also spoke briefly from "The Relation of Missionary Work to Christian Education." Special prayer services were conducted daily by prominent "elect ladies," which brought much spiritual enthusiasm to the convention. The "pioneers" met Saturday evening and filled in the time with thrilling reminiscences.

The great convention closed Monday evening with the grand oratorio given by the seminary chorus, under the leadership of W. W. Cathey. This was a fitting climax to the twentieth anniversary, as Mr. Beers had always taken a great interest in the work of the chorus. Reference has been made in a previous chapter that Mr. Beers seemed to have very limited musical ability, but he was ever a great lover of fine music and found great pleasure in the singers who were trained in the school.

The singing of the famous seminary quartette always delighted him. "The Forest Glee" as sung by them became a classic with him. Some of their beautiful solos will always be remembered. One of these, "The Palace of the King," will ever be associated with the name of Mrs. June Cathey, who sings today in a higher clime.

Printed invitations to attend the convention had been sent to every circuit in the Washington Conference and to the leading preachers in the Columbia River Conference. Many responded and the attendance was very gratifying. Mr. Beers was at his best, presiding over the services, looking after the entertainment of the visitors and inspiring all with hope, faith and courage, by his optimistic spirit. A large sum of money was raised in cash and subscriptions for the college and the blessed Holy Spirit was poured upon the people in every service. The convention was pronounced a glorious success and all dispersed at the close with stronger purpose and loftier faith for the future of the school.

CHAPTER XIV

A CHRISTIAN EDUCATOR AND PREACHER

If we work upon marble, it will perish; if we work upon brass, time will efface it; if we rear temples, they will crumble into dust; but if we work upon immortal minds, if we imbue them with principles, with the just fear of God and love of our fellow men, we engrave on these tablets something which will brighten to all eternity. — *Daniel Webster.*

One who was conversant with the life of Alexander Beers, says he was divinely called to be a Christian educator as well as preacher. Early in his ministry he had a far vision of the necessity of Christian training for the youth. He realized the dangerous influences which surrounded our sons and daughters in worldly schools. He was willing to deny himself any earthly good that our young people might be saved from sin's allurement, from the blasting, blighting effects of a wrong choice and the everlasting regrets of a wasted life. He gave many addresses on the subject of Christian education, which produced conviction of duty in the hearts of parents and brought many students into our Christian schools as a result. While speaking from the text in Psalm 144:12, "That our sons may be as plants grown up in their youth; that our daughters may be as cornerstones polished after the similitude of a palace," he would show the great necessity of early training. The simple verse he had learned at his sister's knee as a child was used very effectively. A small boy carries on a conversation with a crooked tree:

"Old tree, how much your trunk is bent,
Why don't you make a rise and stand up straight as you
    were meant?"
And has the old tree found a voice
Or did a soft wind stir the leaves on high?
The old tree sighed and said:
"Alas, it is too late. When I was young
That was the time you should have come and propped me
    straight."

Dwelling on the formation of character, he would frequently quote from Thackeray: "We sow a thought, we reap an act; we sow an act, we reap a habit; we sow a habit, we reap a character; we sow character and reap destiny." A few paragraphs are here given from his own pen on "Worthy Educational Ideals":

"It is said that during each spring more than one hundred thousand of the brightest youths of America are graduated and given diplomas from the various high schools, academies, seminaries, colleges and universities. Commencement day is the one high day of school life. Every graduate looks forward with bright anticipation to this day as the consummation of a well planned and carefully prosecuted course of study. Fathers and mothers with equal pride and enthusiasm look with rare satisfaction upon the day when their sons and daughters shall receive diplomas.

"This vast army of young people means much to the generations to come. The home, the church, the state and nation will be influenced for weal or woe by the influence exerted by them. That 'knowledge is power' is recognized by all. The mighty influence that this restless company of educated and aspiring people will have is too great for human mind to grasp. As the mighty Gulf Stream can be traced far out into the trackless ocean, so the influence of this army of one hundred thousand young lives will break on eternity's shore.

"The character of the influence wielded by these young people will depend largely upon the instruction received within the educational walls during the four years of school life. This emphasizes the great need of Christian education. Any system of training that leaves God out of its curriculum is sadly deficient. Dr. Hills says, 'True education leads its possessor to love the truth supremely, to pursue it eternally, to yield one's self to it completely and to defend it persistently even at the loss of reputation or life itself. This is to receive from God the patent of nobility.' Our training must be of such a character as to make our young people strong and wise. The conscience must be quickened, the powers of moral and ethical discrimination clarified, the will reinforced and the soul elevated. In tendency it must always point Godward as naturally as the needle points to the pole. No teacher is properly qualified for the task of instructing and training young people who has not a personal knowledge of God. He must know Him as a Creator and Savior, he should be able to say from personal experience, 'Behold the Lamb of God that taketh away the sin of the world.'

"The safety of our young people and the stability and perpetuity of our institutions depend upon the underlying Christian virtues and principles. A victorious life is the product of good judgment, self-control, a clear head and a pure heart. Absolute justice to all, regardless of rank or station in life, must be the watch-word and motto of the properly trained person. The individual must have clean hands and a pure heart. Such a young person is not easily plunged into ruin, nor is he liable to be shipwrecked upon the first rock of temptation that his bark encounters on the voyage of life. We are taught in the Bible that the man who controls his own spirit is stronger than he who takes a city. He who is governed and controlled by Jesus Christ is of necessity a courageous and victorious person. Looseness, infidelity, duplicity, all forms of sham and hypocrisy must be eschewed. It is cowardly to sin and make a mock of God. The truly righteous life is indicative of scientific bravery. The irreligious young person can not be depended upon. The Seattle Pacific College stands first, last and always for Christian education. Not doctors, lawyers, teachers, preachers, missionaries, but men and women transformed by the grace of God and dedicated to the cause of Christ is the object and aim of this institution. The class that is being graduated this year will go out to represent these ideals. The many classes that have been graduated during the last nineteen years are holding up the standard of their Alma Mater most nobly. Are not our Christian schools the pillar of cloud and of fire that must guide our young people safely through the great wilderness of error and bring them into the Promised Land of a useful life?"

The founding of the Seattle Seminary and College at Seattle was the crowning work of Mr. Beers' life. Fine buildings and a beautiful campus remain today as an everlasting monument to his memory. A brother in the ministry writes in regard to his work: "Brother and Sister Beers came to Seattle nearly twenty-nine years ago to take charge of Seattle Seminary (now Seattle Pacific College), which consisted of an unimproved campus site, one building without any furnishings whatever, which was to serve as chapel, class rooms, dining hall and dormitory, with no student body and a debt of more than sixteen thousand dollars on the property, with a total membership in what was then known as the Oregon and Washington Conference (now four conferences) of six hundred and one, and church and parsonage property valued at less than twenty-eight thousand dollars, and in the midst of the most fearful financial panic we have ever known. Under these most discouraging conditions Brother Beers and his noble wife, with faith in God, heroically accepted the heavy burden which they bore for nearly a quarter of a century, and during those years of hardship and self-denial they never murmured or complained. Brother Beers was a man with a broad vision, and the splendid buildings and beautiful campus of Seattle Pacific College are the result of that vision and his untiring labors and self-denial. Many who are now filling prominent places in the business world, others who are preaching the gospel in this and foreign lands, are there because of the influence of this godly man over their lives, and in many cases because of his liberality. He was a friend of the young people; he coveted them for God and lives of usefulness and they loved him, and scores of young men and women who lived in the home of our dear brother bear witness to the pure, clean, Christian character of this man of God. As a family we feel that in the death of Brother Beers we have lost a true friend and brother, and the church one of its most capable, godly, big-hearted and aggressive men. A prince in Israel has fallen."

Hundreds of students may be found in this and in foreign lands whose lives have been transformed through the influence of the worthy life and lofty ideals of this Christian teacher. One of these said of him, "Throughout the years of his educational activities, his broad sympathetic and intelligent understanding of human nature and of the perplexing problems that sometimes confront young people, in their struggle for success, made him a constant friend and an able adviser. Many today who have gained success and honor received through his words of encouragement and personal influence, the first spark of inspiration, the first glimmer of a pure and lofty ideal, and were made to feel that life is real and worth the living."

A bright, intelligent boy just merging into manhood became discouraged when asked to take the part assigned him in the literary society of the seminary. He really thought he *could not* perform *this task* and rather than make a failure took his books and left the institution. Mr. Beers, hearing that he had gone, sent for him to come to his office where he

THE YOUNG LADIES' HALL, ERECTED IN 1907-08

engaged him in pleasant conversation for a few moments, then asked him about his work in rhetoricals. With great frankness the youth told him he did not care for public speaking anyhow, that he was going back to the farm and "he'd let the other boys be professionals if they wanted to." Mr. Beers commended the farmer and showed how dependent we all were upon the tiller of the soil. "But," he said, "before you go I want you to speak a piece I have here that is really quite a take-off on the professional life—it's entitled, 'The Mother's Fool.'" Mr. Beers then produced those humorous lines:

> " 'Tis plain enough," said Farmer Brown,
> As he put his mug of cider down,
> "That book larnin', as sure's you're born,
> Won't sow your grain nor plant your corn,
> Nor mend a rod of broken fence;
> For my part give me common sense."
>
> The wife was bound the roost to rule,
> And John and Henry were sent to school.
> But little Fred was left behind
> Because his mother said he had no mind.
> But somehow, by hook or crook,
> Little Fred mastered many a book.
> With a knowing look his father said,
> "He's getting book larnin' in his head."

and on through the ditty, showing the failure of John and Henry who were sent to school, and the success of "little Fred" who stayed at home and worked on the farm, and later joined the army and became general. Coming back home he went to work on the farm again, planted the corn and sowed the grain. In fact he conducted himself so wisely that **his father said** that he had "common sense."

"Now common sense was very rare,
And the State House needed a portion there."

So "little Fred" moved into town and the people
called him "Governor Brown," and "the two boys
who were sent to the city school came home and
lived with their mother's fool." These lines, a jingle
though they were, pleased the youth very much and
he said: "I'll speak that if I die trying; I'll show
those fellows that farmers are better than doctors
anyway." For days strange sounds could be heard
in the woods back of the school buildings, but it was
nothing alarming, just declamatory exercising on
the part of this youth who was exerting himself to
put all professionals to shame. When the critical
hour arrived for the ordeal that was to mean so
much to him in after life, everybody in the school
was interested to see how he would succeed. Mr.
Beers said afterward that he was praying very earnestly that the boy might not have a lapse of memory. But he went through with flying colors. "Bring
the house down?" Yes, had every one convulsed
with laughter and cheering him on to victory. This
success brought him back into the school filled with
courage. He did not stop with a high school education, but went on through college and was not satisfied until he had fitted himself to act as principal of
one of our seminaries.

In later years when Mr. Beers was granted an interview with the great railroad magnate, James J.
Hill, and presented the financial needs of the institution, he told this incident to show the kind of work
the school was doing in fitting young men for lives
of usefulness. Mr. Hill was visibly affected. With

moistened eyes and a tremor in his voice, he said, "Such work as that will make your dying pillow all the softer."

Words are inadequate to express the struggle, the strain, the stress, that this noble man of God was called to endure that he might fulfil the divine purpose in his life. Nothing but the strength of an Omnipotent arm could have carried him through and caused him to conquer gloriously. A lady who was formerly a member of our faculty writes, "The crowning work of his life was, without doubt, that connected with the development of Seattle Seminary and its merging into Seattle Pacific College, which has contributed so mightily to the spiritual life, the effectiveness, and the prospects of our Zion. The countless lives thus influenced by him and Mrs. Beers are their monument—far superior to an epitaph graven upon stone, for their names will neither be unhonored nor forgotten though their resting places be as unmarked as that of Israel's leader in Moab. With abiding gratitude and benediction the church will think of him who gave this school direction and impetus and laid broad and deep the foundations of the future." The faculty and students of Seattle Pacific College wrote words of appreciation. "We are constantly reminded of the love and devotion of Mr. Beers as we pass the scenes of his many years of labor and sacrifice in connection with the Seattle Pacific College. His vision of the wider field of usefulness for the young people of the Free Methodist Church, and his untiring efforts in the work of Christ inspire us to renew our allegiance to the Master."

Our denominational college of Greenville, Illinois,
had previously conferred the honorary degree of
A.B. upon Mr. Beers in recognition of the splendid
results of his labor for the cause of Christian education and also for his marked literary ability and
fine scholastic attainments. A few months later he
was called to Whitman College at Walla Walla,
Washington, to receive the honorary title of A.M.
We quote from a letter written by the president of
the college, dated June 14, 1916:

DEAR PRESIDENT BEERS :—

I hereby invite you to be present at Commencement on
next Wednesday, June twenty-first, in order that you may
receive this A.M. degree in recognition of your distinguished
services to the cause of education and religion in the Pacific
Northwest. The Commencement exercises occur at 4 p. m.
on Wednesday. Following them is our Alumni dinner at
which I hope you will consent to make a brief speech not
more than ten minutes in length as a new member of the
Alumni body. Looking forward to welcoming you at that
time, I am with cordial regards,

Very sincerely yours,
STEPHEN N. L. PENROSE, President.

The president of Greenville College says of him:
"He seemed to have a wonderfully clear conception
of the real meaning of life and the practical significance of an education. He made wonderful progress in his studies, and with the larger vision and
increasing ability there were depth of conviction
and breadth of sympathy. He was naturally attracted to the field of religious education. He saw
the strategic value of our denominational schools.
His grasp of the fundamental principles of education and his clear statement of the aims and process

of Christian education gave him unquestioned leadership in the educational work of the church. His great natural gifts and genial personality won young people to himself and to the school for which he was so largely responsible, and with which he was so long identified. A noble company of young people, who had caught his vision and spirit, came on to Greenville to pursue their studies, consecrated and blessed, to go out later into the larger fields of Christian service. A wise educator rests from his labors. But he still lives in the men and women, sometime students of his, marked with the impress of his consecrated and noble spirit." Professor La-Due, of the same institution, in a personal letter says, "And so dear, noble Brother Beers is through with it all—the strain and stress and struggle and care. How glorious for him! What an indescribable relief to find himself at home and crowned. 'He asked life of thee, and thou gavest it him, even length of days forever and forever.' 'What rejoicing in His presence.' It is hard for us, but we will thank for his sake the Master who does as we would too if we knew as well as He. His record is on high, above all touch of blame. His work will last forever, and a multitude will be his friends for time and for eternity."

Mr. Beers was not only a successful educator but was considered an able minister of the gospel and an efficient preacher by many of the leading men of the church. Rev. B. Winget, of sainted memory, says of him: "Rev. A. Beers was a noble man of superior physique and pleasing manners—an able minister of the gospel who rightly divided the word of truth.

During the last few years of his life as pastor he greatly endeared himself to his people and his labors were crowned with success. He did not live as long as some of the Lord's servants. However, he was actuated by a high and holy purpose and moved on an exalted plane. He was esteemed very highly in love for his works' sake." One of the members of the First Free Methodist Church of Portland expresses his words of appreciation: "He greatly endeared himself to the First Church society while with us three years. We shall never forget his abundant labor of love and tireless efforts in our behalf, not only with regard to the spiritual interest of the society, but also in putting the church property in good condition, building over the church and erecting a new, commodious parsonage. Both stand today as a monument to his memory. One can hardly look at them now without seeing Brother and Sister Beers. She stood with him in the good work and gave great encouragement to it. God wonderfully used him in building up the work here at First Church and also as an inspiration to the entire Oregon Conference." Not only was his work in Portland as a pastor appreciated, but as a preacher and pastor in Seattle he was highly commended. Rev. A. N. West, former district elder, says: "For a number of years he served as pastor of the Seattle First Church, also Seattle Second Church. He was successful as a pastor and evangelist and at the same time bore almost the entire burden of the seminary. Brother Beers was one of God's great men, a great mind and a great heart, always manifesting a Christian spirit, ever ready to forgive a wrong. We never heard him speak a word to injure the character or hurt the influence of those who wronged him. He was a most liberal man. No appeal for help was ever made to him in vain. He gave until he fairly impoverished himself. His money helped to build nearly every church and parsonage in the Washington Conference. His home was always open to the people of God. Here the missionaries found a welcome and scores of God's saints have been partakers of his hospitality. He gave the best that he had."

In his preaching he ever depended upon the Holy Spirit for inspiration and help; whenever there seemed to be a lack of unction in his messages, he would mourn sincerely until *he knew* that God again endorsed and was leading him. One who was a lifelong friend and as intimate as a brother in the flesh, says, "He was a thorough Free Methodist and a noble Christian. Often have I seen him stand and hold up his hand and praise the Lord, when there was a special outpouring of the Spirit, and remark, 'I feel like honoring the Holy Spirit.' As a preacher he was far above the average. He was devoted to his noble wife. His work in the Seattle Pacific College speaks for itself. And many shall rise up and call him blessed."

He often aimed forcible thrusts against the seductive teachings of Christian Science. He would say, "Christian Science is like an artificial fire which never produces warmth and comfort, while salvation is like the crackling, roaring fire in the fire-place with a big back log and the fagots heaped high, around which the whole family can gather and find cheer in its glowing rays. Christian Science is like a picture of flowers or fruit hanging on the wall, while salvation brings the fragrance and perfume of the beautiful rose from the garden and furnishes food for all who hunger.   Again Christian Science is like cold statuary. You look at the figure of the man so finely modeled by the sculptor and say, 'Why, I can almost hear him breathe, and I almost expect he will walk away,' but you know that this will never be a fact, while the Christian religion brings the liv-ing, throbbing reality into life.   You enjoy its rich perfume, your soul is constantly warmed by the fire of the gospel and you sit down to the table spread with the richest viands that are freely furnished to all of God's children, and eat until you are satisfied, while Christian Science brings only imaginary joy and at last will leave its followers without hope or refuge to all eternity."

He preached a powerful series of sermons on the fulfilment of prophecy as it relates to the end of the age.   The fourth one of this series, "The False Prophet, the Dragon, the Beast, Hell's Trinity in Unity," attracted much attention.   In this sermon he proved that there is an Anti-God, Anti-Christ, and Anti-Holy Ghost as a trinity in unity in direct opposition to the trinity of the God-head and that in the final end all evil will head up or be impersonated in one great demon of wickedness.

The theory of evolution at that time was very pop-ular in the secular colleges.   That the students of the Seattle Pacific College might be enlightened he studied the subject fully, and delivered a series of lectures refuting this great error.*

---

*See Chapter 22, extract from lecture on Evolution.

He also preached a series of sermons from the book of Job, which were considered very instructive by those who heard them. He was later urged to go on the platform of one of the large eastern chautauquas and deliver this series and offered large remuneration if he would favor them. He declined the proposition. He was a man of such lofty purpose, he could not turn aside for gain.

His addresses on the subject of Prohibition were very strong and vigorous. He often illustrated these by the experience of John G. Woolley, whom he had the pleasure of knowing personally after he had been rescued from the depths of sin and had become a famous lecturer on temperance. He traveled from Portland to Seattle with Mr. and Mrs. Woolley and heard from their own lips the awful havoc that the demon drink had made in Mr. Woolley's life, and the wonderful change that came when he had found "the perfect cure" in the blood of Christ. "Mrs. Woolley, how did you feel when you received the telegram from Stephen Merritt that your husband was a saved man?" asked Mr. Beers. "Oh," she replied, "I was taken from the confines of perdition and placed in the realm of Paradise."

When preaching from the text, "Thy gentleness hath made me great," he would use an incident from personal experience. "I had been trying for some time to secure a 'clergy book' for Mrs. Beers from the railroad company. I knew she was entitled to this courtesy, as she came under their rules. While in Chicago I interviewed the chief secretary in the transportation department, but my request was refused and no reason given me for the refusal. The secretary offered to refund the dollar I had advanced, and I declined it, saying curtly, 'No, thank you. You keep that for the good of the cause.' Going to my room, I knelt in secret prayer, not to pray about the episode that had occurred, nor did I hope to have my request granted. As I knelt there, the Spirit whispered to me, 'Thy gentleness hath made me great,' and I saw I had violated this gentleness by my *curt* reply. I went at once to the office and apologized, telling the man I aimed to be a sincere Christian always, and I wished him to forgive me for my unkind manner. The secretary was deeply moved and said, 'I am striving to be a Christian myself. I do not know why I refused your request. I know your wife is entitled to this favor.'" With this he called a clerk and had the required book filled out and handed to Mr. Beers, who left the office with a deep sense of the divine presence.

We have already alluded to Mr. Beers' success in raising money. When preaching on this subject he would appeal to every generous impulse of one's heart, showing the wisdom of laying up our treasures above, where moth and rust can not corrupt and where thieves do not break through nor steal; then he would show the awful danger of hoarding the money that should be given to God's cause. In this connection he would sometimes quote from Joaquin Miller's "The Dead Millionaire".

"The gold that with the sunlight lies,
   In bursting heaps at dawn,
The silver spilling from the skies
   At night to walk upon,
The diamonds gleaming in the dew,
   He never saw, he never knew.

"He got some gold, dug from the mud,
　Some silver, crushed from stones;
But the gold was red with dead men's blood,
　The silver black with groans;
And when he died he moaned aloud,
　'They'll make no pocket in my shroud.' "

Contrasting this rich pauper with the beneficent giver who gave all he had and still possessed his treasures, he would quote:

"Aye, wisest he in this whole wide land,
　Of hoarding till bent and gray;
For all you can hold in your cold, dead hand
　Is what you have given away."

After one of these passionate appeals, a good brother, who was a member of the Baptist Church, informed Mr. Beers that he felt he should give the sum of two thousand dollars to the school on an annuity plan, and requested him to come to his home so that he and his wife could sign the papers. At the appointed time Mr. Beers took a friend with him and made the visit. The legal papers were made out and the brother called on Mr. Beers to pray before he left. During the season of prayer the Baptist brother seemed greatly distressed; they all arose and engaged in conversation for a few moments and he urged Mr. Beers to pray again for him. During the second season of prayer, he still was not satisfied, and urged Mr. Beers to have the third season of prayer; during this last time of praying he got down on his face and agonized—pleading with God to give him the victory. When all had prayed around, he yielded his will and great deliverance came to his soul. He told how God had shown him he should *give* this two thousand dollars to the seminary as a free, untrammeled gift—not an annuity, and he had been unwilling to do so. There was a great shout in that home that morning. His wife said she got the greatest blessing she had received in twenty years.

In Seattle and vicinity Mr. Beers found much in nature to admire. The towering Olympics and the snow-capped Cascades were a constant source of enjoyment to him. He loved to take long walks under the blue canopy of the skies and gather inspiration from the handiwork of God when preparing to preach; then he would bring the perfume of sweet flowers, the music of rippling streams and the sublimity of the majestic mountains into his messages, leading his hearers to love and adore the infinite Creator.

Mention has already been made of his fondness for poetry. It was his custom, when preaching, to quote from passages that he loved and was familiar with. When preaching upon purity of heart and life, he would emphasize the thought by the lines from Sir Galahad—

> "My strength is as the strength of ten,
> Because my heart is pure."

Describing the search for the Holy Grail and making the application to the quest of the soul after the highest ideals, he would often quote:

> "Ah, blessed vision, blood of God!
> My spirit beats her mortal bars."

When preaching on Christian courage and fortitude, Mr. Beers would exhort his hearers to hold the banner of holiness aloft to the world, even as the gallant

British would not permit the banner of England to be torn down in the "Defense of Lucknow."

"Shot through the staff or the halyard, but ever we raised thee anew,
And ever upon the topmost roof our banner of England blew."

Picturing the awful days of the cholera, scurvy and fever, the wound that would not be healed, "Chopping away of the limb by the pitiful pitiless knife."

Looking for General Havelock to deliver them, not knowing but he had been slain, watching night and day for more than twelve weeks. At last victory comes and the welcome sound of the pibroch of England bursts upon their ears as Havelock and his staff break through the mutineers and the people shout:

"Saved by the valor of Havelock,
Saved by the blessing of heaven,
Hold it for fifteen days;
We have held it for eighty-seven,
And ever aloft on the palace roof
The old banner of England blew."

So God's followers should hold their ground when besieged by the devil and harrassed by every foe to righteousness; when men are yielding on every side to the allurements of the world, be a brave soldier and never surrender your charge. Let every man die at his post and God's people shall shout eternal victory.

When preaching with passionate earnestness of the duty of siding always with righteousness, championing the absolute prohibition of the liquor traffic. pleading woman's right of suffrage, he would often quote from Lowell's "Present Crisis":

"Some great cause, God's new Messiah,
  Offering each the bloom or blight,
And the choice goes by forever,
  'Twixt that darkness and that light."

With what eloquence would he espouse the cause of alien nations in our country, the down-trodden and the poor of earth! Wrong and error may seem to triumph and the oppressed still clank their chains.

"Careless seems the great avenger;
  History's pages but record
One death grapple in the darkness
  'Twixt old systems and the Word;
Truth forever on the scaffold,
  Wrong forever on the throne;
Yet that scaffold sways the future,
  And behind the dim unknown
Standeth God within the shadow,
  Keeping watch above His own."

Showing the grandeur, the privilege of siding with truth when unpopular, we hear him saying,

"Then to side with truth is noble,
  When we share her wretched crust,
Ere her cause bring fame and profit,
  And 'tis prosperous to be just."

When discoursing on the prophecy contained in Tennyson's "Locksley Hall," he would call attention to the wonderful fulfilment in the verse,

"Heard the heavens fill with shouting
  And there rained a ghastly dew (explosive gas)
From the nations' airy navies (aeroplanes),
  Grappling in the central blue."

Then referring to the coming pre-millennial reign of Christ upon earth, he would sound the comforting words:

"Till the war drum throbbed no longer,
  And the battle flags were furl'd,
In the parliament of man,
  The federation of the world."

Rev. William Boddy, an alumnus of the institution, calls attention to this great fondness for poetry in a personal letter to Mrs. Beers and also to the spirit of forgiveness so marked in Mr. Beers: "We have all suffered a great loss in the death of Mr. Beers, but no one will feel this loss as you do. The affection and thoughtfulness that Mr. Beers always manifested toward you was one of the things that endeared him so greatly to us all. As I look back over his life, having known him so many years, the things upon which he might be criticised seem very trivial as compared with his great Christian character. I have been thinking of how he loved poetry and how when he discovered my boyish love of verse he desired so much to direct my thought to great poetry. He often took me into his library and read the classics with me. I especially remember his love for Frances Ridley Havergal's 'Compensation.' That poem has been a great source of comfort to me. I first learned to know it through Mr. Beers calling my attention to it. While attending his funeral in the little church at Gresham it seemed that I was reading the last earthly chapter of a great romance —the romance of a consecrated life. I thought of his magnanimity, his humility and his sympathy which included all mankind. As I sat in the little village church, the evening sun streamed through the window and I looked out upon the quiet of the church yard where my friend was to lie at rest. I

thought of the time when he had gone away from
that little town, just a crude country boy. Then I
thought of the culture and refinement that had characterized his life. I thought of his love for poetry
and of all things beautiful. I thought of his masterly preaching of Jesus Christ. I visualized him as
he moved with equal poise among men, both great
and small, and his life seemed to me to be an em-
bodiment of the full redeeming power of Christ's
grace. I think the outstanding characteristic of Mr.
Beers' life was his exalted attitude toward those
who differed with him. I do not believe that Mr.
Beers was capable of holding a feeling of enmity toward any one."

CHAPTER XV

PROMINENT CHARACTERISTICS

No stars shine brighter than the kingly man
Who nobly earns whatever crown he wears,
  Who grandly conquers, or as grandly dies;
And the white banner of his manhood bears
  Through all the years uplifted to the skies.
              —*Mrs. Dorr.*

Dr. Roberts says, "Preeminently, Alexander Beers possessed greatness of soul. His sympathies were as broad as the claims of humanity. To the sorrowing, the needy, he gave a listening ear, and reached out a helping hand. Was it China, Japan, India, whose needs were considered, or was it a crude son of the pioneer's cabin knocking at the schoolhouse door—a friendly smile, a gift not of money alone, but of priceless sympathy, and helpful, interested effort was granted freely, joyously. His sympathies were without limits of race, class or creed. The banker, the merchant, the farm hand alike found him interested to share their burdens. He sowed, others reaped."

A ruling passion of his heart seemed ever to be to help his fellowmen. For this reason he delighted in serving the church as transportation secretary. Never was any one's plea for help in securing courtesies from the railroad passed unheeded unless the case was clearly a violation of the companies' rules;

then he was very loath to ask for consideration, always being very conscientious in his requests. All the officials at the head of the great railroad systems west of Chicago became so confident that this man would never take advantage of them in any way that they were slow to refuse any application he would endorse. A few weeks before he was taken with his illness, he had the privilege of receiving fifteen passes in one morning mail and two more came in the afternoon, making seventeen in one day. A number of these included passes over an entire system for one individual—this success in aiding so many of his brethren made him very happy.

It appears that Alexander inherited his large-heartedness from his father, as like him he was ever contributing of his means to aid some worthy cause. He was never so happy as when bringing help and cheer to some one in need. His wife says, "In our married life I was constantly impressed with the greatness of his compassion toward the unfortunate. I well remember a poor, ignorant fellow who was not normally bright, but had found salvation. No one wanted to invite this disagreeable brother home to dinner, but Mr. Beers would bring him in to dine with us very frequently. Another instance I can never forget—we were preparing to entertain the annual conference at a place where Mr. Beers was pastor. Free entertainment was offered to all, but strange to say, very few families were found who were willing to care for people with children. For several days he had canvassed for places, but found no welcome for the little ones. At last he said, 'When Christ was on earth He invited the children

Alexander Beers

AT HIS BEST

to come, and we will take them all at our house.' So we filled our large home with children. The sister of one of our preachers came with a babe but two weeks old. This infant was very fretful and Mr. Beers spent many an odd moment walking the house with the child, to give its mother rest. She had come a stranger to us all and a professed infidel in belief. The kind treatment she received completely won her heart and she became a firm believer in Christ and was afterward converted."

Instances of Mr. Beers' benevolences have been brought to mind since he went to heaven, which were unknown to many before. One of the brethren in the ministry tells with much emotion how Mr. Beers had found him in financial distress at one time and dropped a twenty-dollar gold piece in his hand. A dear mother says, "I was trying to make a train laden down with baggage and accompanied by four small children. Brother Beers saw my distress, helped me with the baggage, carried some of the children in his arms, and placed me comfortably on the train in good time. I said to him, 'Brother Beers, the widows and orphans will miss you when you are gone.' Smiling, he replied, 'That is all the monument I ever desire.' "

Space will not permit the author to tell of his many loving deeds of generosity to poor students who were struggling to secure an education. If young men and women were worthy, Mr. Beers would devise some way of helping them through school. Former students are still living who will remember the suit of clothes he gave them or the purse he raised privately for them. Some extracts are here given from letters written to his wife: "I have made the company of nearly all of the passengers in my car. The Lord has given me more to do for Him thus far on this trip than on any previous one and I am improving every opportunity." "Yesterday was a great day on the camp ground—fine crowds, very beautiful weather and much of God's presence. Had a great big blessed missionary service in the afternoon. At night the altar was filled with seekers and nearly all got through."

A young lady, a former student in the college, writes: "Many instances of his benevolence have come under my personal observation. While walking down Market Street in San Francisco with Brother Beers and my husband, a lad came through the throng and touching Brother Beers on the shoulder, said, 'Hello, doctor.' Brother Beers said, 'Well, I don't believe I know you.' The boy replied, 'Oh, yes; don't you remember that day in the city of Portland, Oregon, when I was selling newspapers at the Hazelwood, you bought me a dish of ice cream?' When others were ridiculing because of misfortune or perhaps shabby attire, he in pity was ever ready to lend the helping hand. There were none so lowly but they were worthy of his notice and consideration. He was at ease with rich or poor and a big brother to all. His life was one of sacrifice for others. In his daily walk, the Christ life was exemplified and he gave to the church and to the world his best. 'He poured out his life unto death.' "

A consecrated mother, whose sons and daughters were educated in the school, says: "Many a young person could not have had the privilege of an education, especially in a Christian school, had it not been for his magnanimous spirit. The Tuesday evening prayer meetings at the school were characterized by the burden of Brother Beers and his devoted wife for the young people." Among the many testimonies given of his generous help in time of need, comes this from a fine young man who is an accepted candidate for the mission field: "Speaking from a personal standpoint, I am conscious of no other influence or individual sympathy that has done more for me than the warm-hearted encouragements that I have received from you and Mr. Beers. I am sure thousands of others can bear testimony to the same thing. I remember when I was in school and destitute, how Mr. Beers bought me a suit of clothes, two suits of underwear, an overcoat, and several other things I needed very badly. These are not reminiscences for the occasion, but real, red, living heart memories, and I find I am not the only one by far that has a similar story to tell, and a peculiar swelling and throb of the heart as we think of the *debt* we owe Brother Beers."

Many an elderly person was made happy by his thoughtful attention. It was a subject of comment that he always devoted some time to aged persons he found living with friends in the families where he visited. Sitting down by their side, he would encourage them to tell him of their trials and victories, of their hopes and fears. He would entertain them with pleasing incidents that would tend to lift them out of their monotonous lives and lead them on toward heaven. The interview was like a good meeting to them. May the author be permitted to note in passing his great love for Father and Mother Chesbrough? After he became a member of the Executive Committee of the church, which position he occupied for eighteen years, he went to Chicago every fall, and so long as Mother Chesbrough lived he never forgot to take her a beautiful boquet of flowers.

Little children loved him greatly and he was never too occupied to notice them. As he would start from his home to go to Fremont, a distance of one-half mile, the boys and girls would hail him along the way and watch for his smile and words of recognition or a friendly pat on the head. A friend from boyhood, who was a graduate from the seminary, says he will never forget the pressure of Mr. Beers' hand on his head when he was but a young lad. He said he had a way of placing his hand on a boy's head and pronouncing a prayer or benediction which left a holy and lasting impression. No doubt the reason that children were so attracted to Mr. Beers was because he was always so noticeably fond of them—rarely was a child ever passed unnoticed in the homes he visited. A friend in Seattle, who was at one time a member of the faculty, comments on this: "He was so thoughtful of Miriam. I have an account of some of his kind deeds in her baby book. He knelt down by her in his home at a Berean meeting and recited some poetry to her when she was about six weeks old." This poem is given here:

> "Oh, star on the breast of the river,
>   Oh, marvel of bloom and of grace,
> Did you fall straight down from heaven,
>   Out of the sweetest place?

"You are as pure as the thought of an angel,
  Your heart was steeped in the sun,
Did you grow in the Golden City,
  My fair and radiant one?

" 'Nay, nay, I fell not from heaven,
  None gave me my saintly white,
But I slowly grew in the blackness
  Down in the darkest night.

" 'From the ooze of the silent river,
  I won my glory and grace,
White souls fall not, oh, my poet,
  They rise to the sweetest place.' "

A lady, who was formerly an instructor in elocution and the art of expression, writes: "There were none so poor, so lowly, so unfortunate, but what Mr. Beers had for them a cheery smile, a kind word and helping hand. As president of the school, he was never too pre-occupied to talk to the smallest boy on the campus. The children all loved him." One of the prominent preachers says, "The children especially loved him and when we think of him in these relations we are reminded of that scripture which reads, 'Thy gentleness hath made me great.' " A brother in the ministry from Canada also notes this quality, "His greatness was enhanced by the quality of his childlike simplicity. Children loved him because they found one interested in them. His humility was manifest in his acknowledgment of dependence upon God for wisdom and direction, and he was not above bringing small matters to the Lord in prayer." In a personal letter from a friend, we quote, "My little children will never forget, I trust, how Brother Beers used to lay his hand on their heads in blessing and take them on his lap and talk so lovingly and beautifully to them. It always touched Clyde's heart and mine also."

Much has been said about Mr. Beers' habitual optimistic spirit. Among the many fine qualities which he possessed none was more desirable than the ability to make those about him happy. Affectionate, sunny and resourceful in his disposition, he brought hope and gladness into his own home. The humblest spot seemed sweet and bright when he was there. Professor Holtwick, of Greenville College, says: "In connection with work on our general boards, where the lack of funds so frequently produces more or less depression on the hearts of those who have to bear the responsibility, the sunshine of Brother Beers seemed never lacking. More than once has the grip of his strong right hand clasped in mine, and the outburst of some cheerful quotation from the sunshine poets, bursting from his heart of good cheer, helped me to forget the unpleasant things in life and join with him in expressions of gladness." One who was formerly a member of the faculty writes: "At social functions he always brought to every one hearty, wholesome laughter. In the house of sadness he was kind and sympathetic. His sermons were full of beauty and inspiration. If one had wronged him he freely forgave."

A young man came from the State of Kansas whose head was adorned with an abundance of highly-colored flowing locks. He reached the seminary one Sunday afternoon and came over to the president's house at once to see Mr. Beers. In the course of the conversation with the young man, Mr. Beers

asked him if he was a Christian. "Not now," he replied, and began to weep. "Why are you not?"
asked Mr. Beers. He said he had no reason at all,
and as Mr. Beers urged him to surrender to Christ,
he knelt down and was soon rejoicing in the Lord.
Mr. Beers always called him his Kansas sunflower.
The next day he was to meet Mr. Beers down town
to receive help in getting his baggage. At the appointed hour Mr. Beers was there, but the young
man failed to appear. After waiting a while, Mr.
Beers withdrew. That evening the young man from
Kansas asked Mr. Beers why he had not come. "I
was there on time. Where were you?" asked Mr.
Beers. He said he was about thirty minutes late.
Then Mr. Beers gave him his first lesson on keeping
an engagement, the necessity of being punctual, if he
ever hoped to succeed in life. Mr. Beers was unusually exact in this particular.

He was fond of illustrations that showed the humorous side and often revealed the small stream of
Celtic blood that flowed in his veins by his ready
wit. When addressing young people he would give
some pleasing incidents to intersperse with his more
grave teachings. This one he sometimes gave to
illustrate the overflowing of God's blessing on the
soul: "One day my wife was absent and I thought
I'd cook some dried apples, knowing we had a supply
in the house. I was fond of them and so placed a
generous quantity in a saucepan on the stove with
plenty of water and watched the process of cooking
with great satisfaction. Soon the apples began to
swell and were about to boil over. I divided the apples, using another pan and continued cooking them.

To my surprise they kept swelling and swelling and threatening to run over until I had all the pans in the house filled, covering the top of the stove. If we let the Lord have our hearts He will fill them to overflowing, then expand and enlarge them until many others catch the overflow."

Again when showing the folly of being opinionated where principle was not involved, he would give this: "An old woman had a most wonderful salve which she manufactured herself. The recipe was always held with great secrecy. Finally when she realized that she was on her dying bed, she told a friend she could not die without revealing this great secret. She told her that the salve was made from hypopolarum and lopopohyrum barks. When asked where these wonderful barks could be obtained, she said, 'Why, take any tree and strip the bark from the top downward; that is hypopolarum bark; now take the same tree and strip the bark upward, and that is lopopohyrum bark.'" Applying this homely and amusing illustration, he would show them in a way that students would not soon forget the foolishness of obstinacy in holding to unimportant opinions.

Another one equally amusing he would give sometimes when speaking on prohibition as the only consistent political party, the Democrats and Republicans being both allied with the liquor interests: "One day I wished to see a friend, an old schoolmate of mine, who had come to Seattle as a delegate to a Republican convention, so I ventured to visit the convention for an hour or two in order that I might see my friend. Of course the air was blue with tobacco smoke. When I returned home Mrs. Beers began sniffing the air and said very seriously, Where have you been, Mr. Beers, that your clothes are filled with the fumes of tobacco?' For a moment I tried to recall. I had been in so many places soliciting that day. 'Oh, now I remember. I called in at the Republican convention a while to see F——S——.' 'Oh,' said she, 'I never knew that a Republican convention smelled like that before.' About two weeks after this the Democrats held their convention and again I called in to see an old friend, G—— L——. As soon as I entered the house that evening my wife again discovered the objectionable odor and said, 'I see you have been to another Republican convention.' 'No,' said I, 'it was a Democratic convention this time.' 'Well,' said she, 'they smell just alike anyhow.' " Then he would prove that the purposes and morals of these two old parties were identical and one must keep clear of both when casting his ballot.

Mr. Beers felt that the salvation of the rich was neglected and sometimes he said he went "slumming" among the rich and aristocratic. As one of the district elders said of him, "He moved with ease in all walks of life. He was equally at home with the lowly and the high. He always conducted himself with dignity and grace." Another preacher writes, "He had the happy faculty of gaining the good-will of prominent men in the business world." Going into a large bank one day he asked the president of the bank for a private interview, which was freely granted. With tact and wisdom he talked earnestly to the banker about his soul's salvation and then prayed with him. His efforts were received with gratitude—the banker said as he arose to go, "Mr. Beers, you are the only minister who has ever talked and prayed with me," and placed a twenty-dollar gold piece in his hand. He became acquainted with the owner and proprietor of a large hotel in one of our western cities and was solicitous concerning his spiritual welfare. The man became very ill and Mr. Beers called to inquire about him several times. When he was convalescent he asked for Mr. Beers, having been told that he had called several times while he was too ill to see him. Seizing this opportune time, Mr. Beers knelt down by the sick man's chair and talked affectionately to him about his spiritual condition. The man acknowledged his need and seemed to enter into the prayer Mr. Beers offered in his behalf.

CHAPTER XVI

RESIGNS COLLEGE WORK AND TAKES UP THE PASTORATE

He is dead whose hand is not opened wide
  To help the need of a human brother;
He doubles the length of his life-long ride,
  Who gives his fortunate place to another.
And a thousand million lives are his,
  Who carries the world in his sympathies.
    To give is to live.
              —*James Russell Lowell.*

In the spring of 1916, Mr. Beers resigned his position as president of the college, member of the board of trustees, and financial secretary, and prepared to devote himself exclusively to the gospel ministry. Many friends expressed great regret over his resignation. In a personal letter, the mayor of the city writes: "I am mighty sorry to know you are going to leave Seattle. It is but a just compliment to you to say that you have accomplished far more in the years you have lived with us than the great majority of us accomplish in a life-time, and you are leaving us in the very prime of life, and amidst your years of greatest usefulness. I want to congratulate you upon your success. Your thousands of friends here, amongst whom I am honored to be numbered. wish you every success in the world in your new field." A prominent real estate dealer of Seattle expresses his esteem for Mr. Beers: "Learning that

you are leaving the city, I take this opportunity to
wish you the success, in the future, that you have
had since I first knew you, about the time that you
took up your earnest work in the vicinity of Fremont. At the time I first saw your seminary, I did
not think it was possible for it to develop into the
beautiful and successful college that you are now
leaving. During this time, we have had some severe
depressions. The money that I advanced you, from
time to time, was, in those days, a large amount for
me, but I never questioned the payment, feeling sure
that you would make good. I have always found
your representations correct and I do not recall any
time when you ever disappointed me." Honorable
Milo A. Root, ex-judge of the supreme court, writes
his commendation and regrets: "The building up of
the Seattle Seminary, and of its successor, the Seattle Pacific College, and the spiritual reclamation,
uplift and encouragement of great numbers of children, young men and young women, who have been
students in that institution, constitute a monument
to the Christian character and efficiency of Professor Beers and his estimable wife, more worthy and
lasting than any words I might use. The unselfishness which he has always manifested, the warm-
hearted tenderness and patience which character-
ize his dealings with the students, the perseverance
and faithfulness to duty, which has ever led him to
give his great ability to the working out of the financial and other problems of this institution of learning—ofttimes in the face of highly discouraging obstacles—should commend him to every high-minded
lover of Christianity and believer in Christian edu-

MR. BEERS AT HIS DESK

cation. As one having excellent opportunities to thoroughly know the character of the man and his ability as an educator and a business manager, and of his piety, influence and unselfish work as a minister of the gospel, I regret exceedingly to learn that he is thinking of severing his connection with the college mentioned and of moving his residence to some other place." The Associated Student Body passed the following resolutions of appreciation and regret:

"WHEREAS, Our esteemed president is about to sever his official relation to the college, it seems most fitting that we, the Associated Student Body, should give expression to words of appreciation of Brother and Sister Beers for their devotion to the success of Seattle Pacific College and their undivided interest in the welfare of each individual student.

"We shall miss in Brother Beers his encouraging and scholarly addresses delivered in the Assembly Hall, and his fervent and spiritual appeals at the prayer meetings in the Chapel. We shall miss his warm-hearted council and personal solicitation.

"We shall also miss in Sister Beers her unselfish and untiring interest in the comfort and happiness of each student. We shall miss her earnest prayers and ceaseless care for the spiritual uplift of all.

"And as Brother and Sister Beers depart, we, the student body of Seattle Pacific College, extend to them our best wishes and our prayers for their happiness, spiritual welfare, and success in their new field of labor."

When it became known that his services were available, he received many urgent calls to hold evangelistic services. Many wide and effectual doors of usefulness were thrown open to him; but the cordial invitation that came from his own home town, Portland, Oregon, to become pastor of the First

Free Methodist Church there, appealed most strongly to him. He took his standing from the Washington Conference and again joined the Oregon Conference, of which he had been one of the charter members when he first united with the Free Methodist Church. He assumed the duties and responsibilities of the pastorate with his characteristic courage and hearty zeal. He received a royal welcome from the members and friends of the First Church and began at once to make large plans for the improvement of the church property. The church was old and badly in need of repairs. At first it was thought best to sell the property where they were then located and buy a lot and build elsewhere. After much prayer and proper consideration, this idea was abandoned. With clever tact and the wisdom that comes from above, Mr. Beers was enabled to conciliate all objections and harmonize the various conflicting opinions. The old structure was remodeled from the belfry to the basement floor, where the preacher had formerly lived. Every part of the building received a new touch as from an artist's hand until it really appeared like a new church. Beautiful opaque windows, crystalline as the sea in appearance, through which a soft light issued, and chapel-shaped at the top, were substituted for the old square, angular windows through which the light came in a glaring manner.

Mr. Beers became acquainted with the business men of Portland and raised a large part of the funds necessary for this work from among them. When the three years' term had expired the *new old* church was rededicated by Bishop Pearce and all hearts were made to rejoice in the prosperity of Zion. Believing that the pastor should also have a home, and as there was sufficient land upon which to build, Mr. Beers had begun the erection of a parsonage. He had worked very hard in raising the funds and looking after the work of building, but he felt amply repaid on the day of dedication. Every bill was paid on the church and sufficient funds were subscribed to complete the new parsonage. When conference convened, this structure was all ready for the plaster work and the members were very anxious that Mr. Beers should be allowed to stay and complete this work. But the three-year law seemed to be inexorable at this time. And the completion of the work was left to another.

While the building operations had been going on, the spiritual work had not been neglected. The congregation had been greatly increased and the mid-week prayer meeting was well attended. The Sunday-school and the missionary society were in a flourishing condition, quite suited to the atmosphere of a fine new church.

Extract from a letter written by Mr. Beers to a friend, dated March 24, 1919: "God is greatly blessing our work in Portland. My congregations are large—the best I've had since coming here. Yesterday, Sunday, my enlarged church was packed. The church has been rebuilt and now we have one of the most beautiful and modern churches on the coast. Tomorrow we begin work on a new parsonage."

In Joel 2: 28 we read, "It shall come to pass afterwards—or in the last day—that I will pour out my Spirit upon all flesh; and your sons and your daughters shall prophesy, your old men shall dream dreams, and your young men shall see visions and also upon the servants and upon the handmaids in those days will I pour out my Spirit." While recovering from the deadly epidemic of influenza in the winter of 1918, this scripture was fulfilled in the life of Mrs. Beers, and as it relates so closely to Mr. Beers, she gives this experience here: "For several weeks Mr. Beers had been continually exposed to the disease, ministering to the sick and praying for them, and caring for their needs in every way. He also officiated at many funerals of strangers who were stricken down while passing through the city. He had not spared himself at all, but committed his case constantly to the Lord, feeling that he could trust Him better and felt safest while in the path of duty. One evening I saw he was looking very ill and asked him about his health. He said he did not feel very well, but must attend a business meeting at the church that evening. I urged him not to go, but to no avail. He never would yield to physical weakness until the last extremity was reached. After he had left the house and all was quiet, I took this occasion to plead with God for my husband. I do not know how long I had prayed, but at last my prayer was heard. The room where I was lying and the whole house seemed filled with the glory of God. I do not think I shouted, for I was too greatly overwhelmed with the presence of Jehovah. I saw in visions Mr. Beers walking along the street and the path became shining under his feet. It appeared like a silver highway extending in every direction from where he was walking. Angels moved on either side of him and gently lifted him up on this highway. At once I knew he was healed and I was lost in wonder, love and praise. When he returned home he came in with shining face and before I had time to speak, he said, 'I am feeling better. I am healed.' 'I knew it,' I replied. 'I prevailed with God while you were gone, and got the evidence.' Then he told me how sick he had felt when he left home. It seemed there was an immense weight pressing down upon his chest, which he thought would have resulted in pneumonia—so many died of pneumonia from the 'flu' that winter. He said that while he was walking along the streets it seemed that an Almighty hand had lifted this pressure from his chest and made him perfectly well. The work was complete and he was kept from the disease the remaining weeks of the winter. Others around us sickened and died, and he performed the last sad rites for them, but no scourge came near him. I did not tell him of this experience until five days later. It seemed so sacred, so wonderful, to me that I hardly dared speak about it. When I finally related the vision to him, he was awe-struck. He accepted it as from God and said, 'Why, it seems as if I am going to die, doesn't it?' 'Oh, no,' I said, 'it means you will live to preach the gospel.' I know now, it meant both, for he did preach with greater power than ever before for three years, then laid down his cross to receive his crown. The physical healing that was bestowed upon him at the time of this vision was naught compared to the great spiritual uplift that came to him. As I saw him in the vision, lifted up by the angels, and he himself realized that the awful pressure of disease was removed from his body, so from this hour he seemed to walk on a higher plane and to preach with greater unction." He did indeed traverse the streets of Portland in every direction, soliciting funds for the church and parsonage, even as the shining pathway was seen in the vision extending every way from where he was walking. A few weeks later he had the privilege of seeing three souls converted before his preaching service on Sunday morning, as here related:

One Sunday morning a phone message came to Mr. Beers to call on a dying man at once. He found an aged man past eighty who had never been converted. He was attended by a trained nurse, whom Mr. Beers had met a few years before while holding revival services in Snohomish, Washington. He was greatly blessed in talking to the sick man, who soon yielded himself to God and was clearly saved. Like the jailor of old, he called for water that he might be baptized. After Mr. Beers had finished this solemn rite, he began to exhort the niece. Her uncle also joined in the exhortation, and the young lady very soon bowed herself in humble contrition. With earnest pleadings she wept her way to the cross and was soon rejoicing in the knowledge that her sins were forgiven and washed away. With her face illuminated by her new-found joy, she turned to plead with the nurse. Mr. Beers, too, urged the claims of God upon her. She knelt in penitence and began calling on Christ for salvation. The heavenly light broke in upon her soul and she, too, was soon rejoicing in the Savior's love. Mr. Beers came in to his pulpit that morning imbued with the spirit of a conqueror and preached in a wonderful manner. The pilgrims seemed to partake of the same spirit as the three new converts had manifested as the preacher pictured the scene of their conversion.

Mr. Beers seemed to have a special commission to "sow beside all waters." When traveling on the train, he would watch his opportunity to help some one. The porters in the sleeping cars and the colored waiters in the diner were sure to receive a kind admonition, a bit of helpful exhortation or some of his own experience, all tending to lead them upward.

Sometimes he encountered the agnostic in his travels and he was ever ready, armed and equipped to combat false teaching with the sword of the Spirit. On one of his transcontinental trips he found a large group of men one day, gathered in the smoker, listening with great interest to a man who claimed to be a scientist of deep research. Mr. Beers overheard him say as he was passing through, that the word of God, so-called, conflicted with the teachings of up-to-date science. This remark prompted Mr. Beers to join the group of listeners. After a period of subtle reasoning against the Bible, he asked the agnostic if he might say a few words. Permission having been granted, he then proved from the scientist's own line of argument the reasonableness of spiritual laws. "If certain causes produce certain effects and every time specified conditions are met, certain results are sure to be obtained. You will agree *that* is a law, will you not?" The man assented. "Now," said he, "we read in the Holy Scriptures that if a man gives up his sins and believes on the Lord Jesus Christ, he becomes a new creature. Here is a poor drunkard, fallen and debased. He meets the said conditions and is transformed — becomes a sober, industrious citizen. Thieves, gamblers, libertines—hundreds, yea, millions of all classes, have met the requirements laid down in the Bible and have never failed to realize the same wonderful results, honest, upright, pure and clean lives—a new creation." He then gave his own personal testimony to the mighty, transforming power of God. The scoffer was completely silenced. The group of men evinced great respect and several expressed themselves very sympathetically. After returning home, he received a fine letter from the scientist, saying that he had changed his opinions concerning spiritual laws and hoped Mr. Beers would pray for him—he wanted to be good.

The newsboys on the streets, the bootblacks, the taxi drivers, all shared in the interest of this man of God. Eternity alone will reveal the good achieved by this tactful, kindly seed-sowing. As a slight reward for his faithfulness in this respect, an unusual circumstance occurred while he was pastor in Portland. One evening at the close of the prayer meeting, a driver of a taxi called him one side and asked him to perform a marriage ceremony for his sister in a unique spot. He said she was an artist and wished to be married at Crown Point, the summit of the famous Columbia River highway, where the beautiful Vista house now stands. After proper investigation, Mr. Beers was convinced that the singular place chosen was only to gratify the artistic impulse of the bride-elect, and consented to officiate.

The bridal party reached the summit of the charming, panoramic highway when the sun was nearing the horizon. No artist's dream could picture a lovelier scene. Far below them rolled the noble Columbia, while towering, snow-capped mountains rose majestically in the foreground. The sun's departing rays were reflected from hill and mountain peak, and the heavens above were emblazoned with brilliant banners of victory, while the waters of the river shimmered like a sea of gold. Just as the sun sank—a ball of fire in the bosom of the river—Mr. Beers pronounced the words that made the twain one. It was a solemn, a joyous occasion. As the party motored back to Portland, the silvery moon made a witching scene, coquetting with the grand old fir trees along the romantic, winding highway. When they reached the city, the brother of the bride dropped a generous gold piece into the clergyman's hand, and explained that the reason he was invited to perform this ceremony was because he had manifested such an interest in him when his taxicab was in waiting before the hotel, on several occasions.

In the beginning of the year 1919, Mr. Beers was receiving letters from Rev. J. Barnhart, of California, in regard to the Japanese work in the bay cities. He was very anxious that Mr. Beers should come and take charge of this work. For several months Mr. and Mrs. Beers had prayed over the matter of going to help Rev. Barnhart, as he so greatly desired. At the General Conference they met him and his wife, and had several important consultations over the matter. At last they decided to go and take up this work after the board meetings in the fall.

While this subject was pending, they had accepted the work at the Alberta Church in Portland, Oregon, and continued there until they left for San Francisco. They were received with great kindness by the pilgrims at Alberta and greatly enjoyed the work among them. When the time for parting came, it seemed hard to leave them. A beautiful farewell service was held in the church. While Mr. and Mrs. Donald MacPhee were singing one of their matchless songs,

> "Out of the ivory palaces,
> Into a world of woe,
> Only His great eternal love
> Made my Savior go,"

the spirit applied this verse in a prophetic manner to the new white church which Mr. Beers had rebuilt and beautified until it stood shining in ivory whiteness—from this church to the sea of wickedness, the world of woe—which they found in San Francisco. Later when disease fastened itself upon Mr. Beers, and his wife was compelled to see him waste away until he was a mere skeleton, they both felt that it proved indeed a world of woe to them, but at the time of the farewell they little knew of the sorrow that awaited them, and were greatly cheered and encouraged by the love and prayers of the many friends who had assembled to bid them good-by. They left Portland thrilled with bright anticipation, for the Lord had bidden them go—they felt they were going at His behest. They were assured that He would be with them and prove an ever-present help in time of need. They were soon settled in a parsonage in the rear of the Hart Memorial Church.

A small band of loyal, warm-hearted pilgrims, who received them with great cordiality, were found here, and these pilgrims always comforted and supported their pastor with loving cooperation. The dingy surroundings were a great contrast to the beautiful church they had left in Portland, but they were soon so busily engaged in the Lord's work that they found no time for "idle sighing."

They found the new parish in which the Hart Memorial Church was located to be a strong Catholic center. St. Peter's cathedral and schools were but two blocks from the Free Methodist Church. The daily chimes that pealed from the dome reminded them that they were coping with a powerful adversary. The streets swarmed with children, and many of these were very soon drawn to the Junior Mission Band and church services. As was usual in every place where he had lived, they soon learned to love Mr. Beers very much. It was a common occurrence to hear the door bell ring about 7 o'clock in the evening. When the door was opened, a group of eager-faced boys would ask if they might see Mr. Beers. It mattered not how busy he might be nor how weary from the toils of the day, he would invite them into the parlor and talk to them a while. He would tell them stories with a fine moral and inspire them to live good clean lives. Two of such stories as the children loved to hear repeated again and again are here given:

HOW TWO SQUIRRELS LOST PARADISE

"Two little squirrels frisked and played around among the trees in a big city park. They liked best

to play under a great walnut tree where, as soon as
Jack Frost opened the shells and the nuts began to
fall at their feet, they could gather them up and
carry their treasures to a deep hidden nest where
they laid them up for winter—for did they not know
that by and by the sweet summer time, with all of
its warmth and brightness, would be gone, the
ground would be covered with ice and snow, and
there would be no nuts, nor fruits, nor seeds for
them to eat? O yes, they knew they must lay in a
good supply of food, for winter was surely coming.
So they had always worked hard during the summer
hours to fill their little cellar with good things to
eat so they could live and be happy through the long,
dark wintry days ahead. They frisked their tails
and chattered away to each other and were very
happy as they heaped the nuts in their own deep
nest which no one could see nor find.

> 'Work away, work away,
> Yes, we must work
> As well as play.'

But one bright day in springtime, when their nuts
were all eaten up, they came out in the park to find
food and they met a fine gentleman who offered them
food from his hand. They were afraid of him at first
and scampered about him, refusing to eat, although
they were hungry, but he looked and acted so kind,
they could not long resist, and soon ate their fill.
The next day, and the next, this same friend fed
them such delicious food and they ate, and ate, and
ate, without any effort to get the food, and became
very plump and sleek—such happy, happy squirrels.
They forgot that cruel winter was coming and said

to each other, 'We do not need to work any more. This kind man will feed us all the time.' 'Let us play, play, play; no work, no work today; let us ever, ever play.'

"So they gathered no nuts to put in their cellars, no food had they stored away, and finally the days grew shorter and colder, winter was coming—was already here and their friend gone—where had he gone? For several days when they went out to find him and waited around, he did not come and they were hungry. It was hard to find food. Day after day they searched for him, but he never came back, and their nest was cold—they had neglected to line it anew with nice warm moss and sweet, tender grasses, and oh! they were so hungry, and now everything was covered with a blanket of snow so they could find no food. How they cried because they had not worked through the summer hours and gathered their nuts as usual.

> 'Too late, too late,
> No food can be found,
> For wintry snow
> Now covers the ground.'

The poor little squirrels crept back into their cold, cheerless nests and died, and when they were so dead that they *knew* they were dead, they said, 'We lost our paradise because we did not work.' "

The other story:

A BOY LOVES RED APPLES

Mr. Beers would begin, "Well, boys, how many of you like red apples? Now, I will tell you about a boy who had red cheeks, blue eyes, white teeth, and he liked red apples so much. Now, if I tell you his name, will you be sure to remember it?" Of course they would all say they would. It was, "Miltiadese Aristarcus Augustus Paul." Then he would have them repeat this huge name several times, which they greatly enjoyed. "One day in the fall when the trees were hanging full of apples, Miltie's mother (for this is what they called him for short) said to him, 'Miltie, I want you to take this letter down to the post office for me.' 'All right, I will,' said Miltie, and his mother tucked the letter carefully away in his pocket. He started off whistling down the street, when lo! he saw a tree in Farmer Brown's orchard just loaded down with beautiful red apples.

> Miltiadese Aristarcus Augustus Paul
> Wandered down the street one day in the fall,
> And saw a wonderful sight just over the wall,
> Ripe red apples hanging from a tree top tall.
>
> Oh, I wish, I wish I had a few,
> Said little Aristarcus Miltiadue;
> He climbed the wall and the tall tree, too,
> What harm could there be to lay in a few?
>
> To eat them all he then did try,
> But finally breathed a heart-rending sigh,
> 'If I eat any more, I fear I shall die,
> But oh, how good they taste, oh, my! oh, my!'

Just then a frightful thing happened to him—the limb broke and down fell our boy with a bump and a roar.

> But lucky for him he had on a big corded jacket,
> Which his mother had made stout and strong in the backet.

And as he fell he was caught and held by this high in mid-air." Suiting the action to the words, Mr.

Beers would catch hold of one of the boy's jackets in the back and hold him high in the air, much to the amusement of the other boys.

" 'Help, help, help,' cried Miltiade,
Then quickly the old farmer came out to see,
With big bulging pockets hung the boy in the tree.
Looking up with a frown, said the farmer, 'Now, really,
I think you have been helping yourself pretty freely.'

"His mother watched and waited for her boy to come back from the post-office. But no boy came! Where was he—what had become of him? She went down the street a little ways to see if she could find him. She heard a faint cry of 'Help, help, help!' Soon she came to where he was hanging in the tree, and getting a ladder, she helped him down to the ground. 'Oh, Miltie, why did you climb that tree and fill your pockets with apples?' she said. 'It was stealing to take the farmer's apples, did you not know that?' 'Oh, mother,' cried the boy, 'I wanted red apples to eat.' His mother made him give all his apples back to the farmer, and he promised her he'd never steal anything again. Later she taught him to plant apple trees so he could have all the apples he wanted to eat, and when he grew to be a man he had red apples, white apples, yellow apples and green apples to eat and he gave them away to all the boys in the neighborhood and they all said there was nobody so good as Uncle Miltiades." The boys would listen to this story with breathless attention and ask to have it repeated again and again. The charm of these stories lay in the personality of the story-teller. These attentions that Mr. Beers paid them won their hearts and they would steal into the church unknown to their Catholic parents. One boy told Mr. Beers that he came to hear him preach last Sunday and said, "Oh, but I got a good thrashing when I got home, but I am coming again anyhow." As soon as it became known to the parents and the priest that the children were attending these services, they evidently protested, for the children were not allowed to come any more.

The priest thought this would intimidate Mr. Beers, but found him to be as bold as a lion for righteousness. A number of them, with their head prelate, accosted him in a grocery store one evening. "Mr. Beers, what are you here for?" asked one. "I am here to preach the gospel and help people to follow lives of righteousness," replied he. The arrogant prelate said, "We have plenty of men here to do all that. It is not necessary for you to stay here." He seemed to forget that many of his parishioners were leading immoral and dissipated lives. The brave preacher straightened himself up and looking the priest squarely in the eye, said, "I am not afraid of anything you may have coming up the road, and I shall remain just as long as duty calls me here." In this conection we are reminded of the words of John B. Gough:

"Be a bold, brave, true, honest man,
If you know a thing is right, do it.
If you have a solemn conviction,
Dare to utter it in the fear of God,
Regardless of the wrath of man."

CHAPTER XVII

WORK IN SAN FRANCISCO AND AMONG THE JAPANESE

Be still, my soul, and murmur not,
However hard may be thy lot;
Tho' sorest grief now weigh thee down,
Glory ere long thy course shall crown.

O, joy divine, by Christ possessed,
    For which He did the cross endure,
Fill with Thyself and make me blest,
    Contented, restful and secure.
                                    —*Wilson T. Hogue.*

It can not be all loss. There is a just balance wheel that adjusts our measure of weal or woe, compensating springs of joy in every valley of Baca. This was found especially true in the work in San Francisco. While loved friends and companions of other years were greatly missed, the new pastor and his wife soon made many new friends who greatly added to their pleasure. Mr. Beers was especially interested in the wonderful city of San Francisco. He had always been an ardent admirer of fine architecture. The great buildings that surrounded the civic center were of continual interest to him. The majestic city hall with its marble staircases ornamented with real gold trimmings, the elaborate library and other imposing buildings afforded him the keenest delight. Shortly after they were settled in their new home, he insisted on Mrs. Beers going down to see these buildings and pointed out to her the loveliness, the exquisite adornment which he enjoyed so greatly. But magnificent architecture, however splendid, could not turn his heart away from the one transcendent theme of preaching the gospel of Jesus Christ. In addition to his regular church services, he sought opportunity to preach on the streets. Once every week at the noon hour **he** mounted an improvised pulpit at an important street intersection where immense throngs were passing and repassing every moment. Here a large crowd of working men, with their dinner pails in hand, would sit on the curbstone and listen to his declaration of gospel truth, while they were eating their lunch. Others congregated until he would have a large crowd of listeners. Many held up their hands for prayers and some reported afterward that they had found the Savior through his preaching. Mr. Beers never found more delight in anything that he did than in this street work. He would go home afterward, greatly exhausted, as he usually had to preach against the strong trade wind, but it seemed that his spirit had been lifted unto the third heaven. He greatly enjoyed also his ministrations in the Hart Memorial Church, although the membership was small and the congregations never large. He preached some of his finest sermons here—one the writer will never forget, from the subject, "Give Your Soul a Chance." In this discourse he showed how people were robbing their souls of the rich heritage that Christ had purchased for them, becoming so absorbed in money-making, the cares of the house, and vain-seeking after pleasure, that the needs of the soul were entirely neglected. Their immortal natures were crushed, the breathings of the soul after higher things were stifled and quenched. He quoted an incident that he had heard given by a noted divine one Sunday morning, in New York City: "A millionaire was dying in his sumptuous home on Fifth Avenue. Everything that wealth could buy was purchased for his comfort. Fruits and nuts from the Orient and rich viands were ordered by his loved ones for him to eat. The servant, in a very unjust manner, ate the nuts and carried the shells to the dying man; she ate the luscious oranges and carried him the skins; she ate the fine beefsteak and carried him only the bones and the refuse." Then turning to his congregation with a significant gesture, the preacher thundered, "And you are that dying man, and you are that dying man," placing the charge on all parts of his congregation. He said, "Your body is a servant. You have been caring for its needs, feeding it with all the nuts and fruits, while your poor soul has been starving on the husks and refuse of this world. Your soul says, 'I am hungry.' You reply, 'Have I not fed you on all the pleasures of the day—the moving picture, the races, the banquet, and all kinds of entertainments?' The soul wails, 'I can never be satisfied on such food as that. Nothing but divinity, nothing but God's love can ever satisfy the longings of my immortal nature.' Your soul says, 'I am cold, I am shivering,' but you say, 'Have I not bought for you the warmest fabrics, the costliest furs, that money can purchase? Did I not pay ten thousand

dollars for a seal-skin wrap to keep you warm?'
'Oh,' says the soul, 'I can never be warmed by any
costly covering for the body. What I need is the fire
of God's Spirit and the sunshine of His smile to comfort and cheer me.'" Mr. Beers enlarged upon the
above illustration in a most impressive manner until
his listeners felt that the most important work of
all was to look after and care for the development of
the soul—that it was fed and its longings satisfied.

At the General Missionary Board meeting in Chicago, Mr. Beers had been appointed superintendent
of the Japanese work in the bay cities of the California Conference, and was appointed the pastor
of the Hart Memorial Church. Accordingly Mr.
Beers began in addition to his church work to
search out the Japanese in San Francisco. On Mission Street, some eight blocks distant from his home,
were many shops which were kept by Japanese mer-
chants who could speak some English. Mr. Beers
called repeatedly upon these men and carried the
gospel to them. They seemed very grateful and listened with evident interest. He became quite well
acquainted with several of them. One fine Japanese
gentleman wrote Mr. Beers a very striking and peculiar letter which came in the mail. It ran something like this:

"DEAR PASTOR BEERS :—

I call you pastor, for you are the only minister who has
ever talked to me about the true God. I want to tell you,
Pastor Beers, I feel I am a big fool. I spend all my time
selling things they do not need to people who are also big
fools. I should be getting ready for eternity, and your
teaching has shown me what a big fool I have always been.
I feel I must soon die and from this hour I want to get

REV. J. BARNHART

ready. I want to be saved. Will you not pray for me and continue to come and see me?   ————————."

This Japanese afterward professed to be converted and no doubt many others were greatly benefitted by the seed that had been sown. Two friends from Portland, Oregon, visited Mr. and Mrs. Beers during the holiday season, and while out sight-seeing in San Francisco, they visited the Buddhist temple there. How sad that so many Japanese in Christian America should worship idols! But they were even more greatly shocked that many white people are also members of this Buddhist temple and are constant worshippers at this heathen shrine.

Although Mr. Beers had pursued the work very faithfully for several months, there did not seem to be any opening to carry out the plan that Rev. Barnhart had proposed. He had seen in vision a church, Sunday-school and day school for these aliens in our midst. He was the district elder of the San Francisco District and came to them regularly with Spirit-filled messages. Both the church work and the work among the Japanese pressed very heavily upon his heart. He was like a wise, tender father to the pastor and his wife, helping them in every way and always talking about his loved theme, "the betterment of the Japanese." True to his word, the Lord did not keep His servants long without an open door. Dear Mr. Barnhart's prayers were answered and Mr. Beers' expectations fulfilled—a divine providence was leading to success and victory.

Among the honored graduates from the institution in Seattle were Rev. and Mrs. August Youngren, who for several years had been laboring as mission-

aries in Japan. We had always maintained a correspondence with them and this simple fact led to the
establishment of the Japanese work in Berkeley.
One day a letter came from Mrs. Youngren, in which
she called attention to her friend, who was now laboring in Berkeley, California. She said, "I wish
you would look her up. You will find her a woman
of prayer and deeply spiritual; she labored near us
here in Japan for several years, and we had sweet
fellowship together." At this very time Mr. Beers
had another letter from a friend in Washington asking him to call on a sister-in-law who had been a student in Seattle Pacific College, and who was now living in Berkeley.

When Mr. Beers started for Berkeley to make a
call on the latter, his wife said, "Be sure to find Miss
Pool." He did not feel certain that he could, since
Mrs. Youngren had failed to give her street address.
However, he found the sister-in-law without difficulty, and having prayed with her, he inquired for
Miss Pool, and learned that she had a church or mission not far away. Miss Pool and the native pastor,
Rev. T. Misawa, received him gladly and told him
about their work. They had a fine church membership of about twenty members and a good Sunday-
school and a small day school in another denomination. Little did Mr. Beers surmise the deep heart
sorrow that had come to them nor the difficult problems they were now facing. A few hours before Mr.
Beers had visited them, their district superintendent
had called and informed them that the church had
voted to discontinue all work among the Japanese.
The anti-Japanese sentiment prevailed so strongly

among the people they thought best not to sustain
a church among these foreigners any longer. They
could also no longer contribute to the support of
this school and the work. Miss Pool was now cut
adrift with her flock, looking to her for guidance
and comfort. What should she do? Her heart
turned at once to the Free Methodist Church, having had such pleasant companionship with the
Youngrens and the other missionaries of our denomination in Japan. But she said nothing to Mr.
Beers during this first visit. A few days later she
called him over the phone and gave him some intima-
tion of the difficulty she was in, asking if he could
not come over again. He told her that if she was
having any difficulty in her church relationship he
did not wish to interfere because he never believed
in proselyting. However, if he could be of any service to her in the way of advice and comfort, he
would be glad to see her at the parsonage any time.
A few days later she came over to the house, and told
Mr. Beers all of the trouble, and said she and the
pastor, Rev. Misawa, had decided to join us and
wished to know if we as a denomination would wish
to carry on work among the Japanese. She had
never met Mr. Beers before he called at Berkeley,
nor even heard of Mr. Barnhart, but felt led in this
direction. Mr. Beers was just starting for a called
meeting of the Executive Committee in Chicago, and
while there he presented the matter to the missionary secretary, W. B. Olmstead. A meeting of the
Board of Directors was called and a full discussion
of the subject followed. When the vote was taken,
they all agreed it was best to open up work in Ber-

keley and place Miss Pool in charge. Before leaving
for Chicago, Mr. Beers had urged Miss Pool to read
our general church rules to her members and be sure
they understood the import of our issues. Inasmuch
as she had been the instrument used in the conversion of every one of her Japanese members, she felt
that they belonged to her, and when she was compelled to change her church relation, she thought it
was only right and just to take them with her and
still continue to care for their spiritual interests.
Soon after Mr. Beers returned from Chicago, a new
society of about twenty Japanese was organized in
the city of Berkeley. There had been very little difficulty experienced in making this change. Some
artificial flowers and pieces of jewelry were necessarily sacrificed in taking this step, but this was done
joyfully for the most part. One fine business man
brought a box containing his jewels, which were very
valuable, and gave it to Miss Pool. She afterward
sold these for one hundred dollars and turned the
money into the church treasury.

A new difficulty now presented itself. So great
was the prejudice against the Japanese which prevailed among the people, that very soon Miss Pool
was informed that she must vacate the house she had
occupied and she would now be turned out on the
streets. Day after day she tried to find a suitable
building for church purposes, but as soon as the
authorities would learn that it would be for work
among the Japanese, they would refuse very emphatically to rent to her. There seemed to be nothing
else to do at this juncture but to buy some property.
In this case, "the wrath of man was made to praise

God," as extreme necessity pushed Mr. Beers out
and caused his faith to grow exceedingly. He soon
found a handsome property for sale, only five blocks
from the state university. It was a difficult and very
delicate situation to handle. Many of the inhabitants were so prejudiced they would neither rent nor
sell property to be used for the Japanese. He visited the owner in person and with great tact and
diplomacy made the purchase, even though the land-
lord learned that Mr. Beers proposed to make a
home and church of the property for this hated race.
The writer may be pardoned when she says, "The
Lord had given Mr. Beers a wonderful gift in dealing with individuals." Others might have bungled
and failed and the dear Japanese still have been
homeless. This pleasing quality which was so distinctive in his character, has been commented upon
by many of his friends. One preacher says, "He
was a wonderful combination, equally at home in
the association of great and small, college and railroad presidents, state and church dignitaries, and
the students even down to the primary class in his
school." Another writes, "He was a man among
men anywhere, and not out of place among the
great on earth, either from the human or the spiritual standpoint. He moved among men of culture,
wealth or spirituality, with ease and simplicity, and
yet without compromising his character, and as an
earnest Christian and a minister of the gospel. He
conversed with men of wealth and influence at their
places of business about their spiritual welfare, and
asked and was granted the privilege of praying with
them. Though a humble Free Methodist preacher,

yet he was respected and honored by people of all classes in the cities in which he labored in the interests of the cause of Christian education and the salvation of souls at home or abroad." Dr. Benson Howard Roberts says in his tribute, "A few years ago we spent a memorable week with Brother and Sister Beers in their home in Portland, receiving daily inspiration and strength of soul from their loving Christian fellowship. During that week Brother Beers introduced me to more men of standing in business circles than I ever met in the same period. He was a welcome caller on editor, banker, merchant, busy men of great interests." We also quote some kind words from a former district elder: "Alexander Beers was a man of exceptional talent and ability, and rare qualities of character far above the ordinary. He could have filled any position in the church acceptably, from the pastorate to the office of bishop. He was at ease in conversing with railroad magnates, bankers and business men in every line, or with the great educators he was equally at home as when in the class room of Seattle Seminary. He was kind to all and ever ready to help those who were in need."

But the laymen of the church, as well as the preachers, appreciated this quality as shown in one of their tributes: "We all loved him very much and many times he was a great source of inspiration to us. He was ever ready with a word of comfort where it was needed, and his sunny countenance and large, warm heart could be felt for good as he went from place to place on his pastoral calls. He never passed a little child on the street without a word of good cheer. He was also at home with big business men as he called at their offices. They all knew him in Portland and held him in high esteem. It could be truly said of him that 'those that knew him best loved him most.' " One of our Canadian brethren also writes: "His consideration of men who occupied earthly positions of greatness did not cause him to entertain feelings of inferiority because of his faithfulness to Christian principles. He showed no respect of persons, but was as ready to pray with the manager of a business corporation as with a man in the humbler walks of life, and apparently as much at home in the company of one as the other."

Much prayer had been going up to God concerning the purchase of this property, and these prayers were heard and answered—let all the glory be given to God! The building which had been secured was comfortable and commodious, and the little band of Japanese was soon established in its new quarters as happy as though no race prejudice existed. Dear Miss Pool was filled with thanksgiving after having been buffeted about for so long a time. On three different occasions she had been ordered to vacate her apartments because of the deep hatred for the Japanese race, and many times she had been refused permission to rent. She was homeless no longer. Her cries had entered into the ears of the Lord of Sabaoth. At this opportune time the Japanese showed great generosity, which still continues. They came forward at once, pledging themselves to give as much as the General Missionary Board. The pastor, Rev. T. Misawa, raised one thousand dollars among the Japanese, and District Elder Barnhart and Mr.

Beers the other thousand to make the first payment on the property.

With these hindrances removed, the work progressed nicely. Under the spiritual teachings of Rev. Misawa and Miss Pool's wise management, the Sunday-school flourished, souls were saved and added to the church and a good day school maintained. Rev. Barnhart came to hold their quarterly meetings and often brought his band of sweet singers, who would lend the beauty of their songs to enthuse and inspire the Japanese. Mr. Beers was also with them and addressed them frequently. All English-speaking must needs be interpreted by Miss Pool or Rev. Misawa, but heaven-inspired singing went directly to their hearts by the ever-present aid of the Holy Spirit and needed no human interpretation.

Mr. Beers' relationship with the Japanese continued to be very congenial and they showed deep sympathy during his illness. They, too, prayed very earnestly that his precious life might be spared. Like many other friends, they sought to express their love for Mr. Beers and one day sent in a beautiful boquet of flowers by Miss Pool, accompanied by the following letter:

DEAR BROTHER BEERS :—

We have heard from time to time of your weak condition and we have not forgotten you. We have prayed for you and asked the Lord to heal you. "Nevertheless, not our will, but Thine be done."

We are so sorry to lose you from our work. We ever remember your kind assistance, your labor of love, your precious words of advice, and we herewith, as a church, express our feeling of gratitude and also extend our sympathy to you, and may He verify these scriptures in your case: "The

Lord will strengthen him upon the bed of languishing; and thou wilt make all his bed in his sickness" (Psa. 41:3). "Thou art my hiding place; thou shalt preserve me from trouble; thou shalt compass me about with songs of deliverance" (Psa. 32:7). "When I remember Thee upon my bed and meditate on Thee in the night watches" (Psa. 63:6). "May the Lord bless thee and cause His face to shine upon thee and give thee sweetest peace and joy."

Our words are too limited to reveal our sympathy and appreciation so we present these flowers to you. God is now smiling at us and others through your life of love as He is smiling at you through these flowers.

Ever yours to carry on the work,
From the Japanese Free Methodist Church of Berkeley,
TEINOSUKE MISAWA, Pastor.

When Mrs. Beers read this letter to Mr. Beers, he was sitting in his arm chair by the window, great tears coursed down his cheeks, and he said, "Please have that published in the *Free Methodist* paper."

At the time Mr. Beers was appointed superintendent of the Japanese work, he had labored very faithfully to secure the services of the Rev. T. Kawabe, of Japan. He had brought the matter before the General Missionary Board and they were very ready to cooperate in bringing this great evangelist and his wife to America. When the matter was finally settled that they were coming, Mr. Beers rejoiced greatly, but before they had arrived, he was stricken by the hand of illness and was never able to be present at their meetings. He had been watching for their coming and longed to meet them, and when he learned that they were to reach San Francisco at a certain hour and would need his assistance in securing passes, with superhuman strength he went down to the pier to meet them at Oakland and accompanied them across to San Francisco. No one who looked at his white face and saw his trembling step could think that he was physically able to assume any responsibility or carry any burden. As greatly as she longed to help Rev. T. Kawabe and his wife, Mrs. Beers urged her husband not to undertake this task because of his great weakness, but persistence in the face of difficulties was one of the prominent traits of his character. Twice during Rev. Kawabe's stay, he helped him get passes. We insert here the kind words of Rev. T. Kawabe concerning Mr. Beers: "Many years ago I heard of Brother Beers from our missionaries in Japan. They told of his zeal for foreign missions and how he inspired them to give themselves to this work and encouraged them in preparing for service. Many of our missionaries in Japan were thus influenced by him, and thought of him as a father. For more than twenty years he was connected with Seattle Pacific College and his labors for that institution were a great factor in the establishing of this school upon a good foundation. The first direct communication I had with this man of God was a letter I received from him last November. It was an invitation to come to the United States and help him in his work among the Japanese. It showed plainly his love for these people in America. Seeing this, I felt constrained to come and work among my countrymen in America. I first met him in the ticket office in San Francisco on the 30th of last March, the day we arrived, and was surprised to see his pale face and weakened condition. But he kindly secured a pass for me and accompanied us to the station. I can never forget this great kindness to me. Even when he was on his sick bed, twice he helped me get a pass. Because of his interest in and love for the Japanese, in the midst of an anti-Japanese section, the organization of the Berkeley church was made possible."

CHAPTER XVIII

WORK IN OAKLAND— HIS SICKNESS—GOES TO SANITARIUM

Were a star quenched on high,
  For ages would its light
Still traveling downward through the sky
  Shine on our mortal sight.

So when a great man dies,
  For years beyond our ken
The light he leaves behind him lies
  Along the paths of men.   —*Longfellow.*

When the California Annual Conference was held in June, 1920, the work in Oakland was added to San Francisco. The pilgrims there were few in number and were worshipping in a hall which was owned by a secret order. The hall could only be used in the evening, when the order was not holding its sessions. Mr. Beers preached in the morning and held his usual Sunday morning services in San Francisco, then partaking of a hasty lunch, he and Mrs. Beers would hurry off to catch a boat that would bring them to Oakland by 3:30 in the afternoon. The preaching there was followed by class meeting, and then they would hasten back to San Francisco to eat another hurried lunch, and go at once to their evening service there. Holding these three services on Sunday seemed too much for Mr. Beers' strength, but he carried his burdens joyfully and was very happy in his work. He prepared regular addresses or short talks for his mid-week prayer meetings at San Francisco and Oakland, which were gems of thought and inspiration. The members felt they could not afford to miss one of these heart talks.

But the work in Oakland was greatly hindered by the fact that we had no church building. The hall in which the society worshipped was very small in its seating capacity and the congregation had increased until the crowd experienced much discomfort in the way of heating and ventilation. It seemed imperative that they should have a more comfortable place for their services. Truly, the Holy Spirit was poured upon the services from time to time and some said, "We can not bear to leave this sacred spot."

For a long time Mr. Beers and a special committee had been looking for a church building, which could be secured at a reasonable figure. There were several churches in Oakland that had been vacated for different reasons and were now standing empty. There will ever be a sorrowful memory connected with the purchase of the church that the Free Methodist society is now occupying in Oakland. A choice of a church edifice had been made by the committee, negotiations were pending, when suddenly Mr. Beers was stricken with the illness from which he never recovered. He had been over to Oakland Sunday afternoon as usual and preached with unusual liberty and power from the text, "Grieve not the Holy Spirit." We think that no one who was present on this memorable afternoon can ever forget this discourse. This proved to be the last sermon he ever preached when able to stand, although he filled his appointments many times sitting in his chair. That night he was taken very ill from what appeared to be a nervous collapse. In his dream he thought some one knocked him prostrate with a club and he awoke in great pain and distress. Reference has been made in a previous chapter to the great delight Mr. Beers took in street preaching, but he had been compelled to abandon this work for several months before his illness.

To resume the subject of buying the property: the next day after Mr. Beers was taken ill, his friends could see that he was indeed in a serious condition and urged him to remain in bed, but he would listen to no entreaties. He had agreed to meet the authorities concerned, and close the deal for the purchase of the church in Oakland. He insisted on making this trip and finished all the details of the transaction, although so weak he could scarcely get about. This persistent adherence to the call of duty was a prominent characteristic of the man. If he had an engagement to meet any one at a specified time, he would invariably be there on the spot at the time designated. No matter if it were only a small boy he was to assist in getting a job, or some insignificant individual who was applying for a charity ticket, his word was sufficient. He would forsake any pleasure in meeting his friends, or lay aside the most pleasing affairs to keep his promise and be of assistance to any of the Lord's least ones.

The heroic and splendid virtue of this man's character never had shown more brightly than during the long, weary months of his illness. His wife had noticed his failing strength for at least a year before he was stricken and tried in every possible manner to make his work easier. Perhaps he foreknew that his time of service on earth was short, for it seemed his great activity forbade him taking a rest. Many of his friends tried to persuade him to go on a vacation, but he loved his work and the people committed to his care too well to think of leaving them even for a short time. After Oakland had been added to his circuit and he had been appointed superintendent of the Japanese, the work consumed much of his time and strength. He would scarcely admit that he was feeling poorly, even when his friends all knew by his apperance that some dread disease was making inroads upon his once stalwart frame. Even after he was too ill to permit his standing on his feet, he would break the bread of life sitting in his chair, with white-drawn face, and hardly able to talk to his parishioners for a limited time. He insisted upon keeping up his appointment in this manner for several weeks. God very graciously enabled him to impart wise counsel to his people. They received help and inspiration every time he ministered to them from his chair. Their hearts were greatly saddened by his serious physical condition, but they always went home refreshed and cheered in spirit.

For two months he would not yield to the advice of the physician, nor the persuasion of his friends who urged him to take a vacation. It was very fortunate at this time that the general conference evangelist, Rev. B. W. Huckabee, had been secured to hold revival services in the newly purchased church at Oakland. The meetings continued for three weeks, with much of God's blessing resting upon Brother and Sister Huckabee. Almost every evening Mr. Beers persisted in being present, against the strong protest of his friends. Loving hands brought in a Morris chair which he occupied sitting on the platform. When the power of God rested especially on the evangelist and the people were blessed, Mr. Beers' face would light up and he would be strengthened in body—several times it seemed as if he was healed. Through the kindness of the dear Salomonson family, he was carried to and from the services in their auto.

When the revival services closed, Mr. Beers consented to go out to Beulah Heights and seek the quiet atmosphere of "Rest Cottage," which was the property of the Peniel Mission. Mr. and Mrs. Ferguson, of Los Angeles, who were the founders of the Peniel work, had long been close friends of Mr. Beers. Mr. Ferguson attended the revival services held by the evangelists under whose labors Mr. Beers was converted. Several months before his illness, dear Brother Ferguson had been called suddenly from service to reward. When his sorrowing wife heard that Mr. Beers was so seriously broken in health, she wrote him a most urgent letter, entreating him to occupy the "Rest Cottage" at Beulah. She hoped that the invigorating air and the atmosphere of prayer which prevailed in all the surroundings would bring restoration to Mr. Beers.

While stopping in Oakland, Mr. Beers had consulted the best physicians in San Francisco, but received very little encouragement. Many X-rays had been taken, but the seat of the disease could not be located. After he had been moved to "Rest Cottage" and was comfortably settled, he appeared to gain for a short time. Voluntary contributions sufficient to meet all his needs came in from many sources and perfect peace was reigning in all his borders. Kind friends took him out riding in their automobiles, and remembered him constantly with flowers and delicacies. "Rest Cottage" is located across the street from the "Home of Peace," which so long has been a home of refuge for hundreds of people. Mr. and Mrs. George Montgomery came in often to cheer and pray with the invalid. It seemed that volumes of prayer from many friends from all parts of the country were continually ascending to the throne for the healing of the sufferer. As Charles Kingsley writes, "His life was prayed for and God in His great mercy answered all by giving him immortal life." His friends had wished that his life might be spared, that his health should be restored and that he might again be permitted to preach the unsearchable riches of Christ. We are glad to record that these prayers were not offered in vain. He was given wonderful victory and marvelous endurance while compelled to lie patiently and daily see himself grow thinner and weaker. One night while in "Rest Cottage" he had a terrible conflict with the powers of darkness and called on his wife to come in and pray with him. Victory was soon given and he rejoiced as only a conqueror can. His shouts of praise and songs of deliverance were heard by the neighbors across the street.

Again prayer was answered in other ways. Money was continually coming in the mail and this was sufficient to meet all the expenses, which were very great. And his wife was given more than mortal strength to bear the long, severe strain which came upon her. All the last year of his life he had grown in grace so rapidly that it was noticeable. At family worship when no one else was present but Mrs. Beers, he would expound the Scripture with such inspiration of the Spirit that it seemed a pity not to preserve the rich, bright thoughts. When they bowed together in prayer, his petitions were powerful indeed—simple but great in their simplicity and intimate access to the throne. Why did not his friends see then that he was ripening for the sky? Why were their eyes so blind? Even after he had become too weak to kneel, sitting in his chair, his prayers were remarkable—not demonstrative, but bringing God so near. Those present seemed to be brought into the very vestibule of heaven—but in all his prayer he was never heard to ask for healing for himself but a few times during his illness of more than seven months. He seemed to feel that his work on earth was done, and desired only the accomplishment of God's will.

For about two weeks he had suffered greatly from excessive vomiting. A colored evangelist came in to see him and learning of his alarming condition, she prayed vehemently with child-like confidence until she prevailed. He was immediately relieved of this distressing symptom which did not return, and hope sprang up anew that he would now recover.

During his stay at "Rest Cottage" he asked to

have Rev. J. S. MacGeary come and anoint him and pray for his healing. Rev. MacGeary had come up from Turlock to hold a quarterly meeting for Rev. Barnhart, and drove out to Oakland in a driving rain to minister to Mr. Beers. Rev. MacGeary administered the holy sacrament and then held the anointing service as was desired. The whole service was graciously owned by the Spirit, and Mr. Beers received a great blessing in both soul and body.

Another visit made Mr. Beers while at the cottage brought great joy to his heart. Bishop Walter A. Sellew stopped off on his way to hold the Southern California Conference, and went over to Beulah to see his sick friend. He found him, as was Mr. Beers' custom, sitting on the front porch in the sunshine. Bishop Sellew had just come from Seattle, his former home, and had many things of interest to tell Mr. Beers. As he went away, he assured him that he was praying every day for his recovery. A short time before this, the missionary secretary, Rev. W. B. Olmstead, passed through the city on his way to attend the evangelistic services held by Rev. T. Kawabe, from Japan. Arrangements were made so that Mr. Beers had a brief visit with his friend; this interview cheered and comforted his heart, atoning in a slight degree for his not being able to attend Rev. Kawabe's meetings.

When Mrs. Beers saw that her efforts were all in vain, that country air and sunshine, pure jersey milk, perfect rest and quiet availed nothing—that her husband was gradually failing in flesh and strength—she felt keenly that something further must be done for his restoration. Mr. and Mrs.

Montgomery, whose home was next to the cottage, were so kind and tender toward him in this affliction. Mr. Montgomery came in very frequently to bring the consolation of Scriptures to him and to encourage his faith and trust in the Almighty arm. Then he would bow in prayer and with loving entreaty would plead with God to heal this child of His. When they, too, saw that Mr. Beers was surely growing weaker, they advised placing him in the St. Helena Sanitarium, located up in the hills some distance from Oakland. This was an Advent institution, conducted on a similar plan to the famous Battle Creek Sanitarium of Michigan. The members of the church and friends also strongly favored placing him in this sanitarium.

One of their good friends, A. Verkuyl, took Mr. and Mrs. Beers up there in his automobile—a five hours' ride. This was a very tiresome trip for Mr. Beers, but he bore it with great fortitude. After his passing, an intimate friend, one of his former private secretaries, wrote: "I shall always bear in my memory his fortitude, meekness, gentleness, magnanimity and cheerfulness." His wife feared all the time that the trip was too hard for him—too taxing —in his extreme weakness. But he bore every hardship without a murmur, without any complaint escaping his lips.

Mr. Beers was given a pleasant room and every attention paid to him. He enjoyed the fine baths very much and at first seemed greatly benefitted by the special treatments they gave him. The doctors and nurses were very kind and considerate. The praying band put his name at once on their list and remembered him constantly as long as he remained in the institution. It was impracticable for his wife to stay there with him owing to the great expense, and consequently he was left alone with only the frequent visits of the attendants. She visited him nearly every week-end and stayed over until Monday, which cheered him greatly. He seemed wonderfully sustained in his spirit. Whenever she came up she would say, "Do you not get very lonesome up here alone?" He would always reply, "No, the Lord is ever with me." He would tell her of great blessings and victory in the night. He was always very fond of Bishop and Mrs. E. P. Hart. One night he dreamed he heard dear Mother Hart singing one of her beautiful hymns. Several extracts from letters written while at St. Helena are given here: "God is blessing me. Last night the Spirit came upon me at two o'clock in the morning. I praised God on my bed. They are all good to me here. I am slowly improving. No vomiting since I came." (It will be remembered how wonderfully God had healed him of this distressing condition just before he left "Rest Cottage.") From another letter: "Please have Brother Barnhart thank the California Conference for their kind offering of love they sent me. This conference will ever have a warm place in my heart. The dietitian thinks I should have meat, fish and chicken included in my diet and will order them for me" (this was so considerate when the Advent menu was always strictly vegetarian). "God is good to me and blesses me continually, though I miss you greatly. God will take care of us."

One who sat under his preaching, who is now pastor with his wife at Oakland, California, sent these words in a personal letter: "Brother Beers lived a beautiful and useful life, filled with the Spirit. There were many lives made better through his influence and many shall call him blessed. Personally he seemed like a father to us, so thoughtful of the interests of others, so appreciative of every little kindness. While an intellectual giant and possessing so many excellent qualities, he was very humble, which made him truly great. We feel that a *great* man has been called home and that heaven is the richer and this world poorer. We are very thankful that it has been our privilege to know him. We shall never forget him, and his influence helps us to live better lives." Another who was a member of the church in Oakland at that time, sent the following: "We shall always be glad that we ever knew and loved Brother Beers. It has been, and ever will be an inspiration to me, and heaven comes very near to us when we think of his being there just a little sooner than we are. God grant our work may be as well done, when we are called home. A friend from Alameda, California, who often sat under his preaching, said this in a personal letter. "I think I have never known any one who could express his thoughts as well as Brother Beers, and he had thoughts far beyond the rest of the inhabitants of this world."

CHAPTER XIX

IS TAKEN TO PORTLAND—PASSES AWAY

Sure the last end
Of the good man is peace! How calm his exit!
Night dews fall not more gently to the ground,
Nor weary, worn-out winds expire so soft.
Behold him in the evening-tide of life—
A life well spent—whose early care it was
His riper years should not upbraid his green:
By unperceived degrees he wears away;
Yet, like the sun, seems larger at his setting.
High in his faith and hopes look how he reaches
After the prize in view! and, like a bird
That's hamper'd, struggles hard to get away;
While the glad gates of sight are wide expanded
To let new glories in, the first fair fruits
Of the last-coming harvest. Then, oh, then!
Each earth-born joy grows vile, or disappears,
Shrunk to a thing of naught. Oh, how he longs
To have his passport sign'd, and be dismiss'd;
'Tis done, and now he's happy! The glad soul
Has not a wish uncrown'd! E'en the lag flesh
Rests, too, in hope of meeting once again
Its better half, never to sunder more.
Nor shall it hope in vain: the time draws on
When not a single spot of burial earth,
Whether on land or in the spacious sea,
But must give back its long-committed dust
Inviolate.   —*Robert Blair.*

After Mr. Beers had been in St. Helena about a
month, he began to grow worse again. The doctors
and nurses were very solicitous and exhausted their

skill in striving to improve his condition, but to no avail. He missed his wife so greatly it was thought wise to move him down to Berkeley where she could be with him constantly. There was a private sanitarium at Berkeley, the El Reposa, which was conducted on the same plan as that at St. Helena. He was now much weaker than when he came from Oakland, so his friends were compelled to move him reclining on a bed in a large touring car. This was extremely hard for him in his emaciated condition, and one can never forget the patient endurance he manifested during this ordeal. Mrs. Beers rented a room across the street and stayed with him constantly excepting when teaching two hours in the afternoon in a Japanese school. Mr. Beers was made very comfortable at Berkeley and everything was done for him that science and skill could devise. He was happy to have his wife with him, but he grew homesick and said frequently that he was very tired of institutional life. He longed to be at home. Perhaps no one ever appreciated his home life more than he. An old friend says of him: "He was one of the kindest of men in his own home. It was beautiful to see him and Sister Beers so devoted to one another and together so devoted to the work of the Master. He was a great man in every respect. Would that we had many others like him." As was said of one great man, might be truthfully said of Mr. Beers, "His highest virtues were known only to his wife, his children, his servants and the poor." Many of his friends who are living today testify to the beauty of his home life and his ever-tender love for his wife. One says, "Mr. Beers was a devoted husband, a generous friend, an able preacher, a capable executive and a man of large visions." Another says, "If he could speak, he would say that he had become what he was through the grace of God so far as his character was concerned. But his education in our Christian schools and the sympathetic and noble assistance of his wife, did much to help in his achievements and successes." Others, "He was a true and disinterested friend, given to hospitality, an entertaining companion, a model husband, a high-souled and magnanimous man." "He was a very kind and loving husband, and will be greatly missed by his beloved wife."

For more than five months Mr. Beers had been without a home, and now the shadows of life were lengthening, the sun was sinking in the west, he longed once more to be at home surrounded by his loved ones and friends. Calling Mrs. Beers to his bedside one day, he told her he felt he was nearing the end of life. He said he had known from the first that his life-work was done—that he was now ready to depart, but he greatly desired to go back to Portland, his old home, to die. Then he arranged all the details for his funeral—he asked that Rev. David Cathey should preach his funeral sermon and Mr. and Mrs. D. L. MacPhee and Raymond VanValin should sing. He wanted to be buried beside his parents in the old church yard in Gresham. It seemed like an impossible task to take him for so long a trip in his seriously weakened condition. He had ceased to eat solid food and had not been removed from his bed for some time. But while looking to God, a strong assurance was given his wife that he would be strengthened for the trip and would not be injured by the journey. At once she began making preparations for this last mile of the way. Letters were written to Gresham, his old home, to arrange for his burial, and many requests for special prayer sent out. He had many visits from kind friends and members of the church. His sister came over from Lodi and cheered him greatly with her ministeries. When he learned that Professor Mark Hopkins, from the Los Angeles Seminary, was in the vicinity, he asked to see him, and a precious interview followed. During this visit, Mr. Beers made a donation of many valuable books to the Los Angeles Seminary.

During the anti-Japanese campaign which had been carried on vigorously just previous to Mr. Beers' illness, he had been associated in the work with Dr. James Gordon, pastor of the First Congregational Church of San Francisco. They had met several times in their effort to bring deliverance to this persecuted race. As soon as Dr. Gordon heard of Mr. Beers' illness, he came over to Berkeley and called on him. Mr. Beers was greatly helped by this visit. He spoke words of consolation and good cheer to his afflicted friend and prayed with him. As he was about to leave, he requested Mr. Beers to have Mrs. Beers call at his hotel in San Francisco. In answer, to this request, she went over to see him and found him most kind and approachable. He wished to know about Mr. Beers' financial condition and particularly if he would object to receiving money as a gift. She told him that they would regard it as given from the Lord in a pressing time of need. He asked Mrs. Beers to return after the Sabbath, as he said he would try to raise a little fund for Mr. Beers from among the members of his church. When she made her second call, this great-hearted man placed a roll of one hundred dollars in her hand. He seemed so happy to do this—said he wished it were more. May God bless the donors forever!

When at last the journey to Portland was decided upon, even though the doctors feared he would die on the trip, Mr. Beers could scarcely wait the time to go. Mrs. Beers' nephew, Earl B. Newton, who had formerly lived in their home for several years, his own father having died when he was very young, regarded his Uncle Alexander as his father. Now as he would soon be called upon to part with his uncle and it would probably be his last earthly good-by, he wished him to perform the sacred rites of matrimony for him. He and his fiance had planned to wait until Earl had received the degree of M.D. from Stanford University, which would be a year hence, but as they looked into the wasted face and on the emaciated form of their loved one, they realized that when they should part with him at Oakland pier, they would never see him again until they greeted him in the better country. Simple arrangements were made, and the wedding ceremony was held in his room. This marriage was beautifully sacred and solemnly impressive. Mr. Beers was too weak to rise from his couch, but his mind was as clear as crystal. The beloved couple knelt by his bedside, and placing his hands upon their heads, he read the marriage ceremony from memory that made the twain one.

This was his last official act. Mr. Beers was too weak to have any one in the room excepting a young lady friend who acted as witness, but no doubt the heavenly hosts were present and "angels were hovering around us unperceived."

We give extracts from letters received from the bride and groom after Mr. Beers had passed away. From Earl's letter: "My sorrow and great sense of loss could be no greater if he were my father. Sometimes I wonder if he really knew how greatly I loved him. And Florence loved him too. He has been one of my models of character and I feel that whatever little I may have achieved in life, he has contributed in a large part to that. And we have remarked that we could hold no finer ideal of domestic life than we have seen in your ideally long, happy married life. It will always be an inspiration to us, and a constant call to a continued ever-happy, love-filled life. which we both feel is only in the bud now. It brings tears to my eyes to think of his victorious spirit, even though deprived of the luxuries and comforts of his own former cozy home. The way he has mastered the inner fight of mental conflict and soared above all his difficulty is surely a wonderful tribute to the largeness of the man as well as to the power of divinity to rule the heart and head. Few men have been so completely master of themselves in their successes and losses as he. To have had him marry us as the last official act in life was a wonderful benediction and I am sure will hallow our domestic relations to each other forever as the years go by." The bride also writes: "I am so glad we did not put off our marriage for another year, and appreciate particularly the beautiful service. We shall never forget the sanctity of it. God seemed to direct in everything."

We sometimes hear people praying for "journeying mercies"—if ever divine providences were needed it would seem they were absolutely essential in this never-to-be-forgotten trip from Berkeley to Portland. Careful attention had been paid to every detail that could render the precious invalid more comfortable. Even the railroad company entered sympathetically into the arrangements, giving him "the very best porter they had on the road," as they learned afterward. The skilful hands of the ambulance boys lifted and carried him as tenderly as they would their own loved one. A reservation in the drawing room car had been secured and Mr. Beers seemed to enjoy his comfortable bed, during the two nights and one day of travel on the train. He was very happy indeed to be "homeward bound."

His great love for his brothers and sisters nerved him in his last hour to take the weary journey from Berkeley to Portland. He longed to see them once more and was willing to risk dying on the train, as the doctors feared, if he could but clasp their hands and look into their faces again. He was greatly cheered by the thought that some of his brothers and sisters would meet him when his wasted body was carried off the train on a stretcher. He was ever very loyal to his friends and loved them unto the end. The thought of meeting them, too, buoyed him up during this wearisome trip. Thank God, he was not disappointed! Some of his relatives and loved ones were at the train when he reached Portland

and ministered unto him to the last, and his great, loving heart was satisfied. In speaking of his friend-ships, one wrote, "He was a big-hearted man, always ready to help any one who needed help. He loved his friends, as many well know, and it was a very common thing in writing to them to call them his 'precious brothers.'" A former student who is now a trained nurse in Omaha, Nebraska, in a personal let-ter wrote: "I don't believe I ever fully realized how much I owe to Mr. Beers for his life of service and his sweet loving kindness."

His friends hoped when he reached Portland that he might find the same kind consideration in one of the good hospitals there that he had received in both the California sanitariums. But in this they were doomed to disappointment at first, but which proved later a kind providence. "God moves in a mysteri-ous way, His wonders to perform." A room had been previously secured in one of the best hospitals and Mr. Beers was moved from the train to this place, but strange as it may appear, no loving con-sideration was shown him there. He was placed on a most uncomfortable bed and his friends were not permitted to bring in a suitable one for him to lie on. In this extremity a kind friend appeared on the scene and urged Mrs. Beers to move Mr. Beers to her front parlor where she would help her in caring for him. Since this friend was a very fine nurse, this was indeed God's opportunity in caring for His own. How wonderful are His ways! In packing their household goods in San Francisco, Mrs. Beers failed to sell their bed as she had hoped, so shipped it all complete to Portland. Now when a good bed was

so greatly needed, divine Providence had so wisely
planned that all she had to do was to order it
brought up from the freight depot. After a stay of
but thirty-six hours in the hospital, when all the
arrangements had been made, the dear sufferer was
moved on a stretcher once more and carried to the
hospitable home of Mr. and Mrs. J. Wrage. They
placed him on his very own bed in their pleasant
parlor in front of two large windows where he could
look out and see the passers-by and the little children playing in the streets, and could also receive
all the sunshine and fresh air he needed. When they
had gotten him nicely settled, he looked up and said
with a pleased smile: "Oh, this seems like being at
home again." In this homelike atmosphere of love
he received every attention that medical skill and
careful nursing could bring. Many loved friends
came from far and near, bringing sweet flowers and
speaking loving words to cheer him. All of his
brothers and sisters, excepting one sister who lived
in Lodi, and who ministered unto him just before he
left Berkeley, gathered around him, ready not only
to nurse and cheer him, but to help in a practical
way with his personal needs.

His case was taken up by the prayer band and
God's people all over the city were praying for his
recovery. The week before he passed away, on three
successive days kind friends were sent by the Holy
Spirit to hold an anointing service over him. On
one of these occasions a lady, who was a stranger,
came alone. She said she had received a great favor
in former years in the way of transportation priv-
ileges which Mr. Beers had secured for her, and had

never been able to make any return for his kindness. Now, when she learned of his serious illness,
she had spent nearly the whole night before in
prayer and felt she must come and pray for his healing. After very earnest pleadings with God at his
bedside, she received only the answer, "that all was
well—that no mistake would be committed—that it
was either healing or heaven, just as God willed."
In the case of one of the others who had held an
anointing service, after the funeral he felt troubled
because he had performed this ceremony over Mr.
Beers, and in prayer he asked why he had been told
to do this. The answer came quickly from the Spirit,
"I had you anoint him for his burial."

For three weeks this noble man lingered on the
shores of time amid these beautiful surroundings.
At first he appeared to gain a little and the hopes
of his friends were brightened, but only for a brief
moment. He was slowly but surely sinking. Twice
the physician ordered transfusion and his wife
gladly gave him blood from her veins. This process
caused him great mental suffering. He protested as
strongly as he was able against taking the blood
from her, thinking only of her personal comfort. So
long as this new blood was coursing in his veins he
seemed to rally and his friends hoped he was better,
but were encouraged only for a few days. The end
was drawing near and must soon come.

Francois Fenelon says, "If all the riches of the In-
dies or the wealth of the crowned heads of Europe
were given to me in exchange for my love of reading,
I would spurn them all." A characteristic love for
poetry, coupled with a very intense love for reading,

followed Mr. Beers during his entire life. After he was taken ill so that he could no longer endure the strain of holding a newspaper or book in his hand, he called for his friends to read to him every day and kept in touch with the great affairs in the English Parliament and the important decisions in our own senate. Two days before his death he insisted on the reading of the editorial page of the *Oregonian* to him. He did not care to hear anything about the murders, suicides or divorces, but wanted to know what the great men were doing in the world.

The last few days of his life his throat seemed paralyzed so he could not speak without difficulty, and there were not many last words to record. The day before he left his earthly house he spoke of the approaching birthday of his wife and said he would like to get her a nice present. He asked a friend to take her riding, for he feared she was too closely confined. Mrs. Coffin, an old friend who had been one of his teachers in Sunday-school when he was pastor of the First Church, was calling, in company with her mother. He said to her, "The next time you teach your children a new song, I wish you would train them to sing, 'Wonderful Words of Life.'" And as they started to sing this song, he tried to join in the chorus.

On one of his two last evenings on earth, the two young men whom he had chosen to sing at his funeral called to see him. He seemed much pleased to see these loved friends and asked them to sing for him. With great emotion, they complied with his dying request and with loving pathos they sang one of his favorite hymns:

"His eye is on the sparrow,
And I know He watches me."

As they finished the song, Mr. Beers said, with a pleased look on his face, "That was the best singing I ever heard."

These were sad and trying days for Mrs. Beers. A dear friend sent her the following lines to uphold her through the valley and the shadow:

"Child of my love, lean hard,
And let me feel the pressure of thy care;
I know thy burden, child, I shaped it;
Poised it in mine own hand;
Made no proportion in its weight to
Thine unaided strength.

"For even as I laid it on, I said,
'I shall be near, and while she leans
On me, this burden shall be mine, not hers;
So shall I keep my child within
The circling arms of my own love.'

"Here lay it down, nor fear to impose
It on a shoulder which upholds
The government of worlds.
Yet closer come; thou art not near
Enough. I would embrace thy care
So I might feel my child reposing
On my breast. Thou lovest me?
I knew it. Doubt not then;
But loving me, *lean hard*."

While nearly all of his friends had given up hope that Mr. Beers would live, his wife still refused to believe he was really going to leave her. "It could not be. He must live to preach the gospel of Christ," she reasoned. "Why, his sermons had improved so greatly during the last two years of his life, his preaching had been growing richer, more powerful and more effectual." Perhaps, however, selfish considerations also may have influenced her as she thought of her own desolate condition if she should be left to tread life's pathway alone.

On the last morning, loved friends tried to show Mrs. Beers that her husband was already dying and then she relinquished the last hope of his recovery. She says of this last day, "I shall thank God all my life that I spent this last sweet, most sorrowful day talking to my beloved one of the better country. I told him his mansion was awaiting him in the glory world and that I would meet him there. Again and again I poured all the love of my heart into his ears and told him he had always been the best husband in the world. I asked him frequently if Jesus was with him—if Jesus was precious—and received affirmative signs, as he could not now speak. We knew by his shining countenance that he understood and appreciated all we were saying. We sang, 'Jesus, Lover of My Soul,' and Rev. B. C. Dewey prayed aloud shortly before the end came. We realized very much of the presence of God in the room. His mind was perfectly clear to the last moment. A short time before he ceased breathing he kissed me a last farewell. He was quiet and peaceful and seemed to be suffering no pain. How graciously God heard and answered prayer in giving him such a beautiful, triumphant exit from this life. He had gone to be forever with the Lord, as Charles Kingsley says about death. "Death, beautiful, wise, kind death! When will you come and tell me what I want to know?" At last Mr. Beers could solve every perplexing problem that had harrassed his soul here. One of his favorite hymns had been:

> "If we err in human blindness
> And forget that we are dust,
> If we miss the law of kindness,
> When we struggle to be just,
> Snowy wings of peace shall cover
> All the plain that hides our way,
> When the weary watch is over,
> And the mist has cleared away."

The mists had forever cleared away from his vision and he could say, "I know as I am known."

Later the district quarterly conference of Portland, Oregon, sent resolutions of sympathy, from which a quotation is given:

"No man is ever finished. We are here in the making, as a ship we are still upon the stays, with tool, instrument, hammer and saw we are still being wrought upon, sometimes much to our discontent until by the long process man is made and then when the time is come and God is ready He knocks away the underpinning and the ship breaks from its ways out into the element we do not understand, but the very element for which God has been preparing him.

"Pestilence broods over city, the returning husband every night wonders if blooming wife of the morning may not be found stricken. He finds home closed, shades down, no response. He gropes in the dark, his heart sinks, presently he finds note pinned on the door; he reads, 'Friend has come and taken me to the mountains; am safe from the pestilence; I want you to follow me. Here is the means by which to come.' Heart and life spring again to the cheek and bitter sorrow is turned into joy.

"So we come to the house which once held our beloved. It is dark, and out of the windows that shown with the love light, no light is shining; the door is closed; there is no communion, no fellowship. We are heartbroken until we

ALEXANDER BEERS' LAST RESTING PLACE, GRESHAM, OREGON

turn and find this word brought to us, 'The loved one is gone to the mountains with his best friend, Jesus, where there is no pain, no sorrow, no temptation, no disease, but the eternal flowers and the everlasting sunlight; follow thou on, the wail of sorrow is turned to a song of triumph, crape gives way to flowers."

The following poem is a tribute sent by Mrs. Ethel Lawpaugh Klotzbach:

His earthly house has fallen,
  We knew not 'twould be so soon,
But we do know his All in All
  Has prepared for him a room.

And as the golden sun was sinking
  In the rosy-tinted west,
He heard the blessed Lord's "Well done,"
  And entered into rest.

Now he shines in the light of God,
  Christ's likeness stamps his brow,
Through the valley of death his feet have trod;
  He reigns in glory now.

He has reached the joys of heaven,
  And is one of that sainted band;
For his head a crown of gold is given,
  And a harp is in his hand.

He has heard the songs they sing,
  Whom Jesus hath made free,
And the glorious walls of heaven ring
  With his new-born melody.

No sin, no grief, no pain;
  Safe in that happy home;
His fears all fled, his doubts all slain,
  His hour of triumph has come.

Oh, loved ones of mortal years,
  The trusted, the tried, the true,
You are watching still in the valley of tears,
  While he waits to welcome you.

Will he forget? Oh, no!
  For memory's golden chain
Shall bind his heart to the hearts below
  Till they meet and touch again.

Each link will be strong and bright,
  And love's electric flame
Shall freely flow down, like a current of light.
  To the world from whence he came.

Do we mourn when another star
  Shines out from the glittering sky?
Do we weep when the waging voice of war
  And the storms of conflict die?

Then, why should our tears flow down
  And our hearts be sorely riven?
There's another gem in the Savior's crown
  And another star in heaven.

A GOOD MAN GONE

There was nothing small about Alexander Beers. Great
in stature, great in intellect, great in soul, great in spirituality, great in activity, no wonder he excelled. No wonder
he was admired. He was too magnanimous to descend to
anything questionable or unbecoming. He lived in the higher
altitudes.

He loved nature and nature's God. Children were his delight. The unfortunate received his special ministrations.
He lived for others. No sacrifice was too great when the
cause of his Master was in need. No work was too hard if
by its performance others were bettered or made happy.

He reared his own monument. The material part of it is
in the City of Seattle in the form of a Christian school that
has already blessed hundreds if not thousands of the children of men. The immaterial portion of it will abide forever, though the rocks have crumbled and the earth has dissolved.

Earth is always the loser when such a noble character
goes away.   REV. J. T. LOGAN,
                                Editor of the Free Methodist.

CHAPTER XX

TRIBUTES—MEMORIAL SERVICES

The period of life is brief;
'Tis the red of the red rose leaf,
'Tis the gold of the sunset sky,
'Tis the flight of a bird on high;
But one may fill the space
With such infinite grace
That the red will tinge all time,
And the gold through the ages shine,
And the bird fly swift and straight
To the portal of God's own gate.

—Selected.

We live in deeds, not years;
In thoughts, not breaths;
In feelings, not in figures on the dial.

—Philip James Bailey.

Alexander Beers has gone to his eternal reward and it only remains for us who knew him to place our estimate upon his character and his services for the cause of God and humanity. Our conclusions as to these things may be faulty and possibly entirely incorrect, but from our Christ he will receive righteous judgment.

His friendships were very strong. No sacrifice of time or money was too great for him to make in assisting a friend in any interest which that friend might have in hand. He seemed to render such service gladly and willingly.

His mind was a veritable fund of information from history and poetry, which he used very effectively in sermon, address and travel.

As a man among men he was truly great. He could meet and mingle with men of all stations in life. He was particularly kind and polite to the poor and unfortunate people

whom he met. He could also obtain access to those who
were very difficult of approach, and could frequently secure
aid and favors from them when many of us had failed in
our efforts at the same end.

His heart was the biggest part of him. No one who knew
him intimately could doubt this. Tender, considerate, devoted and loyal to his Christ and to every phase of His
cause with which he came in contact, he served his day and
generation.

His services in the cause of God and humanity were too
many and too varied to be mentioned in this brief article.
He was always very successful as a pastor, but all who
know anything about the situation will always associate
Alexander Beers with Seattle Seminary and with Seattle
Pacific College. His heroic efforts for about twenty-five
years resulted in the founding and in the perpetuity of that
institution and those services will never be lost sight of
while the college stands. His desire that the institution
should undertake full college work was finally realized
through his persistent efforts. He secured a large and valuable property to the church, and left his imprint on the institution which will increase as the years go on.

We honor him for what he was and for what he did.

BISHOP WALTER A. SELLEW.

My acquaintance with Brother Beers began almost thirty
years ago. We were then both young men in the full vigor
of maturing manhood. I was impressed then as for years
following with his apparently abounding vitality. He appeared to me to be one of the finest specimens of physical
manhood I ever saw. We were never closely associated in
the work, my field of labor at that time being in the extreme
east and his in the extreme northwest of the United States.
We were, however, frequently thrown together at General
Conference, and at the annual meetings in Chicago, he being
a member of the Executive Committee and I of the Missionary Board. As the years went by our casual acquaintance
ripened into a friendship which remained unbroken until
the end. One could not meet him many times without being

impressed with his geniality. The smile which illuminated his countenance, his cordial greeting, the hearty handshake, all combined to make you feel that he was really glad to see you and at once put you at your ease. This was especially true of his greeting in welcoming you to his home.

He was an able and forceful preacher of the Word. It was the writer's privilege to attend a session of the Colorado Conference at which he presided. His addresses to the conference and his sermons were masterly and would have done credit to the bishopric in any church. On other occasions I was edified and uplifted under his ministrations.

Big in body, big in mind, big-hearted, many knew him to love him and will sincerely mourn his departure. More than one young man and young woman has been helped to a higher and broader view of life by his influence. His help did not stop with encouraging or inspiring words. Substantial aid in preparation for life's work has been rendered again and again.

The sickness which struck him down seemed to come suddenly, but doubtless had been insidiously working for years, undermining his fine constitution. Throughout months of weakness and suffering he never murmured, but calmly, patiently, victoriously awaited the end.

I was glad to call him my friend. I shall miss his genial smile, the grasp of his great hand, his hearty "God bless you," but we shall meet in the morning.

REV. JOHN S. MACGEARY.

Something over six years ago, while helping Rev. T. H. Marsh in revival meetings in the College Church at Seattle, Washington, it was my privilege to become more intimately acquainted with Rev. Alexander Beers than it had ever been previously. Being in his home several times and associating with him in the meetings, I could not help feeling that I was in the presence of a great and good man. His spirit was very precious, his humility and holiness wonderful. I shall always be thankful for the privilege of knowing him, and I feel assured that my life has been made better, my ministry enriched and my heart strengthened by this friendship. Surely in his death, the Free Methodist Church has suffered the loss of one of its great and leading men. The like of Brother Beers are, alas, too few. He has gone, but in the memory of the writer and thousands of others, he will live on, until we, too, are called to cross the solemn river and meet him where tears shall never flow and joys shall never end.   REV. H. O. HUBBARD.

My first acquaintance with Brother Beers was nearly twenty years ago on our coming to the State of Washington. After the session of conference at Tacoma he took us, a family of five, to their pleasant home in Seattle and there entertained us several days with the greatest hospitality and, being strangers and without home in this far-away Northwest, we were strongly impressed with his great-hearted brotherliness.

His great ambition was to serve, to bless, and be a blessing. I have seen times since I first met him when by stepping aside a little from his much beloved work he could have made hundreds of dollars and that legitimately, but it could have been said of him he was a man of one purpose, one ambition, the development and success of Seattle Seminary. He could have said with the apostle Paul, "This one thing I do," or, "The love for Seattle Seminary constraineth me," but we believe the motive force in all he did was divine love. He had an all-consuming zeal to extend the kingdom of God to the ends of the earth.

REV. T. H. MARSH.

Leaving the many outstanding characteristics of a great man for others to mention, I would speak a word in respect to his friendliness.

I first met Brother Beers in Denver, where he was chairman of the annual session of the Colorado Conference. At this conference he preached one of his excellent sermons from the subject which he never tired of, "Friendship." He loved and often quoted those beautiful lines of Tennyson's on being a friend to man.

I was privileged to convey him to the depot in Denver on

this occasion, and as we stopped before the gateway he called my attention to the inscription of that word so full of beautiful thoughts just over the arched entrance to the Union depot, "Mizpah."

I was privileged to associate with him again in the Oregon Conference and always met with a cordial, friendly greeting. During the session of the Oregon Conference, following the terrible winter of the influenza, which left me a sick man for months, Brother Beers met me one day and placing a friendly hand on my shoulder, with a kind, sympathetic tone remarked, "Brother LaRue, I wish you were well."

At the last district quarterly meeting I attended of the Portland District, held on my charge, he related this dream during his sermon: "I dreamed I saw a cyclone approaching and was frightened, and my first thought was to flee. Then something impressed me not to run but stand still. Presently the storm seemed to move directly over my head, and looking up I saw smiling down upon me through the center of the storm the face of my Savior." He has passed through the storm and is at rest near his Friend.

REV. WESLEY LaRUE.

In the passing of Alexander Beers the church has not only lost a loyal and devoted servant, but I feel that I have lost a personal friend. He always treated me like a brother beloved, and I have known him but to love him since I first met him. He was ever cheerful, hopeful and sympathetic. I was with him in revival work while he was pastor of First Church, Portland, in the spring of 1919. He found First Church in the class of the ordinary, and lifted it out and up into the class of the extraordinary during his short pastorate there. I was with him again at Oakland, California, last spring, just after he was stricken with that something which brought him to the grave. I found him there the same aggressive, hopeful worker in the vineyard of the Lord. He had just secured a splendid church property, and had organized a splendid class. I saw him again just a few days before he passed away. That massive frame was reduced to a mere skeleton. He had given up the fight, and was patiently awaiting the end. When I asked him if Christ was still precious, his answer was, "Oh, yes; I have not swerved an inch, nor have I murmured."

Alexander Beers was a big man, big in body, and mind and soul and sympathy, and in vision, and I apprehend his place will not be easily filled among us. It does seem to me that he ought to have lived and wrought among us for a score of years yet, but God knows best, and our loss is his eternal gain. May his good wife be sustained by abundance of grace.   REV. B. W. HUCKABEE.

The memory of Alexander Beers will live long in the minds of the members of the old Western Canada Conference. He presided at three sessions of that conference. His earnest heart-to-heart talks to the conference, his able sermons and his magnanimous, optimistic and humble spirit took root in our hearts and is bearing fruit in many lives. Among his talks to the conference, one on "The Importance of Retaining a Tender Spirit" stands prominently before our memory, while among his sermons, one on "Jesus Christ," which he preached at the Calgary conference, was so inspired with exaltation to the Savior that while repeating the lines, "Oh, could I speak His matchless worth," etc., about one hundred saints unitedly arose to their feet shouting and weeping under the power of the Spirit.

The dear brother is gone, but his memory will long remain green in the hearts of his many friends in western Canada.   R. H. HAMILTON.

Through the years that have so quickly flown I have often been in the home of this departed brother and found in him a large, generous-hearted and broad-minded friend, ready to help and serve others. He and his wife were thoughtful, courteous and "given to hospitality."

While we can not solve the mystery that called him hence when there seemed to be so much he was capable of doing here for the Master's cause, we know divine wisdom makes no mistakes and his home going was marked with tokens of divine love in his being permitted to return to his old home and friends in Portland and Gresham.

On the Saturday before his departure he seemed to be greatly revived and hopeful, and as we talked to him of future plans, he said, "But I came home to die." On Monday, wife and I were permitted to be with him as the things of time were fading and eternal realities were opening to his view. As his spirit took its flight, his wife, with ourselves, were upon our knees in prayer. She was greatly sustained, and triumphant in faith to the last.

As the funeral was being held at Gresham, the home of his youth, the sun from his throne in the sky poured streams of golden light through stained glass upon the scene as if to tell of the glory beyond, and again just as it was fast sinking to rest, it fell in splendor upon the one who had stood so nobly by his side in the battles of life, as she stood at the head of the grave with radiant, upturned face, as if while loving hands hid the mortal form from view, she with an eye of faith was trying to pierce the veil that hid his spirit, in that house of light, where the spirits of just men made perfect are at rest with their Lord.

REV. B. C. DEWEY.

None of us ever knew when Mr. Beers was distressed or in trouble at home, but we were all sure to know when he was unusually happy, for at such times he sang a great deal, although he often apologized for the music he made. He would tell us that we ought to hear how sweetly his heart sang. He loved good music, and always gathered his singers about him wherever he went to labor in the vineyard of the Lord. I shall never forget the animation of his face as Mrs. June Cathey sang in their home and in the school from time to time, and how he would cheer when Will Cathey sang his favorite patriotic melody, "The Old Flag Never Touched the Ground." When he was called to Portland he again found his singers and I heard him say at one time, "I attribute greatly my success in Portland First Church to the beautiful spiritual singing and help I had in Donald and Mrs. MacPhee." When he accepted the call to our lovely,

sunny California, he found Mr. Cochrane and myself glad
to take up our work with him again. He always "boosted"
when we sang and I am recalling with pleasure the times
he shouted the praises of God until we were compelled to
stop until the waves of glory had subsided. I called Mr.
Cochrane's attention to Mr. Beers' broken condition of
health when he came to California and we were both compelled to admit it with a pang that he never knew, and yet
I'm sure that I never heard him preach as spiritual and
uplifting sermons as he did while he was with us here. We
watched him fail as we watch a magnificent sunset fade in
the western sky, and thought with great comfort as we
heard him regularly speak of his favorite hymn, "I have a
Savior, who is mighty to keep." We do not mourn for him
today, but for the loss of him. We are glad that we can
think of him after he has fought through the discords and
enjoyed the harmonies of this life, basking in the full glories of life eternal. And he will find his singers there—a
multitude of them—who have gone on before. Those that
cheered him with their sweet songs during his early struggles with the school problems, and, best of all, he will not
need to listen for fear of missing the parts, but his big voice
will join the chorus in perfect unison with all the harmonies of heaven.   MRS. MABEL BARNHART COCHRANE.

It was my privilege to live in the home of Brother and
Sister Beers for six years, during my connection with the
Seattle Pacific College. These were pleasant and profitable
days to me, and I shall always cherish the memory of the
time I spent in their beautiful Christian home.

Rarely do you find a person so devoted to his home and
its interests as was Brother Beers. He was kind, thoughtful and very appreciative of any attention shown him.

I never knew one more attentive to his companion.
Brother Beers was constantly seeking to lessen the burdens
of Sister Beers, and to bring joy and comfort to her heart.
How he delighted in surprising her when presenting gifts,
or when doing her a favor of any kind. He gave his flowers
while they could be appreciated.

Brother Beers never seemed happier than when he had something to give to others, or could share in their burdens. He took a great interest in the large number of students who lived in their home and every effort was put forth to make them happy and contented.

Whatever the difficulties may have been as he went about his work, he seemed to forget them all when he entered the home at the close of the day, and especially as we gathered around the table at meal time. There he was always cheerful, and by his pleasant conversations helped those who had troubles to forget them. How often he would say, "Well, how I do enjoy being home with you all."

Nothing was allowed to interfere with family worship, but regardless of pressing duties, time was taken both morning and evening for Scripture reading and prayer.

The spirit of kindness, generosity and helpfulness manifest by Brother Beers will never be forgotten by those who were privileged to live in his home.

MISS NETTIE M. TONG.

EXTRACTS FROM PERSONAL LETTERS

From a personal letter from Mrs. Emma Sellew Roberts, A.M., written before Mr. Beers passed away:

"I believe if God should take Mr. Beers to a better, brighter world, you will be comforted by so many, many things: your happy life of concord together; his great usefulness; and what is more—the greater usefulness and service hereafter. We know that this life is but the threshold to the other real life. I believe that such men of talent and self-denial and of holy ambition will be able in that fair land to realize the fulfilment of all these noble desires and ambitions. It is a great comfort to me. Disappointments are ours here. Unfulfilled purposes and ideals—but over there, thank God, our limitations will not be as they have been here. I can not now hold on for people to live as I once did. I have such a sense of the grandeur and beauty of the other life and how soon we shall know as we are known."

From the Educational Secretary, Rev. L. Glenn Lewis:

"Such men as he was are greatly needed in the church. There are many things that we do not understand. 'God moves in a mysterious way, His wonders to perform.' "

One of Mr. Beers' nieces gives this quotation from Charles Fred Gost as her tribute to her uncle:

"If you wish to see the supreme test of character, wait until it becomes plain that upon some hard experience of life the human heart is to be broken; until the man knows beyond peradventure that upon some failure or injustice or misfortune he is to be hung until drop by drop the blood of his courage and hope of success in this world ebbs away. If he picks that cross up without a murmur and bears it bravely up the hill of Calvary, you have seen a man."

From Miss Reed, of Africa:

"May He give you faith to see better plans worked out like the artist instructor who smeared a beautiful painting of his pupil because he saw the student was satisfied with present results. Then he told him to paint again.

"How time flies, and as Cecil Rhodes said in dying, 'So little done, so much to do.' It keeps us astir to keep abreast."

From a graduate who was formerly a missionary to China:

"I shall never, never forget his holy, dignified life, above approach in every way. His influence has been a great blessing to my own soul."

The following tribute was adopted by the Executive Committee of the Woman's Foreign Missionary Society at its annual meeting in Chicago:

"As members of the Executive Committee of the Woman's Foreign Missionary Society, we wish to record our sense of loss in the death of the Rev. Alexander Beers, the husband of Mrs. Adelaide L. Beers, our sister member of this committee.

"Brother Beers always evinced the warmest interest in the work of the W. F. M. S.; he was helpful, wise and loyal to the organization. He advanced the missionary cause, both foreign and home, in his every field of labor. His last work was largely given to the Japanese of California. He was a man of faith, vision and divine love."

During the annual board meetings, which were held in the Publishing House, Chicago, late in October, a memorial service was being conducted for the late Rev. Alexander Beers, who had long been a member of the Executive Committee. The committee room was full. Appropriate scriptures were read and prayer offered for the bereft. Bishop Sellew had given a beautiful tribute to the man who had gone. Our hearts and minds were turned heavenward, while a deep sense of gratitude came over us that another of our number had reached the haven of rest. The audience standing sang that old hymn, which was a favorite of the deceased, "There's a Land Far Away." The day was warm and through the open windows the sweet harmony of that hymn floated out upon the air—air polluted by the smoke grime of the city. Standing near a window, we looked down into the street below. A man with a wagon load of the city's refuse had brought his horses to a standstill, right in the middle of the street. With his face upturned, he sat almost transfixed as he seemed to drink in the music. Perhaps that old hymn brought to his mind, as it did to mine, the days of childhood, back when life seemed pure and sweet. It must have touched a responding chord in his heart or he would not have seemed so enwrapped. As the singing ceased he looked wistfully about him as though he wished that others might have heard. He drove on. We never saw him more. He was lost to us in Chicago's millions. But we could not dismiss from our mind his visage as he listened.

Whoever he was, wherever he went, that song must have uplifted him and brightened his humble labor. Like the song of Browning's Pippa, its influence can never be known.

Mrs. J. B. Lutz.

In recognition of the long services of Rev. Alexander Beers to Seattle Pacific College, the flag on the campus was placed at half mast for the week in which occurred his death and burial.

On Thursday afternoon, September 15, 1921, on which the funeral occurred at Portland and Gresham, the college classes adjourned and teachers and students gathered in the assembly hall, where a fitting service was held.

HE'S GONE

He's gone, our own great-heart is gone.
  Gone to his blest long home of love;
It was but yesterday he smiled
And firmly clasped my hand with cheer—
  Today he walks with hosts above.

I see him in my memory,
  With stately form and ruddy face;
Had I not known his humble heart
I would have classed him as a king—
  Yet like a king he filled his place.

His lips and life poured eloquence,
  Touched with the love of verse and lyre;
In friendly way he labored long—
Perhaps with overzealous plans
  He strove to build God's kingdom here.

For years he served the church and school
  In which he gave his life and all;

With one short mission in the end—
A prophet to the Japanese
  In our own land, he heard the call.

Ah, soulful eyes! big generous heart
  Burdened with some great heavy load
Which seemed to crush his very life;
Today he rests, the toil is done,
  And his great soul is free in God.
        —By W. C. Folsom, a former student.

CHAPTER XXI

TRIBUTES—Continued

Beloved, sleep!
    Thy conflicts now are past,
Life's battles fought,
Thy bliss begun,
    And thou art crowned at last.

We wait in hope
    Till Jesus comes again;
We'll meet thee then,
To part no more,
    Beyond the reach of pain.   —*W. H. Clark.*

The Missionary Secretary, W. B. Olmstead, writes:

I have always been impressed with the greatness of soul and breadth of vision of Rev. Alexander Beers. He had a genuine interest in all of the varied activities of the church and he was especially active in the missionary cause. His work among the Japanese in California revealed the great love he had for the foreign-speaking people of this country. I regarded him very highly and found him to be a true friend and brother.

After Mr. Beers had passed away, the pastor of the Japanese church at Oakland, Rev. T. Misawa, and the members assembled and considered the matter of sending some expression of their sympathy and love to the sorrowing wife. They raised an offering with which to purchase decorations for the grave of their dear departed leader and sent it to Portland, with the following affectionate letter:

DEAR SISTER :—

I am sure human words utterly fail to comfort your heavy soul at this time of sadness. But thanks for the everlasting arm. He will take you through, and make you more than conqueror. "In my Father's house are many mansions; if it were not so, I would have told you; for I go to prepare a place for you—that where I am, there ye may be also."

Our church members expressed themselves with the deepest sympathy and instructed me to send you a token of love. Please accept it and decorate his resting place with it.

His deep voice is still lingering in our ears. It will remain ever as a sweet savor before men and angels.

We pray that the Lord who called him home may bless you and keep your being steadfast in faith until He comes.

Yours in Him,

T. MISAWA.

Two Japanese shrubs have been purchased and placed upon his burial plot in Gresham, Oregon.

An extract from a personal letter:

Knowing of his great labors for the cause of God, I was made very sad by news of his death; and not only I, but all the Japanese of the Free Methodist Church are saddened by it. We feel we have lost a true friend. Twice during his sickness I visited him and always his face was shining. This is a source of comfort to us in the midst of sadness. We can not understand God's providence in thus removing this valiant one from the field of battle, but our loss is his eternal gain. I wish to extend to Sister Beers my heartfelt sympathy and assure her of the prayers of the Japanese Christians in this time of her great affliction.

REV. T. KAWABE.

From Dr. Whitcomb, of University Park, Iowa:

Dear Brother Beers! I am lonely! How I loved him! He was one of God's good and great men. How highly favored you were in that the Father loaned him to you for so many years! But he is not dead! Never! Good men and women never die! Just gone before! Heaven is certainly filling with our list. "The kings of earth shall bring their glory and honor into yon city."

From Francis E. Pond, district elder in the Columbia River Conference:

Brother Beers was always an inspiration whenever he attended our conference. He was a true friend and a great man. I think he was one of the strongest of our leading men.

From Rev. R. A. Zahniser, of Pennsylvania:

Surely a good man has gone to his reward, and he will be greatly missed by the church and world. The great consolation at such times is the assurance that "We can go to him" and that he not only lives on in heaven, but also in the good influences that follow such a life in this world.

Resolutions from the Oregon Conference assembled at Portland, Oregon, May 20, 1921, and sent to Mr. Beers:

Well do we remember your many years of toil and labor among us as an educator, and as a good minister of Jesus Christ; there was no load so great but what you would go under it, and put forth all your strength until it was lifted.

Your pastorate at First Church will not be forgotten soon, as both the people and the fine buildings testify to your wisdom and untiring devotion to the Free Methodist Church, and *Him* whom you *love.* .

> "There is no death!
>   What seems so is transition ;
> This life of mortal breath
>   Is but a suburb of the life elysian,
> Whose portal we call Death."

From a loved cousin in the East:

I have read somewhere that the goldsmith uses only ore of the highest grade for any article that requires the finest chasing. Nothing but the very best material will yield that exquisite result which is worth the labor and pain he must spend. This seems to me to be the most satisfactory explanation of suffering which the Father—who is Love—allows to come to some of the most faithful of His children. He sees that the ore is worthy of His utmost refining into beauty.

From one of his former secretaries:

How words do fail in such hours of sadness. At such times we can somewhat understand the old custom of sackcloth and ashes. I feel as though I would like to be near to express other than in words the heart anguish I feel.

I shall never forget our labor, trial and blessings together, and the wonderfully sustaining love of Jesus. This verse rings in my heart and ears: "That we might know Him and the power of His resurrection, and the fellowship of His sufferings."

I thank God in this connection with him that "If we suffer with Him, we shall also reign with Him."

As a student in the Seattle Pacific College for several years, I became well acquainted with President Beers, and became greatly attached to him.

He was a great lover of young people. His home was a Mecca for them. Nothing pleased him more than the developing of some young man into a polished Christian gentleman. He keenly followed their progress through life. In years after, many longingly looked for the time when they would see him, for there was only one Brother Beers who could shake your hand, and put a world of meaning into it. His burning desire as president was the welfare of the students. He neglected his own need to make more efficient the institution he served.

After I left college his interest in me never ceased. To get acquainted with him was to gain his friendship. As opportunity served him, he spoke a good word for me, which word was as "apples of gold in pictures of silver."

I greatly prize the association of this great man, and ever sacred to me shall be his memory.   REV. L. A. SKUZIE.

A feeling of infinite sorrow and deep personal loss comes to the hearts of legions of friends because the pure, noble and generous spirit of our most highly esteemed friend and brother, Rev. Alexander Beers, has passed away from this earth to the "city of God," eternal in the heavens.

Of him it can truly be said, "He trod the meadows and left the daisies rosy," for his great devotion to God and his fellow men led him to expend his utmost energies, not in "money making," but for "man making." By his zeal and enthusiasm all with whom he came in contact were inspired with higher aspirations and more noble ideals. Every one who was privileged to come under his influence and to be associated with him, was made the better and stronger because of this personal contact.

MRS. ETHEL L. KLOTZBACH.

In the death of Alexander Beers the church has lost one of her ablest ministers, who for many years had been unusually effective in his labors. He had long been a conspicuous figure in the official councils of the church, and his passing is a distinct loss. For many years I have prized him as a warm, personal friend and his death is a distinct loss to me. Our people in southern California greatly loved and prized him, for on different occasions he was with us and always with helpfulness and large vision for the future of the work.   REV. W. W. VINSON.

It would seem a strange neglect if the church where the spiritual as well as the intellectual life of Alexander Beers began should give no expression of the deep loss it has sustained in his going, as well as its great indebtedness to him. The church of his choice, as his cherishing mother, owns a close tie to such a son whom she has seen develop under her care from the untutored rustic youth, with heart all aglow for his Savior, to the Christian gentleman with a supremacy of intellect, diplomacy, eloquence and conscientiousness; which greatness combined of genius, character, manner and achievement, made him a mighty factor in the growth and development of the holy faith of our fathers, both in our own and in foreign lands—a living stream of influence whose fruitage is yet too soon to be fully appreciated.

Girded when he knew it not, in early manhood he was providentially led across the continent where he could the better prepare himself for future work and where the Lord provided him with one of the richest of legacies, a prudent wife, who through all the vicissitudes of life proved herself a true and sympathetic helpmeet. It was soon manifest that he was set apart from most of his fellows by certain superior gifts which he used unreservedly as a laborer together with God. His native talent for organization and able leadership, which were fully consecrated, gave birth and impulse to a number of the church's most important agencies which have brought blessings abundant to so many.

It was with unfaltering trust that he endured all the severe disappointments of life that came to him. But with a grateful sense that he was graciously led, he resigned himself to be made "perfect through sufferings." And when at length the day was far spent for him, the gloaming brought no gloom. In fixed confidence, with brightening, wistful hope, he waited on bravely and patiently till God soothed him to sleep. Surely such quiet resignation can only be explained by close fellowship with God.

NANCY C. MORROW.

BISHOP CLARK'S PRAYER AT THE MEMORIAL SERVICE HELD IN THE PUBLISHING HOUSE, OCTOBER 27, 1921

We thank Thee, our Father, for the privilege of bowing at the mercy seat. We acknowledge Thy greatness and Thy goodness. We thank Thee that Thy wisdom ruleth over all. We thank Thee that Thou art the refuge and strength of Thy people and always a very present help in time of need.

We thank Thee that as Thy children we are not left to solve life's problems and brave life's bereavements alone. We thank Thee that Thou hast promised to go with us all the way. We thank Thee that all of life's unknown future is in Thy hands and overshadowed by Thy promises. We thank Thee that whatever is before us, we are assured that we "can not drift beyond Thy loving care." We thank Thee that in all our afflictions the "angel of Thy presence" saves us. Our short-sighted human wisdom is baffled many times as we meet these strange experiences, but we thank Thee that we can leave it all to Thy great wisdom and love, assured that it is always right, always best, always well.

We thank Thee that, while our hearts are saddened by the absence of our brother, Alexander Beers, from our midst, that Thou didst give him to the church and the work of God. We thank Thee for the life of our Brother Beers. We thank Thee that Thou didst call him to the ministry of Thy word and that in his ministry he was able to accomplish, in a signal way, so much. We thank Thee for the years of service that have been given and for all their gracious results. We thank Thee that Thou wast with him during all the months of illness and that when the end came Thou wast with him to guide him into the haven of rest. We thank Thee that his tears are all wiped away. We thank Thee that never again shall a burden sadden his heart. We thank Thee this morning that, while he is gone from us, we have the assurance that he is with the great white-robed throng, singing Thy praises around the "throne of God."

We commend to Thee our beloved sister, bereft of the companionship of many years, and who must now take the journey of life alone. We thank Thee that Thou hast cheered her heart and kept her head above the waves. As the days come and go, more and more perfectly fulfil Thy promises to her and the comfort of Thy word, and as the sharp recollections come to her afresh, comfort her heart, and speak the words of peace that never were spoken before.

We ask Thy blessing upon all the interests of the church which were committed to our brother and which were dear

to him. Bless those who now have them to look after, and
if he is now permitted to realize earthly events, may his
heart be gladdened in the signs of the advancement of the
work so near to him.

Hasten the return of our Lord and the ushering in of the
everlasting triumph of righteousness, and may we all be
able to sing Thy praises in the city where there is no more
sorrow, where tears are all wiped away and where the glory
of the Lamb is the light thereof. All of this we ask in the
name of Jesus Christ, our Lord. Amen.

Note—The thoughtful and valuable assistant in the missionary
work, who is always strewing flowers in the pathway of her
friends, took this prayer down in shorthand, that the incense and
comfort it contains might be preserved for the bereaved one who
must now "take the journey of life alone." She passes it on to
other sorrowing hearts.

CHAPTER XXII

EXTRACT FROM LECTURE ON EVOLUTION

"Study to show thyself approved unto God, a workman that needeth not to be ashamed, rightly dividing the word of truth" (2 Tim. 2 : 15).

"Heaven and earth shall pass away, but my words shall not pass away" (Matt. 24 : 35).

"Thy statutes have been my songs in the house of my pilgrimage" (Psa. 119 : 54).

"Thy word is a lamp unto my feet, and a light unto my path" (Psa. 119 : 105).

Here are some names of eminent scholars who never embraced the theory of evolution. At the head I place Agassiz, who had more brains in his feet than many of the evolutionists have in their heads, Beale, Carpenter, Dana, Davy, Dawson, Faraday, Forbes, Gray, Herschel, Newton, Lord Kelvin and many others quite as illustrious. The late Joseph Cook of Boston hurled thunderbolts of righteous indignation against this miserable culprit, Evolution.

When the evolutionist speaks of the concensus of scholarship, what he has in his mind is in reality the concensus of opinion of all those who agree with him. Scientific orthodoxy is his little 2x4 doxy and all minds dissenting are necessarily hetrodox. The concensus of opinion involves a summary or a round table of all the different branches of scientific, his-

toric and ethical thought. It includes every branch
of study that the mind of man has had a grasp upon.
It not only includes the different branches of study
and various realms of thought, but must embrace all
periods in the history of the world. Moses must be
reckoned with, Job and the psalmist, David, must
not be left out, Nehemiah is to be regarded with
proper respect, the apostle Paul, the brilliant student from the feet of Gamaliel and philosopher and
orator of Mars Hill must be asked to contribute his
part; statesmen like Gladstone, Bismarck, Patrick
Henry, George Washington, Daniel Webster, Abraham Lincoln and McKinley, all believers in the divinity of Christ, and of the inspiration of the Holy
Scriptures must be consulted and allowed to contribute their part to this concensus of scholarship;
great reformers who have made the world to rejoice
by their benign influences must be reckoned in before we complete our round table of concensus of
scholarship, Savonarola, Luther, Wycliffe, Mary
Lyons, Frances E. Willard, John B. Gough, must be
reckoned when the vote is cast. Instead of the concensus of scholarship favoring evolution, the evolutionists are in a hopeless minority. The greatest
writers and historians of the world, both ancient
and modern, have given all but unanimous verdict
in favor of the Christian's Bible, the Christian's
Christ and the Christian's heaven. If you are contented to wade in the shallow pools of the evolutionists who never get in ankle deep, I prefer for my
own company the association of these mountain-
minded philosophers, statesmen, journalists, orators,
poets and reformers and feel unspeakably honored

for the privilege of sitting down at the feet of the
Master Teacher who spake as man never spake.

EVOLUTIONISTS WRONG IN TEACHING CONSTANT IMPROVEMENT

There is no evidence showing an improvement
through natural selection of anything living, including the human family, which stands at the head of
creation. Birth, growth and decline are nature's
order of things. The best scientists show that multitudes of species, both in the vegetable and animal
kingdoms, show no traces of improvement. Insects
that build the coral reefs of Florida have shown no
advancement in three hundred years. The beaver
works now just as he did in the earliest period of
history. Bees continue to build their combs and
cells just as they have for hundreds of years. It is
said that the fish are not as highly organized now as
they were originally. Prof. Ritter, of the Zoological
Department of the University of California, has
shells thrown up during terrestrial upheavals hundreds of years ago; by comparing these with the
more recent forms, he declares unhesitatingly that
there is no improvement. It is discovered that cats,
birds of prey, crocodiles and the heads of bulls discovered in the temples of upper and lower Egypt
thousands of years ago are identical with the same
animals now.

Man viewed from a biological point shows no improvement. A noted professor, Broca, who made a
critical study of the celebrated Cro-Megnon skull,
belonging to the earliest age, says: "The great volume of the brain, the magnificent development of the

frontal region, the fine eliptical profile of the anterior portion of the skull are evidences of a superiority that are found only in the most highly civilized and educated nations." Huxley himself, after having examined one of the oldest fossil skulls, significantly says, "So far as size and shape are concerned, it might have been the brain of a philosopher. What is true of the brain is equally true of the entire human body." Scientists skilled in comparative biological studies declare that the statuettes recently discovered in Crete show in every respect a development of muscle, sinew and bone at this early age and everything in connection with the arm, to correspond in minutest detail to the forearm of man as found in this age. Many of their theories have been hopelessly exploded of late.

HORSE PEDIGREE

Evolutionists have endeavored to prove that our modern horse is simply the result of an evolutionary process of a similar animal that lived in bygone ages. A Chicago professor in the University of Chicago says the modern horse can be definitely traced through a series of intermediate stages to a primitive species having four toes on each foot. Our good college professor has been much embarrassed on learning that still another animal has been discovered having five toes. No less a scientist than Henry Fairfield Osborne, of the Museum of Natural History, New York, has recently given an account of the possibility of the discovery of another animal having fifteen toes. Our friends of evolution are entitled to our sympathy when they try so hard to toe the mark under such adverse circumstances. It is now learned that the fossils of the four-toed animal, the five-toed animal and the fifteen-toed animal, if such there be, are entirely different and bear no resemblance whatever to the bones of our modern horse. The evolutionist does not know but what the four-toed animal may be a higher order. Indeed there may be some even striking resemblances between the four-toed animal and the modern horse, as there are resemblances between a cow and a crow, a man and a mouse, each having a head, with its eyes, nose and ears, and each having feet with which to walk. I would be ashamed of a grammar scholar in Seattle Seminary who would try to connect these animals on these superficial supposed resemblances. I have the most profound respect and the highest regard for an honest and unbiased mind. Impartial investigation is welcomed by me. I claim that we have every reason to call in question the intellectual honesty of a man who takes only the time to investigate one side. If half the attention was given to the study of the differences between the species that is now occupied in trying to point out resemblances, the entire subject would appear in a different light. The old astronomers, with their preconceived opinions, went to the heavens with their theories and not for them. This one-sidedness has retarded the progress of science for years. We now allow in the evolutionist what we decry in the astronomer. He has his little pet theory of the arrangement of the world, the origin of life, the development of man, and ransacks every field of knowledge, celestial, terrestrial, telescopic, microscopic, philisophic and diabolic, to prove and substantiate the deplorable little theory that he has hatched from his own fancy or plagiarized from some one else. No better specimen could be invented or argument offered against this theory of improvement than the evolutionists themselves— their cheap reasoning, shallow philosophy and illogical conclusions.

THE ABRUPT TRANSMUTATION OF THE SPECIES

This is one of the most vital points in the theory of evolution. It teaches that by natural selection and survival of the fittest, a lower or inferior species by an inexplainable change becomes a species very much higher. This has been studied and an attempt vainly made to discover the link that connects man with the anthropoid ape. The missing link has been the golden fleece after which thousands of evolutionists have gone in quest. Reports have survived and died and were buried, concerning this wonderful link. Thousands of students in our higher universities of learning are taught by eminent professors that this link has been supplied in the famous Java skeleton. A Dutch doctor by the name of Du Bois, near the city of Java was excavating one day, or digging potatoes, and he discovered a tooth. Later on he found the bone of an arm and about thirty feet from this another bone. In a jocular manner he said to his wife, "I have discovered the long sought for missing link. The bones of this animal certainly are what the world has waited for these years." The struggling Darwinites, grasping for a straw, immediately circulated the news throughout the scientific world that the missing link had been discovered. They dignified the bones with the wonderful name "Pithecanthropus Erectus," which in ordinary language simply means the erect ape man. The ape or monkey, becoming tired of walking on all fours, resolved to become a man. He immediately stands upon his hind feet, uses his front feet for hands, sits on his tail until it is worn off because it is a useless appendage, and at once commences to invent machines, writes histories, measures the distance of the sun, travels among the stars, takes excursions to and through the milky way, becomes a preacher of the gospel, or runs for the presidency of the United States, or is crowned king of Great Britain. Indeed this is a most abrupt transmutation of the species, were it not for one simple but embarrassing fact—it never took place. Du Bois found himself famous, and in the writings of such men as Hechel and others, he is called the scholarly Du Bois, the learned Doctor Du Bois, the eminent Du Bois, and other terms of complimentary endearment, sufficiently weighty to sink a ship, but this eminent and scholarly Du Bois was none other than a very ordinary country Dutch doctor. He lived a few miles from Java and attended the sick and to make ends meet, planted a garden and hoed potatoes. These bones were found in his potato patch; they were later sent to Germany and placed in a museum where they are today. Later on, twenty-seven leading scientific men went and examined them. After the most careful scrutiny, ten decided that they were the bones of a monkey and seven that they were the bones of some animal and might possibly be the bones of the Pithecanthropus

Erectus. Later on, however, Dr. D. C. Cunningham, an eminent scientist and one of the highest authorities in Great Britain on comparative anatomy, went and personally examined these bones. He declares unhesitatingly—and challenges the scientific world to prove the contrary—that they were the bones of a man, the bones of an ape or a monkey or the bones of some animal. What seems passing strange to me is that many of our professors in our modern universities are still palming off these bones on the unsuspecting students. For my part, I have something very much more real and satisfactory than a lot of old skeletons or bones that have been wasting and drying for lo, these many years. They are farther trying to palm off this abrupt transmutation of the species by other arguments such as the development of the human hand and eye, rudimentary or useless members, metamorphosis, etc. Volumes are written that the paw of an animal or the hand of a man was at one time the fin of a fish. They have, however, met with a very serious obstruction in the history of a whale. This mammal has been particularly bothersome; in fact, the evolutionist finds himself about as much at sea as does the whale. He does not know whether the whale is a land animal developing into a fish, or a fish aspiring to be a man and get a seat in the U. S. senate, but while he would reject the story of Jonah being swallowed by a whale, he has been contented to swallow this sea monster at one gulp, and say nothing about it. He tells us that the eye, or an eye used to exist on the top of the head, that there is a useless gland or rudimentary appendage to be found there, which shows that an eye formerly existed, when the now man was once a fish or a reptile and went head-first; while not willing to concede that there ever was an eye on the top of a man's head, yet I will be generous enough and sufficiently broad to recognize that there is every evidence of the existence of a soft or silly spot in the brain of the evolutionist. I have referred to the monkey sitting on its tail until it was worn off. Much has been written on this subject of the rudimentary appendages. The range of investigation has covered all the fields from whales to snails and from men to midgets, but in all this talk, satisfactory argument is sadly lacking. Pigeons have been experimented with, butterflies have been transported from one climate to another and very great changes produced thereby. The insect becomes larger, the wings longer and the hues much more rich and beautiful and the power of locomotion greatly accelerated in a tropical climate. It is even called a different species, but that does not make it such. The explanation is obvious and can be understood by all. A rather amusing story is told, the truth for which I will not vouch. An evolutionist conceived the idea that by cutting off the tails of mice and propagating new races, eventually he would produce a mouse without a tail. He cut off and propagated, but the tail kept growing; cut off and propagated, and yet the tail grew—again cut off and propagated and still the tail appeared; cut off and propagated, and yet my tale is not told; cut off and propagated, and still the wonder grew and the tail appeared, until at last, baffled and discouraged, he gave up the job, remarking that "Fate is against me, and that old adage is true, 'There is a divinity that shapes our ends, rough hew them as we will.' "

The foundation principle and predominating idea of this transmutation theory is to prove that Genesis is scientifically inaccurate. Everything after its kind is a statement in the old Book, and the test of ages has proven it to be indisputably true. Fish after its kind, fowl after its kind, fool after his kind, evolutionist after his kind. This gulf between the species is so broad and so deep that it is impassable. "The only attempt that we have in the Bible to cross it was made by Balaam's mule, who tried to cross over and speak with man's voice, but the angel of the Lord, with drawn sword, stopped the long-eared evolutionist then and there." This principle in Genesis of everything after its kind is the basis for all human knowledge that is recognized in every branch of scientific usage. In no other branch is it recognized more than in materia medica. Each germ produces a specific disease; the typhus germ could not produce small-pox or scarlet fever. Every disease germ in the universe, every atom of matter in the world, every law by which this great world is governed, flies directly in the face of the evolutionist. Lord Lytton very pertinently asked the question, "Why strive where the gods must yield, why fly in the face of facts, in the face of the laws of our own being, in the face of the laws of our universe, in the face of the teaching of the Holy Bible and of demonstrated facts of a thousand years?" The world in which we live was not evolved, but created by the touch of the divine hand. He is found in every atom, flashes in every wave, shimmers in every dew drop and scintillates from every star.

"There is a God that fashions all that is,
Whose glory crowns the rugged mountain heights,
And echoes in the anthem of the seas."

Final recommendation as to its treatment:

1.   Bury it in the Sahara Desert, face downward.

2.   Take it to the North Pole and put it under ten thousand fathoms of ice.

3.   Sink it in the depths of the ocean.

4.   Send it in exile to Siberia, and its promoters along with it.

5.   Take all the books and make a pyramid as high as the snowy crest of Mt. Rainier, take all of J. D. R.'s oil and pour it over them and set fire to it. Take all the promises of the blessed old Book and read them during the conflagration, then join in singing,

"Praise God from whom all blessings flow."

CHAPTER XXIII

EXTRACTS FROM SERMONS—ORIGINAL POEMS

WE KNOW

There is "a God who fashioned all that is,
Whose footprints shine upon the milky way,
Whose glory crowns the rugged mountain peaks,
And echoes in the anthems of the sea."
This is His glorious world, made by that loving hand,
That binds every broken heart-string.
And guides every burdened spirit
To that place of "perfect rest."
There is a God whose resplendent glory
Streams through every upturned face
And fills each trusting soul
With hopes of immortality.
We know.

The black angel of night called Death ends not all;
A childlike trust in Him whose "lips of love
Kiss away" all tormenting fear,
That we shall forever sleep in nameless dust,
And ever points with greatest joy
To a higher life beyond this vale of fleeting phantoms.
The unfolding of which scarce begins
From childhood to the grave,
From youth to hoary age,
To that endless life, measured not by the flight of years,
But by the endless cycles of eternity.
We know.

We know that from the arcana of each and every heart
There radiates a hope divine, too intense to be

Smothered by the agnostic's piteous wail of doubt.
"The dove flying forth from the ark of each individual life"
Returns again, bearing in triumph the olive branch of hope,
Piercing the clouds of doubt and error,
And brings back the blessed truth.
                              We know.

We know—this is the voice of God,
Which from the Delphic cave within
Speaks to every heart in accents sweet,
Telling the savage wild of that glorious life to be,
The tissues of which we weave in colors more radiant far
Than the rainbow's brightest hues,
More glorious than the roseate sunset's glow
That gilds the western sky.
                              We know.

"We know," sound forth the words of Holy Writ divine,
Spoken by the inspired writer, lifted from the mists of
        doubt,
If this house of clay in which I have tented long
Should by the ravages of time be dissolved,
I have another building fair, a glorious house,
By hands not made, in that "better country"
Where Death a stranger is and doubt never enters,
Where the bloom of eternal youth paints every cheek.
                        We know, we know.
                              —*Alexander Beers.*

Extracts from the last sermon preached by Alexander Beers on January 23, 1921, at Oakland, California:

This is the last meeting in which I shall have the privilege to preach, and I am sure it is a privilege to speak to you dear people. I enjoy having you precious people with us. Brother Barnhart will be here on Thursday. On Friday the Sunday-school conven-

tion will meet here, and on Thursday Brother Mac-
Geary will speak to us.

(Here Mr. Beers read the fourth chapter of Ephe-
sians.)

I desire to use the thirtieth verse of this chapter
which I have read in your hearing: "Grieve not the
Holy Spirit of God whereby ye are sealed unto the
day of redemption."

If you could trace the tragedies that have been
enacted from the time of the slaying of Abel to the
present time, you would find that it has all been due
to the fact that men have grieved the Holy Spirit
and have not listened to the admonition given in this
chapter, "grieve not the Holy Spirit." All the tragedies of the world have come from grieving the Holy
Spirit. The tragedies of individual lives come from
individuals grieving the Holy Spirit. The tragedies
of countries and nations come because of grieving
away the Holy Spirit.

It has been said by one man that God has been
crucified in every age. The first dispensation was
that of God the Father. God the Father was crucified, and the antediluvian world closed up that reign
with the tragedy of the flood. Secondly came the
dispensation of God the Son. Jesus Christ was
crucified on the cross, and Calvary's scene closed the
dispensation of God the Son. We are now living in
the dispensation of the Holy Spirit.

The sin against the Holy Ghost is the greatest sin
of the world. Jesus said, "All manner of sin and
blasphemy shall be forgiven unto men, but the blasphemy against the Holy Ghost shall not be forgiven
unto men. And whosoever speaketh a word against

the Son of man it shall be forgiven him; but whosoever speaketh against the Holy Ghost it shall not be forgiven him, neither in this world, neither in the world to come." I believe that the antediluvians committed the unpardonable sin; that Ananias and Sapphira committed the unpardonable sin; that the cities of the plain committed the unpardonable sin; that the cities of Pompeii and Herculaneum, and the nations of Greece and Rome, with all their power, wealth and grandeur, committed the unpardonable sin. I believe that Oakland is in danger of committing the unpardonable sin. I think that the United States is in danger of committing the unpardonable sin; and that San Francisco is in danger of committing the unpardonable sin. I believe that churches are in danger of getting into forms and ceremonies and grieving away the Holy Spirit.

There is great danger of sinning against the Holy Ghost until you are lost. I could use all of my time in relating tragedies of wrecked lives and homes because young people have had the light of God on their hearts and have rejected it.

At one time we had two children in our school, and both were in the grade department. The girl was a very fine elocutionist. The mother saw that the child was talented, and she also saw that the Spirit of God was working on the hearts of her boy and girl. Finally she took them out of school and had them prepare for the stage, where she thought they could make big money. I remember the mother asking me to buy the furniture necessary to give them lessons in theatrical art. In a short time they were both on the stage. But judgment seemed to fall and came in a very short time. The son lost his health and had to go to California. I remember the girl came to our home and wanted some help. We helped her to get down to see her brother. He finally became able to get around again and she came back, only to go down a little later and see him die. One of the last things he said was, "I think that if we had stayed in the school, things would have gone better with us." Later the girl got sick and died without God. I received one of the saddest letters from this mother. Among other things she said, "Here are my children both dead because of what I did." We all knew what she had done.

I am not going to turn this service into a class meeting, but I am going to call you to witness if there has not been a time in your life—I don't mean a general time—but if there has not been a special time when the Holy Spirit strove with you. I believe people have but three or four times when the Spirit really strives with them. When I refer to strivings of the Spirit I refer to Genesis 6:3, "My Spirit shall not always strive with man." The Holy Spirit will grapple with you. When Jacob wrestled with the angel there was real striving. The angel wanted to get away. Jacob said he would not let him go until he blessed him, although when the angel saw that he prevailed not against him he touched the hollow of Jacob's thigh, and the hollow of his thigh was out of joint as they wrestled. There are certain times and certain places where the Spirit comes and battles with you.

I can go back in my own life and see three wrestlings. I was a lad of eight when the blessed Spirit first strove with me. I had not been taught the Bible. It is wonderful how the Holy Spirit will talk to us about the Bible when we have not the knowledge of its truths. Oh, the blessed Spirit will guide you into all truth. You take the thought of wrestling mentioned in the chapter, there is the thought of bringing the bottom of your life up, doing all that God would have you do.

Time went on until I was fourteen years of age. Then I felt another mighty striving of the Spirit, and, in a sense, gave myself to God. My father was taken sick and we thought he was going to die. The doctor told mother that he would not recover, and I knew that mother was anxious to have the preacher do something for him. The preacher was called and prayed for him, then father wanted him to sing,

> "Come ye sinners, poor and needy,
> Weak and wounded, sick and sore;
> Jesus, ready, stands to save you,
> Full of pity, love and power.
> He is able, He will save you."

They sang that song all the way through. As I listened to that my whole life came before me. I slipped away from the place of prayer and went back in the woods and prayed to God for myself, and my father, and earnestly confessed my sins. As I came back from where I had been praying, I met my sister who had also been out in the bushes praying. That was the Spirit of God speaking to us.

When I was nineteen years of age, under the mighty preaching of the Word, the Spirit strove with me again and warned me to seek God. I do not know that I should have had another warning. I might have had another, but it seemed to me that that was the last call. It was now or never. I tell you, getting to God is a very serious thing, and it is a very serious thing when you trifle with the Holy Spirit. When He knocks at your heart's door and tells you what to do, walk in the light, but do not grieve Him.

There are many ways of grieving the Holy Spirit. I grieved Him by not going far enough when only eight years of age. When fourteen I grieved Him again by not going far enough. I might have grieved Him again in 1881 by not going far enough. Very often people come up to the parting of the ways because they do not go far enough. They do not meet the conditions. I am getting at the necessity of our coming to God, putting self into the hands of the Spirit and our whole being absolutely into God's hands; yielding ourselves to God entirely and com pletely until we know that we have given ourselves to God, and that there is not one single thing that we have not surrendered. We must give ourselves unreservedly to Him.

A man sees a fine field. He likes it and says, "My, I wish I had that field." But wishing for it does not bring it to him. He has to pay the price. He goes to the owner and tells him that he wants it and asks the price. "I want ten thousand dollars." "Won't you take nine thousand dollars?" "No." "Won't you take nine thousand nine hundred dollars?" "No." God gives His price and he won't change it. How many people think they can get through to heaven by going the cheaper way. This man is going to buy the ten thousand dollar farm

and he has nine thousand nine hundred and ninety-
nine dollars. He hands this to the owner and says,
"I believe the place is mine." "No, you pay the full
price and the land is yours." When you have paid
the whole price you do not have to guess or think
that the desired article is yours.

I believe that faith is the evidence of things not
seen. It is the absolute evidence of things that are
not seen in your own life and heart, and, dear ones,
if you are giving the Holy Spirit an opportunity He
will lead you into all truth. Praise God! Hallelujah! He will lead you into a good place where you
will not be doubting what the Lord will do for you.
He will lead you into a deeper and more blessed experience.

We can grieve the Holy Spirit by not saying "Yes"
to everything the Lord tells us. We can grieve the
Holy Spirit by not receiving the light that the Lord
gives us. I think that a great many people come up
to the parting of the ways there. Then again, there
is something more the Bible says, "Put off concerning the former conversation the old man, which is
corrupt." The "old man" is as old as the human
family. He is as old as the fall. He is in every human heart. He is the stronger man and he is hunt-
ing you up. You feel your need of entire sanctification. There is something in your heart that will
spring up and trouble you until you have it taken
out by the Lord.

You say when you are saved and sanctified that
is all there is for you. Oh, no! no! I would not say
that! You are just engrafted in the vine. When
you are sanctified you are just purged. That is the

starting point. God wants you to grow. The only way to do that is to follow the Holy Spirit, and not grieve or quench Him. A great many people fear to give themselves over to God for fear they will become fanatics. We are not in very grave danger of fanaticism. We should praise the Lord at all times, and especially when we enter into His sanctuary. Why do we allow demonstrations at university games? But when it comes to praising God, we are very modest and want everything to be quiet and nice. Why do we allow men on the football field to yell? They have their rooters and we can hear them for miles, but we forbid any shouting in religious meetings. But I say when the Holy Spirit comes there will be a demonstration in some manner, and you will be so full that you can't help demonstrating in some way.

I remember hearing of an incident that occurred in Libby prison during the Civil War. One day two of our men were to be executed. The sentences had been passed and the time had been set for the execution. Everything was as gloomy as the grave, and every one was mourning. They had been given time to prepare for death, and the hour had arrived for their execution. The scaffold had been erected and the two men stepped up to seal their doom. Just as the time had come for the execution, a messenger came in and handed a telegram to the executioner. It read, "We have captured Fitzhugh Lee, and if you have these two young men executed we will execute Lee." What did these men say when they heard the contents of the telegram? Do you suppose they said, "It is very nice that we are not to be executed"? Why, every one in the jail demonstrated in some way. They laughed and cried, shouted and kissed each other. Then they carried these young men around the jail on their shoulders and sang everything they could think of. The funeral was turned into a song service, and patriotic and religious songs were lustily sung.

I tell you, my dear ones, God Almighty came into my heart and took away my sins, and said He would remember them never again, and then the blessed Holy Spirit took the efficacy of the shed blood and applied that blood to my heart, and drove out that "old man"—drove him clear out beyond the border line, to be gone forever, and God the Father came into my heart and filled me, and I know that He dwells in me now, and enriches me, I know I am a child of God, a sanctified man! And then you tell me to keep still? No! No! Bless the Lord! I am going to have my *Amen!* my *Praise the Lord!* my *Hallelujah!* my *Glory!* my *"Oh, give thanks unto the Lord, for He is good, for His mercy endureth forever.* Let the redeemed of the Lord say so, whom He hath redeemed from the hand of the enemy." Hallelujah to our God!

Grieve not the Spirit of God. Let Him have His way with you.

There are two ways to shut off the fire. First, put no more coal on. Many people don't put enough fuel on their souls to keep them from freezing. Put on fuel. Put on the anthracite of God's great promises. Get one of the great salvation back-logs and get some of the promises, and then get the baptism of the Holy Spirit and have a big fire. Praise God!

The second way to quench the fire is to just shut off the draft. Simply neglect the means of grace and fail to do your duty. If you get to praising the Lord, there will be a sound of abundance of rain, and sinners will be converted. I want more coal. Bless God!

"He shall baptize you with the Holy Ghost and with fire." Hallelujah! Praise God! We want the holy refining fire from heaven. You say, "Brother Beers, you are getting on dangerous ground." Oh, no, dear ones; I am getting on the safest ground. I am not going to live without the presence of the Holy Spirit in my life. And if you are going to heaven, the devil will be after you with all the arsenal of the army of the flesh.

I think the devil has a great big arsenal and he has captured the salvation flags of many churches. His imps say, "We have captured the preachers' 'Amens.' We have captured a Free Methodist's 'Amens.' We have captured some of the 'Glorys' of others. We have captured the 'Hallelujahs' of that brother. We have stilled the shouts of those pilgrims. They haven't shouted for a long time." Let us see that the devil does not get our "Hallelujahs." Let us go in for good old-fashioned religion. I am for it. You say, "Brother Beers, you are beside yourself." No! Bless God! I am with the Lord. I feel like singing with David, "Bless the Lord, O my soul, and all that is within me bless His holy name." Hallelujah!

Let us go in for the riches of His glory, for the outpouring of His Spirit. We can all have that. Praise God!

Grieve not the Holy Spirit. Let Him lead you.
Let Him have His way with you, dear ones. Amen.

NOTE—The notes of this sermon were taken in shorthand
by Miss Vera Salamonson and were transcribed nine months
after Mr. Beers' death. The Holy Spirit was so abundantly
poured out during the preaching that it was utterly impossible to get all the points of the sermon, so only a brief ab-
stract is here offered.

A SONG OF REDEMPTION

Look, behold our Christ in heaven,
  As He sits upon the throne.
Clothed in robes of dazzling splendor
  And the glory all His own!
On His brow a royal halo,
  In His hand the sceptre true,
He has swayed through countless ages,
  Over worlds all to Him true.

He is clad in kingly beauty
  As He stands before the throne,
Countless myriads of all ages
  Laud and praise the Mighty One.
He's the chiefest of ten thousand
  In His majesty and might,
And the altogether lovely
  In His robes of spotless white.

To this Son of rarest beauty
  Angels, cherubs, seraphs bright
Make to Him their glad obeisance,
  For Him take their swiftest flight.
Myriad worlds roll on in splendor
  At the mandates of Him still,
On and on in silent homage,
  Glad for aye to do His will.

Vast creations none can number,
  From unfathomed depths of blue,
Wheel along in solemn grandeur
  To their Maker always true.
But, alas, one world so favored
  From its course has turned aside,
Plunging down, still down in darkness,
  Into sin's most fearful tide.

Farther on from God, their Maker,
  On, away from Christ their friend,
Ever on through darkest midnight,
  Till they reach doom's bitter end.
Heavens draped in deepest mourning,
  Justice says they all must die,
For the law of God is broken,
  God, Jehovah, can not lie.

Mercy stands upon the threshold,
  Pleads and pleads with tear dimmed eye,
"God of justice, canst Thou save them,
  For their sins I'd gladly die.
Shall this world be lost forever?
  Sink beneath sin's threatening wave?
Can you find no eye to pity?
  Is there now no arm to save?"

Justice speaks in tones most solemn,
  "Knowest thou not Mercy fair,
That my law can not be broken,
  But demands obedience rare?"
"If we find a being holy,
  Full of life and kingly grace,
Could he satisfy you, Justice?
  Could he take the sinner's place?"

Justice says, "My law is holy,
  And to meet its just demands
None of all created beings
  In man's place can ever stand."

Then the Lord of life and glory
  Speaks to Justice at His side,
"I to earth will go to save them,
  I will stem sin's awful tide."

Turns He then from heaven so glorious,
  Turns from crowns and throne on high,
Lays aside His robe and sceptre,
  Comes to earth to bleed and die.
From the mansions high in heaven
  To a manger He descends,
And the King of life immortal
  Now a servant lowly bends.

Hear Him groaning in the garden,
  See Him dying on the tree,
Drink the dregs of bitterest anguish,
  Bringing joy to you and me.
From the cross they bear Him gently,
  Lay Him low in Joseph's tomb,
All their fondest hopes lie buried;
  Settles on them deepest gloom.

But the bands of death can never
  Hold the mighty, conquering One,
See, He breaks them all asunder,
  Victory gains for every one.
Now He walks the earth in triumph,
  Won the battle fought so well,
Sending dread and consternation
  Through the very gates of hell.

Oh! my soul, thou hast a Savior,
  One so mighty, so divine,
Saving ever to the utmost
  Every power and gift of thine.
Of His love so pure and tender
  Thou to all the earth must tell
That the nations now in darkness
  In His light may ever dwell.

Sing it forth with joy and gladness,
  From the hilltops to the plain,
Shout it from the highest mountain,
  Tell of your eternal gain.
First at home we speak the tidings,
  Our Jerusalem so dear!
Then still farther in Judea
  Ring it out in accents clear.

Sail beyond the surging billows
  Of the ocean's restless tide,
Bearing news to every nation
  Of our Christ, the crucified.
To the sunrise kingdom hastening,
  This salvation loud proclaim,
Speeding on to China's millions,
  Tell with joy the Savior's name.

Tell it to thy dark faced brother
  By the Congo's mournful roar,
To thy sad-eyed sister weeping
  On the sacred Ganges shore.
Every isle shall hear the tidings,
  All oppressed at last go free,
Every prison house must open,
  Earth will chant her jubilee.
                    —*By Alexander Beers.*

"America for Americans" is supreme selfishness. This principle carried out, would mean dry rot, political, social and religious disintegration. Our motto must be "America for Christ," and, "Christ for the World." We have been highly favored and richly blest of God, and we must bless others. We are exalted in point of privilege, and must uplift those below us. We are blessed with earth's bounties, that we may bestow benefactions upon others. No man is blessed for the sake of himself alone, but that his blessing may bless another. A nation is not prospered and exalted for its own glory and advancement, but for the sake of helping others not so highly favored. If the man who has been trusted with money does not understand the sacredness of stewardship, and do his duty by way of helping others, his gold is cankered and his garments motheaten. His wealth will become an unmitigated curse instead of a blessing. The rich person who allows the yellow gold in molten form to so fill his ear as to make it impossible for him to hear the cry of want, is poor indeed now, and will be a pitiless pauper in the world to come.—*Extract taken from one of Mr. Beers' sermons.*

TO OUR SOLDIER BOYS

Welcome home, our gallant heroes!
  Bravely did you fight and well,
All your noble deeds of valor
  History's pages soon will tell.

Welcome home, our own brave warriors,
  Wear your laurels proudly won,
Laurels richer and more glorious,
  Than were won by Spartan son.

Welcome home, the winds repeat it,
  Welcome home, the waves reply,
Welcome all ye brave defenders
  Of a people doomed to die.

Welcome home, our hearts keep saying,
  Welcome back, ye boys in blue,
Bearing high our glorious banner,
  Never trailed in dust by you.

Welcome back, "Old Glory," welcome!
  Thou shalt ever be unfurled,
Floating in thy triumph proudly,
  Bringing freedom to the world.

Welcome to each town and hamlet,
  To each village and each plain,
Welcome to our homes and firesides,
  Welcome, welcome, home again.

Welcome, welcome, swell the chorus,
  Waft it out upon the breeze,
Let it echo, ever echo,
  Through our islands of the seas.

Let the welcome reach fair Cuba,
  Rescued from the power of Spain,
Sound it forth in Porto Rico,
  Welcome, welcome, once again.
          —*Alexander Beers.*

"PEACE AND GOOD WILL"

Most precious are these words. They are wafted to us from heaven and bring with them the aroma of the skies. They fell directly from the lips of angelic visitors as they sang over Bethlehem's manger on the night of the Nativity. "Peace on earth"—our language would be impoverished without these words, which originated in heaven.

The world is far from this ideal condition now. Hate, discord and unrest are found everywhere. The time will come, thank God, when things will be changed. The Prince of Peace will return and reign without a rival from "the rivers to the ends of the earth."

Ruskin caught the vision of the millennial glory and describes it as this literary artist alone was capable of doing:

"They come, they come, how fair their feet,
　Their glistening hosts increase
Upon the glassy mountain paths
　They come who publish peace.

"And victory, fair victory,
　Our enemies are ours.
For all the earth is clasped in light
　And all the world with flowers.

"Ah, still bedimmed and wet with dew
　But wait the little while,
And with the radiant deathless rose
　The wilderness shall smile.

"And every tender living thing
　Shall feed by streams of rest;
Nor lamb shall from the fold be lost
　Nor nursling from the nest."

　　　—Extract taken from one of Mr. Beers' Sermons.

VIRGINIA

Dear Virginia! Land of beauty!
On Potomac's crystal shore,
Where Mount Vernon's sacred story
Speaks thy praises evermore;
Of thy glory I am musing,
As the golden setting sun
Throws a beauty and a halo
On the tomb of Washington.

CHORUS

Dear Virginia! land of beauty!
Gem of southern states so fair;
Land of love, of youth, and childhood,
Oft my heart still wanders there.

Oh! the grandeur of thy forest,
On the mellow autumn days!
Heavens filled with richest splendor,
And the earth with golden rays!
Teaching us of life immortal
In our heavenly city there,
Gates of pearl and walls of jasper,
Shining with a radiance fair.

Snowy lilies, sweet magnolias,
Send their perfume everywhere,
And thy lovely mountain laurels
Shed a fragrance rich and rare;
Feathered songsters of thy pine groves,
Make the leafy temples ring
With their choruses of music,
Telling of eternal spring!
—*Alexander Beers.*

BEAUTIFUL WASHINGTON

I would sing of a state of fairest renown,
  Nestling close by the shimmering sea,
One far more resplendent in beauty her own
  Than all of her sisters to me.

CHORUS

Dear Evergreen State, how I love thee,
  Oh, Washington, Washington, dear;
The queen of this glorious Union,
  The fairest art thou of the fair.

Thy snowy-capped mountains, whose heights most sublime
  Tower up to the azure above,
Proclaiming in accents that never were told,
  That the Builder and Maker is Love.

How glorious thy sun as it sinks 'neath the sea,
  Outrivaling an artist's best dream,
Tinting heaven and earth with a glory divine,
  Proclaiming a beauty supreme.

Thy proud flowing rivers, transparent and pure,
  Roll on in their courses so grand;
Thy silvery brooklets dance in their glee
  To gladden this fair promised land.

The proud ships of commerce from far-away shores
  Drop anchor within our fair bay,
To court our rich treasures of forest and mine,
  And bear them in triumph away.

                              —Alexander Beers.

"THE CHRISTMAS SPIRIT"

Text: Luke 2:13, 14.

"And suddenly there was with the angel a multitude of the heavenly host praising God, and saying, Glory to God in the highest, and on earth peace, good will towards men."

"That night when in the Egyptian skies
 The mystic star dispensed its light,
A blind man turned him in his sleep
 And dreamed that he had sight.

"That night when shepherds heard the song
 Of hosts angelic choiring near,
A deaf man lay in slumber's spell
 And dreamed that he could hear.

"That night when in the cattle's stall
 Slept child and mother in humble fold,
A cripple turned his twisted limbs
 And dreamed that he was whole.

"That night when o'er the new-born Babe
 A tender mother rose to lean,
A loathsome leper smiled in sleep
 And dreamed that he was clean."

If we could all catch the sentiment of this heavenly strain and properly interpret the spirit of the text, we would be better Christians, and the world greatly enriched by our lives. Christianity is a message of good cheer to a lost world.

Standing one beautiful Sunday morning in London near St. Pauls on my way to attend church at the Spurgeon Tabernacle, the celebrated chimes commenced to play. The great city was brought under the magic spell of worship and reverence. I felt like standing with uncovered head as I listened to the sacred strains raining down upon me from the dome above. "Nearer, My God, to Thee" and other sacred hymns were played, and my soul was inspired by the music, and bathed in the atmosphere. I thought of Joaquin Miller's poetic gem, "the silver spilling from the skies at night to walk upon." The music from the silver toned bells distilled like a benediction from the skies. Old London seemed to forget her sin, and the mighty pulse of commerce apparently ceased to beat for the time. It prepared me all the better to "worship the Lord in the beauty of holiness." Our text brings heaven very near to earth, and lifts earth near the border-land of heaven. The vault of God's infinite sky of divine love encircling a lost world constitutes the belfry, and sweet and melodious angelic voices chime forth to a discordant world the praises of God.

I would that all the members of this church, and that Christians everywhere, would learn the significance of this message, and carry it forth not on Christmas day only, but throughout the entire life. God grant we may learn from this message the true spirit of Christmas.

DIFFERENCES MELT AWAY

For a number of years I have tried to be a close student of human life. I have been interested in watching the manifestations of a Christmas spirit as Christmas day approaches. I have been impressed with the rising of the tide of sympathy akin to the coming in of the irresistible tides of the ocean. People think less about themselves and more of others; a spirit of democracy is felt; good cheer and best wishes fill the atmosphere. Little differ-

ences that had hitherto existed between friends melt
away as icicles melt before the genial rays of the
sun. Old grudges are forgotten and wounds are
healed. Things that have separated men and com-
munities, give way and are buried in tombs of forgetfulness, with no tombstone to mark the burial
place. Gifts are sent to friends, and the poor and
needy are not forgotten. There is a feeling of genuine kinship, as though every one recognized the
Fatherhood of God. The rich and poor meet together on a common level in contemplating the goodness and love of God. All are thankful to the generous Benefactor. Kindness is king, and sways a
royal sceptre.

Is it not a pity—if not a tragedy—that this spirit
does not predominate during the entire year? What
a change would take place if the Christmas spirit
should be projected into the following twelve
months! Who can prophesy as to the changes that
would take place? The world would witness a revo-
lution that would find no parallel in the annals of
history. Many would be willing to affirm that the
millennium had come, and that Christ's kingdom
had really been established upon earth.

NATIONAL POWER NOT MISUSED

A rich nation has a responsibility toward the
poorer nations. America has in many respects been
an object lesson to the world. With all of our
faults, we have had crowning virtues. The national
greatness and wonderful power has not been used
for selfishness. China takes off her hat to America's

generosity. A few years ago other nations were looking upon China with greedy eyes, and planning the dismemberment of that great empire. Our country had the opportunity of joining the vandal nations in this conspiracy, and of being rewarded by a generous slice of territory. She positively refused the temptation, and said to the nations of the world, "No, stand back; hands off!" The nations wisely took the hint, and China was not dismembered. Thank God for this spirit! Missionaries from the United States are thrice welcome in China. The Gospel is well received in the Celestial Empire, and our country looked upon as the one that China will desire to pattern after as her civilization advances. England must account yet for forcing the opium traffic upon China. America must be careful, as she is in danger of losing prestige with China by permitting tobacco syndicates to flood her people with the deadly cigarette. We are informed that more than fifty-one million of these cigarettes were recently carried in one boat to a Chinese port. Let us awake and beware. Now is the time to act.

We demonstrated to the world our unselfishness in our generous attitude toward Cuba when Spain had her bloody hands upon the throat of that island and others. Uncle Sam sent a Dewey and a fleet of battleships to Manila and demanded that Spain release her grasp. The entire world knows full well that there was no ulterior motive back of our freeing Cuba. The work was done in the interest of humanity, and not for the sake of territory or for the purpose of colonization. This is the practical manifestation of the Christmas spirit by a nation.

OUR DUTY TO STRICKEN EUROPE

No logic save the logic of need is required to show our obligations there. Poor devastated Belgium, lying prostrate before our eyes, and stretching forth her helpless hands to us. This country must be the Good Samaritan, and show her greatness by pouring in the oil and wine for the necessary relief. Would it not enhance our greatness, and add to our glory, if we as a people would largely forget ourselves this Christmas time, and make our gifts as generous as possible for those who are so needy? Our generosity and kindness should be manifested alike to all the stricken and suffering nations of the earth. What can be done now by way of temporal relief, will add immeasurably to our influence when the time comes for negotiations of peace. "Not to be ministered unto, but to minister" would look well in the dome of our National Capitol. Our country must be the Polar Star of nations, a true example to all who aspire. Old glory will shine with a heavenly glory when she stands for "peace on earth and good will toward men."

A PROPHECY FOR THE FUTURE

We are not skeptical concerning the outcome of Christianity. That Christ will triumph over every foe is clearly prophesied. The kingdoms of this world will become the kingdoms of our Lord and of His Christ.

Many would have us believe that the ghastly European war has sounded the death knell to Christianity. Nothing could be more foolish or superficial.

This horrible war does not sound the death knell of Christianity, but it does mean the utter collapse of imperialism. No longer will we hear of the "divine right of kings." The star of true Christian democracy has arisen, never to go down. The common people will soon come into their own. The oppressor will be banished forever to some island of forgetfulness. Thrones are tottering and kings are trembling; crowns are making heads very uneasy. Christianity has begotten a civilization that has outgrown old forms. The mighty dynamic force of the gospel is bursting its way through obstacles of centuries. The hand writing of dissatisfaction of old conditions is plainly seen on the wall. The blazing finger of justice points with unerring accuracy to an outraged humanity, and God is saying, "Let my people go."

Christianity is throwing off the embarrassing increments of the past. The church of the living God is catching the spirit of her leader. She is going on steadily to the immortal and eternal victory. Let no pessimistic wail be heard or discordant note sounded during this glad Christmas time. Let no prophecy of doubtful things concerning the cause of Christ be heard.

Thest strains of celestial music still cheer and inspire the church on her glorious mission—the conquest of the world. She will continue with her task until the world with all of its sorrow will have been brought to the feet of Christ. She will soon reach the shore of that realm where her victorious host will camp, and before an assembled universe raise the white banner of eternal victory.

"Jesus shall reign where'er the sun
Doth his successive journeys run.
His kingdom spread from shore to shore,
Till suns shall rise and set no more."

Sermon delivered by Rev. Alexander Beers, pastor First Free
Methodist Church, East Ninth and Mill Streets, Sunday, December 24, 1919.

ALEXANDER, THE GREAT BUILDER

There came a voice to Alexander,
   "Hasten westward with your queen,
O'er the tops of Cascade Mountains,
   In a valley ever green,

"Upon a slope close by the water
   Stands a structure new and bare,
Where will gather many children,
   Fit them for the mansions rare.

"Stumps enclose the view around you,
   Logs lie scattered all the way,
Right and left and on before you,
   As you go to lake or bay.

"In that valley where I send you
   Are bright jewels for your crown,
And that building has a future
   Standing there upon the Sound."

Then aboard the train they hastened;
   To this wilderness they came,
Found the task to them appointed
   For the Master's precious name.

Students crowded to the campus,
   All the rooms upon it filled,
Till the voice again from heaven
   Said, "Alexander, rise and build

"Another hall upon the campus
   And other structures in the town,
For still with favor on your future
   Will I send my blessings down."

In their season these were finished,
  Fitted for their service bright,
But the needs kept on increasing
  To conduct the work aright.

The cry again went up for buildings,
  Fully furnished for the cause
Of Christian education, having
  Full equipment for each course.

He knows 'tis better to go forward
  When the voice from heaven calls,
So today he builds a structure
  Greater than the former halls.

Twelve years have passed since first they heeded
  And came westward to this shore.
God has given them many jewels,
  And will grant them many more

In the future that's before them,
  Comes with an assurance bright
As they upward press and onward
  In the battle for the right.

Let us pause a while in honor
  Of our builder true and brave,
Bring him now a glad thanksgiving,
  Not "strew roses on his grave."

Scatter flowers along his pathway,
  Make him bearer of the palm,
Cheer his heart with joy and gladness
  As those who sing the sacred psalm.

Three and forty years he numbers
  As he "pitches now his tent
Farther on" life's rugged pathway
  Labors with a heart content.

Honor then to our great builder,
  To the pastor of our flock,
To the financier, the poet;
  His labor shall not be forgot.

Let us strew his path with blossoms,
　Let us sing the joyful psalm,
And take up his birthday chorus,
　Make him bearer of the palm.
　　　　　　　—Mrs. Laura Millican Appleton.

The above poem was written in honor of Mr. Beers' birthday when a fine growing palm was to be presented to him by the students. Mrs. Appleton was asked a short time before the dinner to prepare a suitable presentation speech. She responded with this poem, which of necessity was written hurriedly.

THERE'S A LAND FAR AWAY

There's a land far away 'mid the stars we are told,
  Where they know not the sorrows of time,
Where the pure waters flow thro' the valleys of gold,
  And where life is a treasure sublime;
'Tis the land of our God, 'tis the home of the soul,
Where the ages of splendor eternally roll,
Where the way-weary traveler reaches his goal,
  On the evergreen mountains of life.

Here our gaze can not soar to that beautiful land,
  But our visions have told of its bliss,
And our souls by the gale from its gardens are fanned,
  When we faint in the deserts of this;
And we sometimes have longed for its holy repose
When our hearts have been rent with temptations and woes,
And we've drank from the tide of the river that flows
  From the evergreen mountains of life.

Oh, the stars never tread the blue heavens at night,
  But we think where the ransomed have trod,
And the day never smiles from his palace of light,
  But we feel the bright smile of our God;
We are traveling home through earth's changes and gloom,
To a region where pleasures unchangingly bloom,
And our guide is the glory that shines through the tomb,
  From the evergreen mountains of life.

The above poem was one of Mr. Beers' favorites.
He would call for this hymn to be sung in his congregation at least once every Sunday.

THE BLESSED HOPE

BY ADELAIDE L. BEERS

Oh, happy day when Christ shall come,
And take His ransomed treasure home;
He long hath waited for this day,
For this He gave His life away.

CHORUS

Oh, happy day, oh, happy day,
When Christ shall catch His bride away.
He soon will come to claim His own
And reign with her upon His throne.

He's ransomed her from every sin,
And decked her for His diadem,
In richest robes He clothes His own,
And soon He'll take His treasure home.

Oh, glorious day so long foretold
By prophets, bards and seers of old,
Millennial morn forevermore,
When Jesus reigns from shore to shore.

Ten thousand saints and thousands still,
Shall sit with Him on Zion's hill;
His kingdom stretched from sea to sea
Shall reign throughout eternity.

Written by Mrs. Beers while recovering from small-pox, and later set to music by the Rev. I. G. Martin, pastor of the First Nazarene Church in Chicago.

THE HOUSE BY THE SIDE OF THE ROAD

There are hermit souls that live withdrawn
   In the peace of their self-content;
There are souls, like stars, that dwell apart,
   In a fellowless firmament;
There are pioneer souls that blaze their paths
   Where highways never ran;
But let me live in a house by the side of the road
   And be a friend of man.
    *   *   *   *   *   *

I know there are brook-gladdened meadows ahead,
   And mountains of wearisome height;
That the road passes through the long afternoon
   And stretches away to the night,
But still I rejoice when the travelers rejoice,
   And weep with the strangers that moan,
Nor live in my house by the side of the road
   Like a man that dwells alone.
    *   *   *   *   *   *

Let me live in my house by the side of the road
   Where the race of men go by;
They are good, they are bad, they are weak, they are strong,
   Wise, foolish—so am I;
Then why should I sit in the scorner's seat,
   Or hurl the cynic's ban?
Let me live in my house by the side of the road
   And be a friend to man.
               —Extract from Sam Walter Foss.

Note—This extract illustrates the ruling principle of Mr. Beers' entire life after his conversion—"to be a friend to man."

THE SIMPLE FAITH

O give me yet the simple faith in which the fathers trod,
The gospel of the rugged paths that lead our feet to God;
The blood-red road of cross and pain that we must go—and
    then,
That doctrine of forgiving love for men that war with men.

I want that faith that makes no qualm of creed for you and
    me;
That doctrine of old-fashioned trust in saving grace and
    love;
The Scripture truths that children learned at some old
    mother's knee,
The lessons that the Bible taught of realms of grace above.

Men mock such simple faith, I know, and jeer at those who
    pray;
But somehow it seems sweeter here to live our lives that
    way;
To try to keep the golden rule, and help as best we can
To gain a little joy ourselves and help our fellow-man.

And so beyond the stilly deeps of wisdom and its scorn
Sometimes unto my ears it seems a sweeter music's borne,
Because that hunger in my heart turns everything to gold
Beneath that sweet old-fashioned faith to which I long to
    hold.   —*Selected.*

A favorite poem.

www.ingramcontent.com/pod-product-compliance
Lightning Source LLC
LaVergne TN
LVHW011216080426
835509LV00005B/153